First published by Shaurya Nandecha 2025 First edition ISBN: 9789334192056

SAY SOMETHING!

Say Something!

Shaurya Nandecha

SHAURYA
NANDECHA
EST 2025

Contents

Why I Am Writing This Book

Alright, let's cut to the chase. You picked up this book for one of two reasons: Either you're tired of sitting in the corner at parties, clutching your drink like it's a lifeline, or you're genuinely interested in understanding how the other half of the population functions. Either way, welcome. My name is Shaurya Nandecha, an engineering student turned CEO of a startup. I've been an extrovert since childhood—a loud, social animal who thrives in the hustle and bustle of human interaction. I've mastered the art of the handshake, the wink, the "how's it going?" conversation starter, and the oh-so-casual lean against the bar counter.

Now, let me tell you why I'm writing this book. Many of my friends are introverts—shy, reserved, and, to put it bluntly, allergic to people. They sit quietly during team meetings, avoid eye contact in elevators, and would rather drink bleach than engage in small talk. I've watched them struggle through social scenarios, feeling like a spectator at a silent movie, and I've often thought, "Why the hell are you guys doing this to yourselves?"

So, here I am, an extrovert on a mission to convert a few introverts. I'm like that friend who drags you to the dance floor when you'd rather be texting in the corner. But don't worry; I'm not here to bully you into becoming a social butterfly or to shame you into doing tequila shots at the next office party. This isn't some weird extrovert cult initiation. Instead, consider me your sarcastic mentor, your humorous guide to navigating the strange world of social interaction with a little more ease, confidence, and—dare I say it?—fun.

And before you roll your eyes and slam this book shut, let me clarify: Introverts are awesome. Seriously. You guys think before you speak (imagine that), you're fantastic listeners (I never have to repeat myself), and you possess a mysterious aura that we extroverts will never have. But being an extrovert has its perks too. So, why not explore what it means to dip your toes into this world?

This book isn't about transforming you into someone you're not. It's about showing you that with a few practical exercises, a bit of humour, and some painfully real-life examples, you can navigate social settings without feeling like you've been dropped into a gladiator pit. I'll share my experiences, sprinkle in some science (don't worry, no equations), and give you a toolkit to manage, and maybe even enjoy, social interactions. Who knows? You might even make some new friends along the way.

Now, let's get started. Don't worry. This won't hurt a bit—well, maybe just a little. But hey, no pain, no gain, right?

1

So, You're an Introvert – Now What?

Alright, my introverted friend, let's have a little chat. So, you're an introvert. You prefer quiet corners over crowded rooms, meaningful conversations over meaningless chatter, and your idea of a fun Friday night might involve more Netflix and less networking. I get it. I really do. And while there's nothing wrong with that, we've got to talk about the big, awkward elephant in the room: society doesn't always know what to do with you.

The world seems to be designed for the extroverts—the loud, the chatty, the "let's do lunch" kind of people. They thrive on energy exchanges, eye contact, and enthusiastic handshakes that could double as a competitive sport. Meanwhile, you're over here wishing that meeting new people didn't feel like preparing for a job interview where you're underqualified and also, for some reason, slightly damp with sweat. Don't worry. We're not here to throw you into the lion's den. I'm here to guide you gently, maybe with a nudge or two (but I promise, no shoving).

INTROVERT MYTH-BUSTING 101:

First things first, let's bust a few myths about introversion. Contrary to popular belief, introverts are not just extroverts who malfunctioned. You're not broken, defective, or missing some key social gene. Introversion isn't about being socially inept or shy—though, let's face it, those do tend to hang out together like peanut butter and jelly. Introversion is more about where you get your energy from. You see, extroverts get their buzz from social interactions, while you might feel like your life force is being syphoned away when you're stuck in a room with too many people for too long. And that's okay! It's called energy management, my friend, and it's a survival skill.

But here's where it gets interesting: Society's misconceptions about introverts are, in fact, kind of hilarious when you think about it. Some people think you're like some mystical creature that survives on books, coffee, and avoiding human contact. They picture you lurking in libraries or typing furiously on a typewriter like some 19th-century novelist. And hey, maybe some of you are. But introverts come in all flavours—quiet but adventurous, reserved yet bold in thought, or, my favourite, the introvert who's a party animal at heart but only after five drinks and an inspirational pep talk.

THE SUBTLE JOYS OF SOCIAL ANXIETY:

Ah, social anxiety, the classic partner to introversion's awkward dance. If you're reading this, you probably know what it's like to rehearse a conversation in your head a dozen times before speaking, only to forget all your lines when it's showtime. Social anxiety is like that friend who shows up uninvited and eats all your snacks, making itself at home in your mind, convincing you that every "Hi, how are you?" is a potential minefield. But here's the kicker: Everyone experiences social anxiety to some degree. Yep, even those loudmouth extroverts who seem like they've got it all together. They're just better at hiding it—or better yet, ignoring it altogether.

Let me tell you a secret. Social anxiety is just your brain's way of over-preparing you for what it thinks is a potentially life-threatening event. Your brain thinks it's helping you out by running disaster scenarios like "What if you say something stupid?" or "What if you spill your drink on your boss?" But guess what? 99% of the time, none of that happens. And the other 1%? Well, it's probably going to be a funny story later (way later).

THE WEIRD WORLD OF EXTROVERT EXPECTATIONS:

Now, here's a fun twist: Extroverts often don't understand why introverts act the way they do, which leads to some classic moments of miscommunication. Like when you're invited to a group dinner and you think, "Great, I'll just sit quietly, eat my food, and nod along." But then your extroverted friend decides it's karaoke night and signs you up to sing a duet of "Don't Stop Believin'." And suddenly, your life is flashing before your eyes.

The truth is, most extroverts are genuinely trying to help you "come out of your shell," but what they don't realise is that your shell is a carefully curated safe space. To them, social interaction is a game; to you, it's like trying to diffuse a bomb without the manual. The good news is that learning to navigate these situations doesn't mean you have to become an extrovert or sacrifice your comfort zone on the altar of social norms. It's more about learning the rules of the game so you can play it on your own terms. And maybe even have a little fun along the way.

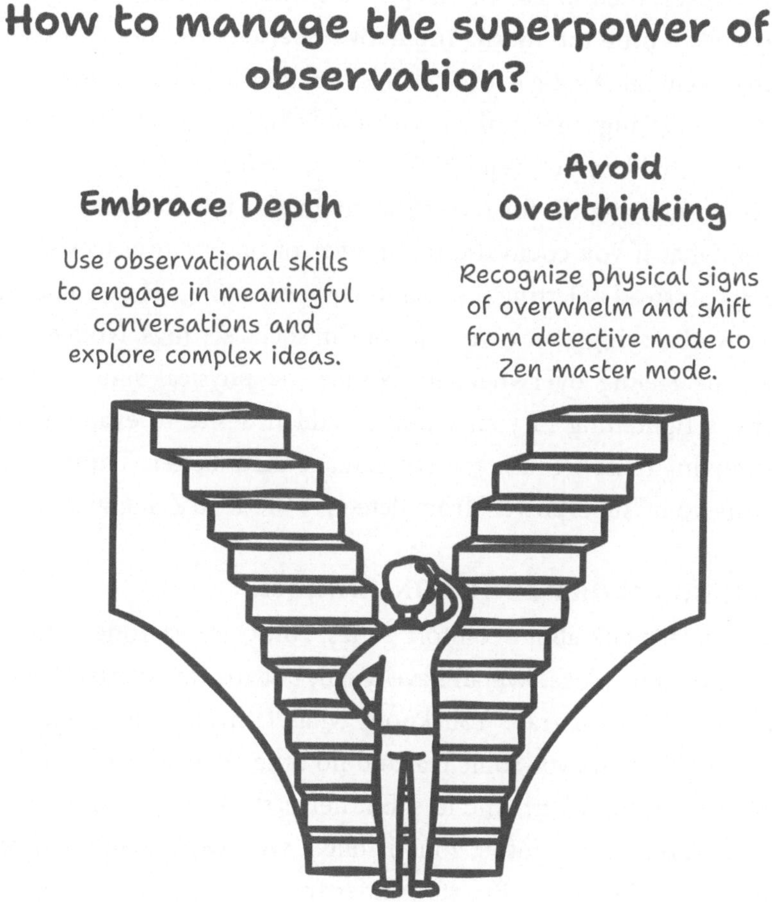

THE "SECRET POWER" OF INTROVERTS:

Here's the thing they don't tell you: Introverts have a superpower. No, it's not invisibility—although you guys do have a knack for blending into walls at parties. Your real power is **depth**. While extroverts are off collecting friends like Pokémon cards, you're diving deep into meaningful conversations, exploring complex ideas, and observing things others miss. You see the small details—the twitch of an eye, the shift in tone, the little nuances that reveal the truth behind words. That's powerful.

However, the flip side of this power is that it can also keep you in your head a little too much. You're like Sherlock Holmes at a speed-dating event, analysing every word, every gesture, every microscopic shift in body language until you've built a complex psychological profile that would make Freud blush. It's great for writing a detective novel but not so great for relaxed, spontaneous interactions.

So, what if you could use that power of observation to your advantage, instead of letting it spiral into overthinking? Here's a pro tip: Start by observing your own reactions in social settings. Notice when you start feeling overwhelmed. Notice the physical signs—sweaty palms, a tightening in your chest, a sudden desire to evaporate. By recognizing these signals, you can manage them better. Think of it as turning your "superpower" from detective mode to Zen master mode.

THE COMFORT ZONE CONUNDRUM:

Now, let's talk about comfort zones. Ah, comfort zones—the introvert's happy place. We all have them, but for introverts, they can become a bit of a trap. You know what I mean: the couch, your favourite book, maybe some tea, and no other human being in sight. Sounds nice, doesn't it? And it is. But here's the kicker—nothing ever grows there. Your comfort zone is like a well-worn blanket; it feels safe, cosy, and familiar. But stay under that blanket for too long, and you'll start missing out on the wonders of the outside world, like sunshine, fresh air, and the occasional awkward but potentially life-changing social interaction.

I know, I know, the thought of stepping outside your comfort zone feels like being asked to walk barefoot on hot coals while juggling flaming swords. But remember, growth doesn't happen when you're comfortable. It happens when you're stretching, testing your limits, and occasionally making a complete fool of yourself. And that's okay! Newsflash: We all do it. Extroverts are just better at pretending they meant to trip over their own feet while introducing themselves.

So here's a challenge for you: Step outside that comfort zone, but in small, manageable steps. Think of it like dipping your toes in the pool before you cannonball in. Try saying "hello" to someone you see regularly but never talk to—the barista, the guy at the gym, the colleague who sits three desks away. You don't need to launch into a TED Talk; just a simple "hi" will do. You might be surprised at how a tiny step can lead to bigger, more comfortable strides.

THE BEAUTY OF AWKWARD MOMENTS:

And let's get one thing straight: Awkwardness is inevitable. Yes, even for extroverts. The difference is, extroverts embrace awkwardness like an old friend. They laugh it off, move on, and sometimes even use it as a conversation starter. "Hey, remember that time I spilled coffee all over the CEO's new suit? Good times, right?" You, on the other hand, might replay that moment in your head for the next decade, questioning every choice that led up to it.

But here's a little secret for you: Awkward moments are gold. They're what make us human. They're relatable, endearing, and most importantly, they're forgettable (except for you, but we're working on that). No one else is thinking about how you stumbled over your words three months ago at Janet's birthday party. In fact, they've probably forgotten it already. So, let it go.

Think of every awkward moment as a deposit in your "I'm just like everyone else" bank. Everyone makes mistakes, everyone gets embarrassed, and everyone has that one story they wish they could erase from the social record. So, wear your awkwardness like a badge of honour. You're out there trying, and that's more than a lot of people can say.

SOCIAL ANXIETY EXERCISE #1: THE 10-SECOND RULE:

Here's a fun little exercise to start stretching your social muscles. I call it the **10-Second Rule**. Next time you find yourself in a social situation—a meeting, a party, or even a casual conversation—force yourself to say something within the first 10 seconds. Anything. A comment, a question, a witty observation, or even just a "Hello, I'm [Your Name]." Why? Because the longer you wait, the more your brain starts to overthink, analyse, and convince you that you have nothing valuable to say. It's like jumping into cold water: Do it quickly, and you'll adjust faster. Linger too long on the edge, and you'll psych yourself out.

You'll find that the more you practise the 10-Second Rule, the less intimidating those first few seconds will feel. And before you know it, you might just be...dare I say...enjoying yourself. Crazy, right?

Look at you, still here and ready for more. That's the spirit! Now that we've talked about stepping out of your comfort zone, let's tackle the next hurdle: **small talk**. For introverts, small talk is often viewed as the lowest form of human communication, right up there with grunts and smoke signals. But let me let you in on a little secret: small talk is not about the weather. Well, sometimes it is, but more often than not, it's about something much deeper—connecting with another person in a low-stakes environment. Think of it as social stretching before the real workout.

THE ART OF SMALL TALK WITHOUT LOSING YOUR SOUL:

Now, I know you might be thinking, "Small talk is pointless and boring! Why can't people just get to the good stuff?" I hear you. And you know what? I kind of agree. Small talk can feel like trying to swim in the shallow end when you're dying to dive into the deep, meaningful conversations where you truly shine. But here's why small talk is actually important: it's the gateway. It's the bridge between strangers and friends. You don't start a conversation with "So, what's your stance on the meaning of life?"—unless, of course, you want that person to start backing away slowly. Instead, you start with a gentle "Hey, how's it going?" or "Crazy weather we're having, huh?"

The key to mastering small talk as an introvert is to see it as a game—a game you can win without having to fake enthusiasm or be something you're not. The trick is to turn small talk into a springboard for more meaningful conversation. You see, small talk is like an appetiser. It's not the main course, but it sets the stage. You're not supposed to fill up on breadsticks, my friend.

CONVERSATION STARTERS THAT WON'T MAKE YOU CRINGE:

So, how do you play this game without feeling like you're wearing a mask? Simple: focus on **authentic curiosity**. People love to talk about themselves—newsflash, I know. Use this to your advantage. Ask open-ended questions that require more than a "yes" or "no" answer. Instead of the classic "So, what do you do?" try "What's the most interesting part of your job?" Instead of "How was your weekend?" go with "What was the best part of your weekend?" These kinds of questions invite stories rather than just facts, and stories are where real connections happen.

Another tactic is to sprinkle in a little humour. Nothing disarms people more than a well-timed joke or a self-deprecating comment. People appreciate someone who doesn't take themselves too seriously. So if you spill your drink on yourself (because, let's face it, it's bound to happen), make a light-hearted comment about your own clumsiness. People will remember the laugh more than the spill.

THE "ELEVATOR PITCH" STRATEGY (FOR INTROVERTS, BY INTROVERTS):

Here's another trick: prepare a few go-to conversation starters, much like you'd prepare an elevator pitch for a job interview. Think of a few interesting anecdotes, quirky facts, or observations that you can pull out of your back pocket when the conversation starts to lag. For example, share a funny story about the last awkward situation you found yourself in. Not only does it make you relatable, but it also takes the pressure off the other person to carry the conversation. Plus, self-deprecation is charming when done right—just don't overdo it, or people might start to worry about you.

But what if you get stuck? What if, God forbid, there's a pause? Don't panic. Silence is not the enemy. Use those awkward silences to your advantage. Smile, make eye contact, and show you're comfortable with a little quiet. If anything, it gives the other person space to think and come up with something new. If you panic and fill the void with nervous chatter, you're only putting more pressure on yourself.

BUILDING THE CONFIDENCE MUSCLE:

Now, let's talk about confidence. You may think confidence is some kind of mystical aura that only certain people have, but let me tell you, confidence is a skill, not a trait. And like any skill, it requires practice. So here's your next exercise: Start treating conversations like mini experiments. Each time you step into a social setting, whether it's chatting with a colleague, talking to a neighbour, or even making small talk with a cashier, view it as a chance to practise your skills.

The goal is not to become the life of the party overnight. Start small. Engage in conversations with people you encounter daily. Make a genuine observation or ask a question that shows you've been paying attention. The beauty of this practice is that the stakes are low. The cashier isn't going to remember if your joke fell flat. The neighbour won't write you off forever if your conversation is a little awkward. Over time, these small interactions will help you build confidence in your ability to talk to anyone, anywhere, without feeling like your soul is being slowly drained out of your body.

SOCIAL ANXIETY EXERCISE #2: THE COMPLIMENT GAME:

Here's another exercise to put in your social toolbox: **The Compliment Game**. The rules are simple: Every day, give at least one genuine compliment to someone. Not a cheesy or forced one—something real. It could be about their shoes, their smile, their choice in books, whatever. The point is to focus on the positive and make someone's day, even if it's just a little bit. Compliments are like social currency; they open doors and build bridges. And the best part? You'd be surprised how quickly a compliment can turn into a full-blown conversation.

Don't believe me? Try it out. Compliment that colleague on their presentation skills or the barista on their tattoo. It doesn't have to be elaborate; it just has to be sincere. You'll find that not only does it make you feel good, but it also makes you more approachable. Suddenly, people start seeing you as friendly and easy to talk to, and guess what? They start opening up more too. Who knew you had that kind of power?

REFRAMING YOUR MINDSET – FROM SURVIVING TO THRIVING:

By now, you might be wondering, "Why am I putting myself through all this social callisthenics? Why can't I just keep to myself and live my life in peace?" Valid question. Here's the deal: The goal here isn't to make you someone you're not. It's to help you see that with a few small tweaks and a little bravery, you can actually thrive in social settings instead of just surviving them.

Imagine walking into a room and not feeling that rush of panic. Imagine making connections that feel genuine and real. Imagine being able to navigate a party or a networking event without feeling like you're running an emotional marathon. This isn't about faking it; it's about finding a version of yourself that is comfortable, confident, and capable of handling any social situation. And trust me, that version of you exists—you just have to be willing to look for it.

So, take a deep breath. Give yourself permission to be a little awkward, a little unsure, and a lot more open to the possibility that social interactions can actually be—dare I say—fun. And if it's not fun, well, at least you'll have a good story to tell.

Alright, introvert-in-training, let's keep this momentum going. We've covered the basics: you know that small talk doesn't have to be soul-sucking, you've got a couple of conversation tricks up your sleeve, and you're learning to see awkward moments as nothing more than opportunities for personal growth (or at least comedy). Now, it's time to address the next big, looming hurdle in your social journey: **group settings**.

NAVIGATING THE GAUNTLET OF GROUP CONVERSATIONS:

Group conversations are a whole different beast. If one-on-one conversations are a game of tennis, then group settings are more like a chaotic, multi-ball dodgeball match. Suddenly, there are more voices, more dynamics, and more potential for disaster. You're not just thinking about what to say next; you're also trying to track who's speaking, who's interrupting, who's nodding, and who's discreetly eyeing the exit. It's like trying to follow five different TV shows at once without a remote control.

For introverts, group settings can feel like a minefield. Do you jump in with your thoughts, risking interruption or, worse, being ignored? Do you hang back and wait for a clear opening, only to find the conversation has moved on to another topic entirely? The frustration is real. But here's the thing: you don't have to be the loudest voice to be heard. You just need to learn how to **insert yourself strategically**.

THE STRATEGIC INTERRUPTER METHOD:

Okay, let's talk about strategy. One of the best techniques for navigating group conversations is something I like to call the **Strategic Interrupter Method**. Before you gasp in horror at the idea of interrupting, hear me out. I'm not talking about being rude or bulldozing over people mid-sentence. I'm talking about finding the right moments to make your voice heard in a way that feels natural and confident.

Here's how it works: Instead of waiting for the perfect pause (which might never come), look for natural conversational beats—moments when someone finishes a thought, when there's a brief lull, or when someone else has just wrapped up a comment. That's your window. Jump in with a comment, a question, or a quick "I totally agree" before smoothly transitioning into your point. It's less about interrupting and more about inserting yourself just as the next breath is being taken.

And here's the kicker: The more you do this, the more natural it will feel. You'll start to notice that group conversations aren't nearly as intimidating as they seem. They're more like a river with currents—sometimes fast, sometimes slow, but always moving. Your job is to learn how to swim with it instead of fighting against it.

CREATING A PRESENCE WITHOUT A MEGAPHONE:

For those of you who prefer a quieter approach, fear not—you don't have to become a master interrupter to be effective in group settings. Sometimes, the most powerful voice in the room is the one that doesn't speak constantly, but speaks **strategically**. Here's a trick: use your observational skills to your advantage. If you're not naturally inclined to dominate the conversation, focus on becoming a **connector**.

What's a connector? Think of yourself as the glue that holds conversations together. While everyone else is busy making their points or arguing over who has the best take, you're there to weave threads between them. Listen carefully, pick up on recurring themes or points of agreement, and then bring them together. For example, you might say, "That's interesting, what you said about X—because it ties in with what Sarah mentioned earlier about Y." Suddenly, you're the person who's listening, synthesising, and adding value without shouting over everyone else. And trust me, people notice that.

THE POWER OF THE WELL-TIMED QUESTION:

Another secret weapon in your group conversation arsenal? **The well-timed question.** You'd be amazed at how much weight a good question carries. While everyone else is busy trying to showcase their knowledge or crack the next joke, you can wield your curiosity like a sword. Not only does it show that you're engaged, but it also shifts the focus onto someone else, which is a great tactic when you want to steer clear of the spotlight but still make an impact.

Here's the trick: Your question needs to be specific enough to add depth but open enough to invite a discussion. For instance, instead of asking, "What do you think?" try "How do you see this playing out in the next year?" or "What do you think is the biggest challenge with that?" Questions like these show that you're not just passively nodding along—you're genuinely interested. And in a world where everyone's trying to be heard, being the one who truly listens is a superpower.

EMBRACING THE ROLE OF THE "WILD CARD":

Now, if you're feeling a bit braver, consider this: Sometimes the best way to make your mark in a group is to embrace the role of the "wild card." This doesn't mean you have to be unpredictable or outrageous. It means you bring something to the table that's a little different from the norm. Maybe you throw out an unexpected perspective or a funny anecdote that lightens the mood. Maybe you're the one who asks the thought-provoking question that shifts the entire direction of the conversation.

Being a wild card is about breaking the monotony and injecting a bit of originality into the mix. It's about playing to your strengths—whether that's your sense of humour, your deep insights, or your ability to look at a problem from a totally unique angle. Just because you're an introvert doesn't mean you have to blend into the wallpaper. Sometimes, the most memorable person in the room is the one who brings a fresh flavour to the conversation.

SOCIAL ANXIETY EXERCISE #3: THE GROUP CHAT CHALLENGE:

Okay, time for another exercise. This one is called the **Group Chat Challenge**. Here's what you're going to do: The next time you're in a group setting—whether it's a meeting, a study group, or a social gathering—I want you to set a goal to speak up at least three times. It doesn't matter what you say or when, as long as you contribute three different times. This could be a question, a comment, an observation, or even just agreeing with someone and adding your own spin. The point is to get comfortable with the rhythm of group conversations.

And don't overthink it! You're not trying to deliver a TED Talk. You're just practising inserting yourself into the flow of conversation. The more you do it, the less you'll feel like you're walking a tightrope without a net. And who knows? You might even find that you start enjoying the dynamic nature of group discussions. Or, at the very least, you'll have a few more social tools in your kit.

REWIRING YOUR SOCIAL BRAIN – IT'S POSSIBLE:

Finally, let's talk a bit about rewiring your brain. Yes, that's a real thing. Neuroplasticity is the fancy term for it, but all it means is that our brains are adaptable. They learn, change, and grow based on our experiences. So, every time you step out of your comfort zone, try a new conversation tactic, or experiment with a new social strategy, you're literally training your brain to be more comfortable in those situations.

Think of it like this: Your brain is a muscle, and just like any other muscle, it needs exercise to grow. You're not going to become a social superstar overnight, but with consistent practice, you'll start to notice subtle changes. You'll feel less drained after social interactions, you'll start to anticipate rather than dread them, and eventually, you might even find yourself seeking them out. Imagine that.

So, keep at it. Embrace the awkwardness, play the social games on your terms, and don't be afraid to stretch those comfort zones just a little more each day. You've got this. And remember, we're just getting started. There's a whole world of social adventures waiting for you, and it's not nearly as scary as it seems.

Alright, here we are at the final page of Chapter 1, and you're still with me. That's commitment! You've already taken some brave steps: understanding the social dynamics, learning to wade into small talk without wanting to dive out a window, and figuring out how to navigate group conversations without having to shout over everyone else. Now, let's finish strong with a little pep talk about **reframing how you see yourself** in social situations and why it's okay—no, actually, it's pretty damn great—to be an introvert who's willing to dip their toes into the extroverted pool.

OWNING YOUR INTROVERSION LIKE A BOSS:

Let's get one thing clear right off the bat: Being an introvert is not a flaw. It's not a personality defect. It's not some curse that's going to prevent you from living a fulfilling life. On the contrary, being an introvert comes with a set of powerful traits that the world needs more of: empathy, depth, listening skills, and a thoughtful approach to relationships and decisions. While extroverts might be the flashy headline-makers, introverts are the ones writing the compelling story behind the scenes.

So, here's your next mission: **Own your introversion like it's a superpower.** Because it is. You're not just someone who's "bad" at socialising or "awkward" around new people. You're someone who brings a unique perspective to every conversation, who sees beyond the surface, and who doesn't settle for shallow interactions. When you walk into a room, you have the potential to shift the energy by simply being present, observant, and engaged.

But—and this is a big but—that doesn't mean you can't benefit from picking up a few extroverted tricks along the way. The goal isn't to change who you are; it's to **expand who you are**. Think of it as upgrading your social toolkit. You're adding a few new skills, not replacing the ones you already have. Because let's face it, even Batman had a utility belt.

TURNING SOCIAL ANXIETY INTO SOCIAL CURIOSITY:

If there's one thing I want you to take away from this chapter, it's this: **You don't have to fear social interactions.** You don't have to see them as battles to survive. Instead, try viewing them through a different lens—one of curiosity. Social anxiety, at its core, is just fear dressed up in different clothes. It's the fear of being judged, the fear of saying the wrong thing, the fear of making a fool of yourself. But what if, instead of fearing these things, you got curious about them?

"What does that even mean, Shaurya?" you ask, probably rolling your eyes. Well, it means approaching social situations with a mindset of discovery rather than dread. Instead of worrying, "What if they don't like me?" ask, "I wonder what I'll learn about this person?" or "What interesting conversation could we have?" Curiosity is a powerful antidote to fear because it shifts the focus away from potential failure and toward potential growth.

You see, when you're curious, you're open. You're more willing to take risks, to ask questions, and to engage with others without the crippling fear of what might go wrong. And here's the beauty of it: When you approach people with genuine curiosity, they respond in kind. It's like giving them permission to relax and be themselves. You'd be surprised how many "awkward" situations can be defused simply by showing genuine interest.

THE ART OF BEING "SELECTIVE SOCIAL":

Now, just because you're learning to step out of your comfort zone doesn't mean you have to do it all the time. That's where the concept of being "selective social" comes in. Not every social engagement is worth your time or energy. You don't have to accept every invitation or engage in every conversation. Remember, your energy is valuable. Spend it wisely.

Being selectively social means knowing when to lean in and when to step back. It's about choosing the social situations that are most likely to be rewarding or meaningful for you. This could be a small gathering with close friends rather than a massive party, or a one-on-one coffee date rather than a crowded networking event. And when you do decide to engage, go all in. Be present. Be engaged. Bring your full self to the table, and see what happens.

This approach also helps prevent social burnout, which is a real thing—especially for introverts. The more you practise being selectively social, the more you'll start to notice which types of interactions energise you and which ones drain you. And that awareness is key to navigating social life without feeling like you're constantly running on empty.

SOCIAL ANXIETY EXERCISE #4: THE "SELECTIVE YES" STRATEGY:

Time for another exercise. This one is called the **"Selective Yes" Strategy**. Over the next week, I want you to make a list of the social opportunities that come your way—everything from casual invites to formal events. For each one, ask yourself: "Does this feel like a genuine opportunity for connection or growth?" If the answer is yes, commit to going and being fully present. If the answer is no, don't be afraid to politely decline. The key here is to be intentional about where you invest your social energy.

And here's the fun part: For every event you say "yes" to, set a small goal for yourself. Maybe it's to strike up a conversation with someone new, or maybe it's to practise one of the social skills we've talked about—like the 10-Second Rule or giving a genuine compliment. The point is to use these opportunities as low-pressure practice grounds to build your confidence and refine your social style.

REIMAGINING YOUR SOCIAL STORY:

Finally, let's talk about the story you tell yourself about who you are in social settings. Too often, introverts fall into the trap of labelling themselves as "bad at socialising" or "socially awkward," and guess what? The more you repeat that story, the more it becomes a self-fulfilling prophecy. It's like typing out a script for yourself before you even walk into the room.

What if you rewrote that script? What if, instead of seeing yourself as someone who struggles in social settings, you saw yourself as someone who's learning, growing, and getting better every day? What if, instead of dreading the next party or meeting, you saw it as another chapter in your evolving social story—a story where you're the hero, not the side character who hides in the corner?

Start telling yourself a different story. One where you're not just an introvert but a **social explorer**, someone who's navigating the landscape of human interaction with curiosity, humour, and a few clever tricks up their sleeve. Because that's who you really are—a work in progress, and that's perfectly okay.

A FINAL WORD FOR CHAPTER 1:

So here we are at the end of Chapter 1, and if you've made it this far, give yourself a pat on the back. You've taken the first steps toward understanding how to navigate the world of social interaction on your terms. And guess what? It's only going to get better from here. We're just getting started, my friend. There's a lot more to explore, and I promise it's going to be a fun ride.

Remember, this isn't about changing who you are—it's about unlocking new parts of yourself, parts you might not even know exist yet. So, take a deep breath, keep an open mind, and let's see where this journey takes us next. You've got this. And I'll be right here with you, cheering you on every awkward, amazing step of the way.

2

How to Talk to Humans Without Feeling Like a Alien

Welcome to Chapter 2, dear introverted reader. You've made it past the initial hurdles—accepting your introverted superpowers, learning to dip a toe into the chaotic world of social interactions, and figuring out that small talk doesn't have to feel like a slow death. Now, it's time to get to the meat of the matter: **how to talk to humans without feeling like you've just crash-landed on an alien planet.**

I know, I know. Talking to humans sounds like something we should all inherently know how to do. After all, we're humans, right? But for introverts, it often feels like speaking another language—one where you missed all the classes and forgot the textbook at home. Suddenly, you're surrounded by people who seem to effortlessly glide through conversations while you're standing there, nodding like a bobblehead, trying to think of something clever to say.

THE "CONVERSATION FLOW" MYTH:

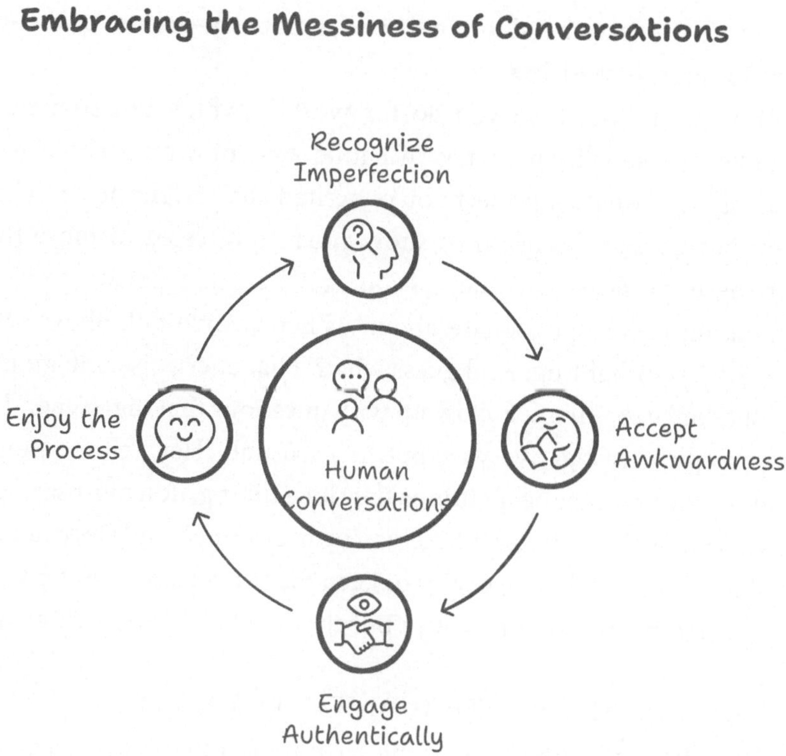

Once you accept that conversations don't have to be smooth and polished, you can start relaxing a little. You don't have to come up with the perfect line every time someone speaks to you. You just have to show up, be present, and be willing to engage. You know, like a normal, awkward human being. And that's where the fun starts.

HOW TO ASK QUESTIONS WITHOUT SOUNDING LIKE A DETECTIVE:

If you remember from Chapter 1, asking questions is one of the best ways to ease into conversations. But there's an art to it. Ask the wrong kind of question, and you sound like you're conducting a police interrogation: "Where were you last night?" "What's your deal?" "Are you hiding something?" People don't like feeling cornered or probed. So, what's the secret? **Ask open-ended, curiosity-driven questions that invite storytelling.**

Instead of "What do you do for work?" (which can sometimes feel like a personality test), try "What do you enjoy most about what you do?" or "What's a project you're excited about right now?" These questions do two things: they show you're interested in more than just the basic facts, and they encourage the other person to share something they're passionate about. When people talk about what they love, they light up. And guess what? That energy is contagious.

But don't stop there. Follow up with questions that dig deeper. Not in a creepy, investigative way, but in a natural, "Hey, tell me more!" kind of way. If someone mentions they love hiking, don't just say, "Oh, cool." Try, "What's the best hike you've ever done?" or "Do you have any favourite spots?" The goal is to keep the conversation going without feeling like you're throwing a bunch of darts and hoping one hits.

THE ART OF THE "THROWAWAY COMMENT":

Now, let's talk about one of the most underrated tools in conversation—**the throwaway comment**. What's a throwaway comment, you ask? It's a small, seemingly insignificant observation or joke that you toss out there to see if it sticks. It's low-risk, high-reward. If it lands, great! You've got a new thread to pull on. If it doesn't, no harm done—you just move on.

Throwaway comments work best when they're light, observational, and a bit offbeat. Imagine you're at a boring networking event (because, let's be real, they're mostly boring), and someone's droning on about quarterly sales reports. You might casually say, "Ah, yes, nothing like a thrilling Q1 analysis to get the blood pumping," with a slight smile. If the person laughs, boom—you've just created a moment of shared humour. If not, well, they probably weren't your kind of person anyway.

BUILDING CONVERSATIONAL BRIDGES:

Another essential skill is learning how to build **conversational bridges**. Think of these bridges as little connectors that help you smoothly transition from one topic to another. For example, if someone mentions they just got back from a trip to Italy, you could jump from "Oh, I'd love to hear more about your trip!" to "Did you try any weird foods while you were there?" or "I've always wanted to visit Florence—what was it like?"

Bridges help keep conversations dynamic and prevent them from dying out in awkward silence. They also show that you're engaged and genuinely interested. The key is to listen for keywords or topics that naturally lend themselves to a new angle or follow-up. This might sound complicated, but it's not—it's all about being present and letting your curiosity lead the way.

THE "YES, AND" TECHNIQUE:

Let's borrow a classic from the world of improv comedy—the **"Yes, And" technique**. In improv, this technique is used to keep a scene moving forward. You never shut down a scene partner's idea; instead, you build on it. In conversation, "Yes, And" is about agreeing with what's being said and then adding something new to it.

For example, if someone says, "I've been binge-watching old sitcoms lately," you could respond, "Yes! There's something so comforting about them. And have you noticed how they always have that one weird neighbour who steals the show?" This keeps the conversation flowing and gives it new life.

The beauty of the "Yes, And" technique is that it helps you avoid the dreaded **conversation killers** like "Oh, really?" or "Cool." Those are dead ends. Instead, "Yes, And" keeps the ball rolling, adding a layer of creativity and engagement to every exchange.

SOCIAL ANXIETY EXERCISE #1: THE "YES, AND" CHALLENGE:

Time for a new exercise: **The "Yes, And" Challenge.** For the next week, practice using "Yes, And" in every conversation you have—whether it's with a friend, a colleague, or even a random person you meet while waiting in line for coffee. The goal is to agree with what's being said and then build on it with a new thought, observation, or joke.

You'll find that this technique makes conversations feel more natural and less like a Q&A session. It creates a sense of flow, and before you know it, you're no longer searching for things to say—they're just coming to you. The more you practise, the more it becomes second nature. And who knows? You might even start having fun with it.

WHY AWKWARD SILENCES AREN'T THE END OF THE WORLD:

Let's address one of the biggest fears of introverts: the **awkward silence**. For some reason, we've been conditioned to believe that every conversation must be a non-stop marathon of words. But here's the truth: Awkward silences aren't the end of the world. They're just pauses—nothing more, nothing less. In fact, some of the most meaningful conversations happen in those quiet spaces.

Think of awkward silences as a breather, not a disaster. They give both parties a chance to collect their thoughts, reflect, and maybe even take the conversation in a new direction. Instead of rushing to fill the silence with meaningless chatter, try embracing it. Smile, take a sip of your drink, or simply nod. You'll find that the more comfortable you become with silence, the more others will feel comfortable, too.

REFRAME: YOU'RE NOT AN ALIEN, YOU'RE AN EXPLORER:

Here's a little mindset shift to carry with you: You're not an alien trying to blend in with the humans. You're an explorer navigating new territories. You're out there collecting stories, learning about people, and finding connections where you least expect them. Every conversation is an adventure—some will be more exciting than others, but all have the potential to teach you something.

So, stop worrying about being perfect. Stop worrying about saying the wrong thing or looking foolish. Instead, focus on being genuinely curious, open, and willing to roll with whatever comes your way. Because the truth is, the more you engage with others, the more you realise that everyone is just as weird, awkward, and wonderful as you are.

Alright, social explorer, let's continue our journey into the wild world of human conversation. You've got a few tricks up your sleeve now: asking open-ended questions, tossing in throwaway comments, and building bridges between topics like a seasoned conversational architect. But there's more to this game than just clever techniques. Today, we're diving into the realm of **active listening**—the secret sauce that transforms a good conversation into a great one.

THE DIFFERENCE BETWEEN HEARING AND LISTENING:

You've probably heard this one before: There's a big difference between hearing and listening. Hearing is passive; it's what happens when someone's talking at you and all you're thinking is, "Please, for the love of everything holy, stop talking." Listening, on the other hand, is active. It's about being fully present, engaging with what the other person is saying, and responding in a way that makes them feel heard.

Here's the thing: Most people are bad listeners. Like, really bad. They're too busy planning what they're going to say next or waiting for their turn to jump in with their own story. But not you. You, my friend, are about to become an active listening ninja. Why? Because being a great listener is a game-changer. It's the ultimate introvert superpower.

When you listen—really listen—you give people the rare experience of feeling understood. And that's worth more than being the funniest, most charming person in the room. Think about it: Would you rather be around someone who always has something witty to say but never remembers anything about you, or someone who genuinely listens, remembers, and responds thoughtfully? Exactly.

HOW TO LISTEN LIKE YOU MEAN IT:

So, how do you practise active listening without looking like you're trying too hard or, worse, like you're a therapist analysing their every word? Here are a few simple tips to get you started:

1. **Maintain Eye Contact (But Don't Stare Them Down):** Eye contact shows you're engaged, but there's a fine line between friendly and freaky. Aim for a balance—make eye contact when they're speaking, but don't forget to blink or glance away naturally every now and then.
2. **Use Nonverbal Cues:** A nod here, a smile there, a raised eyebrow when they say something surprising—these small, nonverbal cues show you're following along and invested in the conversation. Just don't overdo it, or you'll look like a bobblehead at speed.
3. **Reflect Back What You've Heard:** This is a classic trick that therapists use all the time, but it works wonders in everyday conversation. Simply paraphrase what the person has just said and repeat it back to them. For example: "So, if I'm hearing you right, you're saying that your cat knocked over your coffee and ruined your favourite book this morning? Man, that's rough."

Reflecting shows that you're paying attention and that you care about what they're saying.

4. **Ask Follow-Up Questions:** If you want to take your listening game to the next level, follow up with a question that digs a little deeper. If someone says they just got back from a trip, instead of moving on, try asking, "What was the highlight of your trip?" or "Did anything unexpected happen while you were there?" Follow-up questions show that you're not just listening, but you're genuinely interested in learning more.

THE BEAUTY OF SILENCE IN CONVERSATIONS:

Let's talk about silence again—but this time, not as an awkward space to be feared, but as a powerful tool in your conversational toolkit. You see, most people are terrified of silence in conversations. They think it means something has gone horribly wrong. But here's the truth: Silence can be a good thing.

When you're actively listening, sometimes the best thing you can do is...nothing. Give the person a moment to collect their thoughts or expand on what they've just said. Silence gives space for deeper reflection. And here's the magic: When you're comfortable with silence, it often prompts the other person to fill it with something more meaningful. It's like you're saying, "I'm here, and I'm giving you the floor." This builds trust, rapport, and the feeling that this conversation isn't just filler—it's valuable.

HOW TO HANDLE PEOPLE WHO WON'T STOP TALKING:

Now, let's address the flip side of listening—what do you do when you're stuck in a conversation with a **chronic talker**? You know the type: the person who goes on and on, barely stopping to breathe, much less let you get a word in. As an introvert, this can feel like social quicksand—you're sinking fast and there's no way out.

Here's a pro tip: Don't panic. Instead, use what I call the **"Redirect and Reclaim" strategy**. When you find yourself trapped in a monologue, look for a natural pause (they have to take a breath sometime, right?) and jump in with a redirecting comment like, "That's really interesting! It reminds me of something I experienced..." and then share a related story or question. This not only shifts the focus but also subtly signals that it's time to switch gears.

If that doesn't work, don't be afraid to **assert yourself** gently. You can try, "Hey, I love hearing about this, but I'd also like to get your thoughts on [new topic]." This shows that you're still engaged but also need a change of pace. It's polite, direct, and effective.

THE "PAUSE AND PIVOT" TECHNIQUE FOR WHEN YOU'RE STUCK:

But what if you're the one who's stuck? What if you've run out of things to say, and suddenly you're floundering in the deep end of the conversation pool? That's when you use the **"Pause and Pivot" technique**. Here's how it works: Take a small, intentional pause—don't rush to fill the silence—and then pivot to a new, loosely related topic.

For example, if you've been talking about movies and the topic is starting to die out, pause for a beat and then say, "Speaking of movies, I've always wondered—what's your favourite book that's been adapted into a film?" Boom—you've just pivoted the conversation smoothly without making it feel forced.

This technique is great because it gives you time to breathe, recalibrate, and steer the conversation in a direction that feels more comfortable or engaging. It also keeps things fresh and prevents those dreaded lulls where everyone starts glancing at their phones.

SOCIAL ANXIETY EXERCISE #2: THE "PAUSE AND PIVOT" CHALLENGE:

Here's your next challenge: Over the next few days, whenever you're in a conversation that feels like it's losing steam, practise the

"Pause and Pivot" technique. Take a moment to think, then shift to a related but new topic. Notice how the conversation flow changes. Does it feel more natural? More engaging? Use this exercise to become more comfortable with those pauses and to see them as opportunities rather than obstacles.

LEARNING TO ENJOY CONVERSATIONS, NOT JUST SURVIVE THEM:

Here's a radical idea: What if you could actually **enjoy** conversations? What if they didn't feel like social labour, but more like little adventures—each one offering a new perspective, a new story, or a new laugh? I know it sounds crazy, but it's entirely possible.

The secret lies in changing your mindset from "What do I have to say?" to "What can I discover?" When you approach conversations with a sense of curiosity and a willingness to see where things go, you stop feeling like you have to perform. Instead, you get to explore. And that shift is what makes all the difference.

So, let go of the pressure to be perfect, to always have the right thing to say, or to impress anyone. Instead, focus on connecting. Be present, be open, and most importantly, be yourself. Because guess what? People are more drawn to authenticity than they are to cleverness. And who knows? You might just surprise yourself by how much fun you can have when you stop worrying and start listening.

You're not here to be the loudest or the wittiest in the room. You're here to learn how to navigate social interactions in a way that feels genuine and true to who you are. And that's something worth celebrating. So, keep practising, keep experimenting, and keep leaning into the discomfort. Because on the other side of that discomfort is a version of you who's confident, curious, and maybe even enjoying the ride.

Alright, conversational ninja, let's keep sharpening those social skills. By now, you've learned the power of active listening, how to handle both awkward silences and overly chatty folks, and how to pivot conversations smoothly without feeling like you're doing verbal gymnastics. So what's next? It's time to learn about **storytelling**—one of the most powerful tools in the art of conversation.

WHY STORYTELLING MATTERS (EVEN FOR INTROVERTS):

Let's face it: humans are hardwired for stories. Since the dawn of time, we've been gathering around campfires, sharing tales of heroism, tragedy, and even the occasional fart joke. Stories aren't just for writers or grandpas who love to talk about "the good ol' days." Stories are for everyone. And when you master the art of storytelling, you unlock a superpower that makes conversations richer, more memorable, and—dare I say—fun.

But here's the kicker: storytelling isn't just about entertaining others. It's about connecting. When you share a story, you're not just throwing information out there; you're inviting someone into your world, giving them a piece of yourself, and creating an opportunity for them to relate. Even a simple story about a weird thing that happened to you at the grocery store can turn into a shared laugh or an "Oh, I've been there" moment. And those moments are gold.

Alright, you storytelling extraordinaire, let's push ahead and dive even deeper into the world of conversation mastery. You've learned how to use storytelling as a tool to connect with others and how self-deprecating humour can turn awkward moments into golden opportunities. Now, let's shift gears and focus on a skill that's often overlooked but incredibly powerful: **reading the room**.

WHY READING THE ROOM IS A GAME-CHANGER:

Have you ever walked into a room and immediately felt like you've just crashed a party you weren't invited to? Or maybe you've started telling a story, only to realise halfway through that no one is listening, and you're pretty much talking to a wall? That's where **reading the room** comes in.

Reading the room is all about understanding the social dynamics at play—the energy, the mood, and the unspoken rules. Think of it like being a social detective. You're picking up on clues: Who's engaged? Who's checked out? Who's itching for a change of topic, and who's looking for an opening to jump in? When you get good at reading the room, you can adapt on the fly, steer conversations more effectively, and avoid those dreaded moments where you feel like you're bombing on stage.

HOW TO READ THE ROOM WITHOUT LOOKING LIKE A CREEPER:

So, how do you read the room without coming across like you're analysing everyone's every move? It's simpler than you might think. Here are a few quick tips:

1. **Observe Body Language:** Take a quick scan around the room. Are people leaning in, making eye contact, and nodding along? Or are they shifting in their seats, looking at their phones, or staring blankly into space? These nonverbal cues tell you everything you need to know about whether the conversation is hitting or missing the mark.
2. **Listen to the Tone:** Is the conversation light and fun, or is it more serious and subdued? You don't want to be the person cracking jokes when everyone else is discussing deep, emotional topics. Match your tone to the room's energy. If it's light, feel free to keep things breezy. If it's serious, tread carefully and be more thoughtful with your words.
3. **Watch for Social Dynamics:** Pay attention to who's dominating the conversation, who's staying quiet, and who seems to be waiting for a chance to speak. If you notice someone hasn't had a chance to talk, you can create space for them by directly asking, "Hey, what do you think about this?" It shows you're aware of the group dynamic and that you value everyone's input.

4. **Adapt and Adjust:** If you sense that the room's energy is starting to lag, don't be afraid to pivot. Maybe it's time to wrap up a story that's dragging on or shift to a new topic that might be more engaging. Flexibility is key. Conversations are fluid, not set in stone.

NAVIGATING DIFFERENT TYPES OF PEOPLE:

Reading the room also involves understanding the different personalities you might encounter in social settings. Here's a quick rundown of some common types and how to engage with them:

- **The Talker:** This person loves to talk and usually dominates the conversation. To handle a Talker, use the "Redirect and Reclaim" strategy we discussed earlier. Let them have their moment, but don't be afraid to steer the conversation back to a more balanced dialogue.
- **The Listener:** They prefer to observe rather than participate. The trick here is to draw them out gently. Ask open-ended questions and make them feel safe to share without pressure. For example, "I'd love to hear your thoughts on this—what do you think?"
- **The Joker:** They crack jokes non-stop, often to the point of derailing meaningful conversations. The best way to handle a Joker is to laugh along (if it's funny), but also subtly bring things back on track. "Haha, that's a good one! But seriously, what do you think about...?"
- **The Analyzer:** They're deep thinkers and often get lost in intellectual discussions. To engage them, ask probing questions and be prepared for a deep dive. "That's an interesting point—can you elaborate more on that?"
- **The Awkward One:** This person might struggle with social cues or feel out of place. Help them by being inclusive, friendly,

and supportive. Small gestures, like smiling or making eye contact, can go a long way in making them feel comfortable.

THE ART OF CHANGING THE SUBJECT GRACEFULLY:

At some point, you'll find yourself in a conversation that's hit a dead end or, worse, veered into uncomfortable territory. Maybe someone's droning on about their collection of vintage spoons, or maybe the topic has taken a turn for the awkward. Either way, it's up to you to **change the subject** without making it obvious or awkward. Here's how you do it:

1. **Acknowledge What's Been Said:** You don't want to make the person feel like you're ignoring them or dismissing their story. Acknowledge it with a quick comment like, "That's really interesting!" or "I never knew that!" This softens the transition and shows respect.
2. **Use a Segue:** A good segue is your best friend. For example, "Speaking of collectibles, have you ever been to that quirky flea market downtown?" or "That reminds me of something I read the other day about..." This gently nudges the conversation in a new direction without a jarring shift.
3. **Ask a New, Engaging Question:** If the conversation has lost momentum, revive it with a fresh question that sparks interest. "So, I'm curious—what's the weirdest food you've ever tried?" or "If you could teleport anywhere right now, where would you go?" Fun, unexpected questions can quickly change the energy and get people talking again.

HANDLING TOUGH TOPICS WITH GRACE:

Let's be real: Not all conversations are rainbows and sunshine. Sometimes, tough topics come up—politics, religion, money, you name it. These are the conversations where things can get heated, awkward, or downright uncomfortable. So, how do you navigate these murky waters without capsizing?

1. **Stay Neutral and Curious:** If someone brings up a controversial topic, don't feel pressured to pick a side or offer a strong opinion right away. Instead, stay neutral and ask questions to understand their perspective. "That's an interesting viewpoint. How did you come to that conclusion?" This shows you're open to discussion without diving headfirst into conflict.
2. **Know When to De-escalate:** If things start to get tense, it's okay to de-escalate. You can use humour to lighten the mood ("Well, we've solved world peace—what's next?") or gently shift the topic to something lighter. Remember, it's not your job to referee every debate or keep everyone happy, but you can guide the conversation back to safer ground.
3. **Set Boundaries If Needed:** If a conversation becomes too uncomfortable or inappropriate, don't be afraid to set boundaries. A simple, "I'd rather not get into that right now," or "Let's agree to disagree on this one," is perfectly acceptable. Protecting your energy and comfort is key.

SOCIAL ANXIETY EXERCISE #4: THE "ROOM READER" DRILL:

Time for another exercise. This one is called the **"Room Reader" Drill**. The next time you're at a social event, make it your mission to read the room. Spend a few minutes observing the dynamics—who's talking, who's listening, who seems engaged, and who seems like they'd rather be anywhere else. Then, challenge yourself to adapt based on what you see. Maybe you draw in a quieter person with a question or help guide the conversation when it starts to stall.

Reflect afterward: What did you notice? How did you adapt? The more you practise this, the more it will become second nature. Soon, you'll be navigating social situations like a pro, adjusting on the fly, and leaving people thinking, "Wow, that person really gets it."

MASTERING THE SUBTLE ART OF PRESENCE:

Finally, let's talk about **presence**. Presence isn't about being the loudest or most charismatic person in the room. It's about being fully there—engaged, attentive, and responsive. When you're truly present in a conversation, people feel it. They feel heard, seen, and valued. And that's something you can't fake.

Being present means putting away distractions (yes, that includes your phone), making eye contact, and really tuning in to what's being said—not just the words, but the emotions behind them. It means being open to wherever the conversation goes, without an agenda or script. When you bring this level of presence to your interactions, you create a space where genuine connections can happen. And isn't that what this whole journey is about?

So, there you have it—another layer of social mastery added to your growing arsenal. Remember, reading the room, adapting to different personalities, and handling tough topics with grace aren't skills you master overnight. They take time, practice, and a willingness to learn from every interaction. But you're on the right track. Keep pushing those boundaries, keep experimenting, and most importantly, keep being your wonderfully introverted self. Because trust me, the world needs more of that.

CRAFTING THE PERFECT "MINI-STORY":

"But Shaurya," I hear you saying, "I'm not a natural storyteller. My life isn't that interesting!" Well, first of all, nonsense. Everyone has stories worth sharing—you just have to know how to frame them. The good news is, you don't need to be a stand-up comedian or a best-selling author to tell a good story. You just need to know the basic formula of a "**mini-story.**"

A mini-story is a short, relatable anecdote that has three simple components:

1. **The Setup:** Start by painting a quick picture of the scene. Where were you? What was happening? Keep it short—nobody needs a full backstory, just enough to set the stage.
2. **The Conflict or Twist:** This is the hook. What went wrong, or what was the surprising thing that happened? This is where you grab the listener's attention and make them want to hear more.
3. **The Punchline or Insight:** Wrap it up with a funny, thoughtful, or surprising conclusion. This is the part that sticks with people—whether it's a laugh, a "wow," or a "me too!"

Here's a quick example: "So, I'm at the grocery store the other day, right? And I'm trying to choose between two brands of almond milk, which shouldn't be a life-altering decision, but here we are. Suddenly, this guy next to me picks up a gallon of regular milk, looks me dead in the eye, and says, 'Real milk's for real men.' I just smiled and said, 'Well, I guess I'm just a fake man with great cholesterol.' And he actually laughed!"

See what happened there? Simple setup, a relatable twist (because we've all met that guy), and a punchline that turns the moment from awkward to funny. It's not Shakespeare, but it works.

FINDING STORIES IN EVERYDAY LIFE:

The beauty of storytelling is that it doesn't have to be grand or dramatic. Some of the best stories come from the most mundane moments—because they're relatable. So, start paying attention to your day-to-day life. Did something unexpected happen at work? Did you have a strange interaction with a stranger? Did you try to parallel park and end up looking like you were auditioning for a comedy sketch? These are all stories waiting to be told.

Keep a mental (or even physical) log of these little moments. Over time, you'll start to see patterns—what works, what gets a laugh, what falls flat. And remember, the goal isn't to impress anyone; it's to connect. A good story makes people feel something, whether it's amusement, empathy, or just the simple joy of a shared experience.

HOW TO USE STORIES TO CONNECT (NOT DOMINATE):

One of the biggest mistakes people make with storytelling is turning it into a one-man show. You know the type—the person who hijacks every conversation to talk about themselves, their amazing life, and their 17 near-death experiences. Don't be that person. Instead, use your stories to **build a bridge**, not a spotlight.

Here's how to do it: When you share a story, keep it brief and leave room for others to jump in. Think of it as setting the ball in a volleyball game—you're not trying to spike it every time; you're just setting it up for someone else to contribute. After your story, ask a question or make a comment that invites others to share their own experiences. For example, "That's my weird grocery store story—has anyone else had a strange encounter with a stranger recently?"

By making your story a conversation starter rather than a conversation ender, you create space for others to share, engage, and connect. And that's where the magic happens.

THE POWER OF SELF-DEPRECATING HUMOR:

Now, let's talk about one of the most underrated storytelling techniques out there—**self-deprecating humour**. If you're worried about coming across as boastful or if you just want to lighten the mood, there's no better way to do it than by poking a little fun at yourself. Self-deprecation is disarming. It shows humility, relatability, and, most importantly, confidence. Because here's the thing: People who can laugh at themselves are automatically seen as more likeable.

So, don't be afraid to share a story where you're not the hero. Maybe it's that time you confidently walked into a glass door in front of a crowd. Or when you tried to impress someone with your knowledge of wine and accidentally described a cabernet as "spicy." These moments of vulnerability make you human. They make people feel like they know you, and they create instant rapport.

The trick, of course, is balance. You don't want to turn every story into a pity party or make people think you're secretly loathing yourself. The goal is to find the humour in your own mishaps and use them to make others feel at ease. And trust me, when you're comfortable laughing at yourself, you give others permission to do the same. It's a win-win.

SOCIAL ANXIETY EXERCISE #3: THE "STORY SWAP" GAME:

Let's add another tool to your social toolkit with the **"Story Swap" Game**. Here's how it works: The next time you're in a social setting—whether it's a gathering with friends, a family dinner, or even just hanging out with a coworker—try initiating a "story swap." Start by sharing a light, funny, or interesting mini-story, then invite the other person to share one of their own.

This does two things: It creates an instant bond over shared experiences, and it gives you practise in both telling stories and listening actively. You'll find that people often love this game because it allows them to talk about themselves (which, let's face it, we all enjoy) and creates a memorable interaction. Try it out and see how it goes. The more you practise, the more you'll start to feel at home in your own stories.

WHY YOUR STORIES MATTER (EVEN IF YOU DON'T THINK THEY DO):

Finally, let's address a common fear: "What if my stories are boring?" Listen, I'm going to say this as gently as possible—**everyone thinks their stories are boring**. But that's because we live in our own heads. What's mundane to you might be fascinating to someone else. It's all about how you frame it.

The key is to tell your story in a way that highlights the universal themes—awkwardness, surprise, humour, fear, joy. These are the emotions that connect us as humans. So, stop worrying about whether your story is "good enough." If it's honest, if it's real, and if it shows a little piece of who you are, it's worth sharing.

A FINAL NOTE ON FINDING YOUR VOICE:

The more you practise storytelling, the more you'll find your own unique voice—the way you naturally convey humour, emotion, and insight. And guess what? That voice is already inside you. It just needs a little encouragement to come out and play. So, keep experimenting, keep sharing, and most importantly, keep enjoying the process. Because at the end of the day, the best conversations aren't about being perfect. They're about being human.

You've made it this far, and you're becoming quite the conversation pro. So let's wrap up Chapter 2 by diving into some advanced techniques that will turn you from a good conversationalist into a great one. Today, we'll focus on the art of **mirroring and matching**, **managing social energy**, and **closing conversations gracefully**—because, let's be real, knowing when and how to exit a conversation is just as important as knowing how to start one.

THE SCIENCE OF MIRRORING AND MATCHING:

Let's talk about one of the most fascinating psychological techniques you can use in conversation: **mirroring and matching.** This technique is about subtly reflecting the other person's body language, tone, and pace to build rapport and create a sense of connection. It's something you've probably done without even realising it—when you're talking to a friend, and you both start nodding at the same time or leaning in closer. That's mirroring.

The reason mirroring works is simple: People like people who are like them. When you mirror someone's behaviour, you're signalling, "Hey, we're on the same wavelength." It's like social super glue. But here's the trick—you want to do it naturally and subtly. If you overdo it, you'll come off like a weird mime, and that's not the vibe we're going for.

HOW TO MIRROR AND MATCH WITHOUT BEING OBVIOUS:

1. **Body Language:** If the person you're talking to is leaning back and relaxed, mirror that by also leaning back slightly. If they're leaning in and animated, match their energy by leaning in too. Small adjustments can create a big impact.
2. **Tone and Pace:** If someone is speaking quickly and excitedly, try matching their pace. If they're speaking softly and slowly, bring your tone down to match theirs. This creates a rhythm that feels comfortable for both parties.
3. **Word Choice:** Pay attention to the types of words they use. If they're using a lot of descriptive language or specific jargon, sprinkle a bit of that into your responses. It shows you're tuned in and helps bridge any conversational gaps.
4. **Facial Expressions:** If they're smiling, smile back. If they look thoughtful or serious, adopt a more neutral or contemplative expression. These micro-expressions help establish trust and make people feel understood.

Remember, the goal isn't to mimic like a parrot; it's to align yourself subtly with the other person's style. The more you practise this, the more natural it will feel, and the deeper your connections will become.

MANAGING YOUR SOCIAL ENERGY: THE INTROVERT'S SECRET WEAPON

As an introvert, one of the biggest challenges in social interactions isn't just what to say or how to behave—it's **managing your energy levels**. You see, introverts are like smartphones with a battery that drains faster in social situations. Extroverts might be those weird phones that charge up in the sunlight of social interaction, but introverts need a plan to make sure they don't burn out before they're ready to head home.

TIPS FOR MANAGING YOUR SOCIAL ENERGY:

1. **Pace Yourself:** You don't have to be "on" all the time. Give yourself permission to take small breaks. Step outside for some fresh air, head to the bathroom for a moment of peace, or just find a quiet corner where you can recharge. These little resets are crucial for maintaining your energy.
2. **Quality Over Quantity:** Focus on deeper, more meaningful conversations with a few people rather than trying to work the entire room. Not only is this more enjoyable for most introverts, but it's also less draining.
3. **Create an Exit Plan:** Have an exit strategy prepared before you arrive at an event. It's not about bailing early but about knowing your limits. When you feel your energy dipping, don't force yourself to stay longer than you're comfortable. A polite, "I've had a great time, but I've got an early morning," is all you need.
4. **Strategic Partnering:** If you're going to a social event, consider bringing along a "social buddy"—someone you're comfortable with who can help you navigate conversations and give you a break when needed. It's like having a wingman, but for introverts.
5. **Practice Self-Compassion:** Understand that it's okay to feel drained after socialising. It doesn't mean you're bad at it; it just means you're human. Give yourself the grace to recharge in

whatever way works best for you—whether that's quiet time alone, a good book, or a comforting cup of tea.

HOW TO CLOSE CONVERSATIONS GRACEFULLY:

We've all been there—stuck in a conversation that's going on just a bit too long, or maybe it's winding down naturally, and you're ready to move on, but you don't know how to end things without being abrupt. This is where the art of **gracefully closing a conversation** comes in. It's like the closing act of a play—leave them with a smile, a good impression, and a sense of completion.

Here's how to do it:

1. **Summarise and Compliment:** A great way to wrap up is to summarise something meaningful from the conversation and give a compliment. For example, "It was really interesting hearing about your trip to Japan. Thanks for sharing those stories!" This leaves them feeling appreciated and acknowledged.
2. **Offer a Future Connection Point:** If you enjoyed the conversation and want to leave the door open for future interaction, offer a specific point of connection. "Hey, let's grab coffee sometime and talk more about that project!" This makes it clear you'd like to continue the relationship.
3. **Use a Polite Transition:** If you need to move on, use a polite transition phrase like, "I don't want to keep you from mingling, but it was great chatting with you!" or "I'm going to grab a drink, but I'd love to catch up again later." This lets them know you're moving on without making it awkward.
4. **Exit with a Smile and a Thank You:** Always end with a genuine smile and a "Thank you" or "It was nice meeting you." It's simple, but it leaves a positive impression and shows you're polite and appreciative of the interaction.

THE "GRACEFUL EXIT" TECHNIQUE: WHEN YOU'RE REALLY DONE:

Sometimes, you're just done. Maybe the conversation's gone on too long, or maybe you're out of social energy. It happens. That's when you need the **"Graceful Exit" technique.** Here's how it works: Wrap up the conversation with a kind, but firm closing remark that signals it's time to part ways.

You might say something like, "I've really enjoyed our conversation, but I need to step out for a bit. Hope to see you around!" It's clear, polite, and doesn't leave any room for the conversation to drag on. The key is confidence—say it like you mean it, and they'll get the hint without feeling snubbed.

SOCIAL ANXIETY EXERCISE #5: THE "THREE EXITS" CHALLENGE:

For your final exercise of this chapter, try the **"Three Exits" Challenge**. At your next social event, practice gracefully exiting three different conversations. Use the techniques we've discussed—summarising and complimenting, offering future connection points, polite transitions, and the Graceful Exit technique.

Pay attention to how each one feels and how the other person responds. This exercise will help you get comfortable with the idea that not every conversation has to go on forever and that it's perfectly okay to move on when you need to.

WRAPPING UP CHAPTER 2: MASTERING THE ART OF HUMAN INTERACTION:

So, here we are at the end of Chapter 2, and you've covered a lot of ground. You've learned to navigate conversations with ease, read the room like a social detective, manage your energy like a pro, and exit conversations without awkwardness or guilt. These are powerful tools that can help you connect with others on a deeper level while staying true to yourself.

Remember, the goal isn't to become someone you're not. It's to refine and expand the social skills you already have, so you can feel more confident and comfortable in any situation. Keep practising, keep experimenting, and most importantly, keep having fun with it. Because the more you embrace these techniques, the more you'll discover that talking to humans isn't as alien as it seems.

You've got this. And there's a whole world of conversations out there just waiting for you.

3

Why You Should Make Friends

(Even If It's Just for the Free Pizza)

Welcome to Chapter 3, my fellow introvert adventurer! By now, you've learned how to navigate conversations, read the room like a social ninja, and gracefully exit when you've hit your social limit. You've got some solid tools under your belt, and now it's time to tackle a topic that can make even the bravest introvert break into a sweat: **making friends**.

"Wait, Shaurya," you might be thinking, "Do I really need more friends? I've got a small circle, and I like it that way." Fair point. But let's look at this from a different angle. Friends aren't just there to crowd your calendar or drag you to places you'd rather avoid—they're also the key to a richer, more fulfilling life. And yes, sometimes they come with the added bonus of free pizza. Let's explore why that matters more than you might think.

WHY FRIENDS MATTER (AND NOT JUST FOR THE PIZZA):

Friends are more than just people you hang out with; they're your support network, your confidants, and your sounding boards. They're the ones who will tell you if that new haircut actually works, who will listen to you rant about your annoying coworker, and who will split a large pizza with you at 2 a.m. when you're feeling existential. And let's not forget the scientifically backed benefits of friendship: reduced stress, longer life spans, and a boost in overall happiness. Who doesn't want a piece of that?

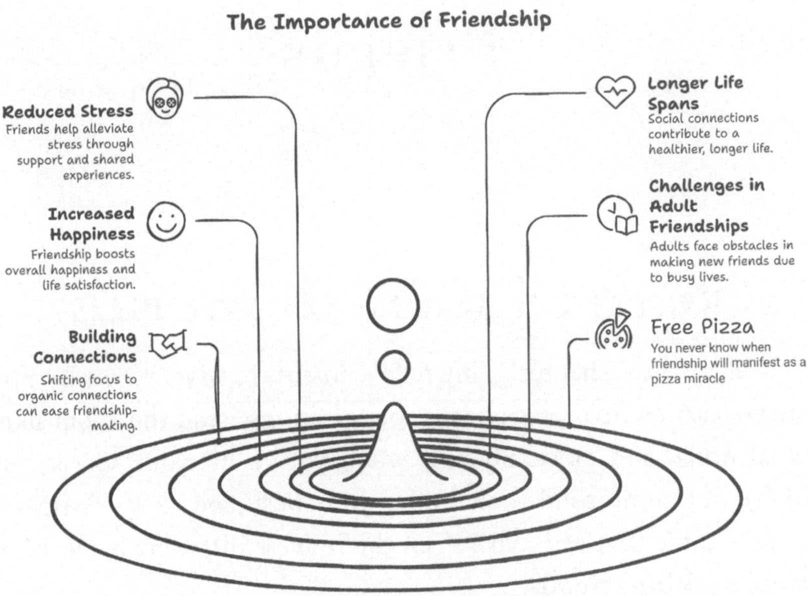

THE MYTH OF THE "BEST FRIEND":

One of the biggest barriers to making new friends is the myth that every friend has to be a **"best friend"**—you know, the person who knows all your secrets, finishes your sentences, and is basically your soulmate. Let's bust that myth right now. You don't need to find a "best friend" to have meaningful friendships. In fact, most people have different friends for different purposes. You might have a friend who's great for deep talks, another who's your go-to for concerts or hikes, and yet another who's your Netflix-and-chill buddy.

So, let's reframe our thinking. You're not out there hunting for a "best friend" like some rare Pokémon. You're simply looking to build a **diverse network** of connections that enrich your life in different ways. And guess what? That takes the pressure off. No need to worry about whether this new person is "The One" who's going to be your friend for life. Just focus on making meaningful connections in the moment, and the rest will follow naturally.

HOW TO MAKE FRIENDS WITHOUT FEELING LIKE YOU'RE SPEED DATING:

Now that we've covered the why, let's talk about the how. How do you make friends without feeling like you're on some awkward speed-dating circuit where you have to sell yourself in 30 seconds or less? Here's the secret: **Take the pressure off and focus on shared experiences.**

Shared experiences are the foundation of most friendships. Think back to your closest friends—chances are, you bonded over a shared activity, interest, or even a mutual dislike of something (like that one awful teacher in high school). So, instead of approaching new social situations with the mindset of "I need to make a friend," shift to "I'm here to have a good time and see what happens." Here are a few tips to help you do just that:

1. **Join Activities That Interest You:** Whether it's a book club, a hiking group, a cooking class, or even a board game night, choose activities that genuinely interest you. This way, you're more likely to meet people who share your interests and values. And even if you don't make a new friend right away, you're doing something you enjoy.
2. **Be a Regular:** One of the easiest ways to build connections is to become a "regular" somewhere—a coffee shop, a fitness class, a local park, you name it. Familiarity breeds comfort, and over time, you'll start to recognize faces, exchange nods, and maybe even strike up a conversation or two. It's like a slow-burn friendship waiting to happen.

3. **Start Small and Casual:** You don't need to dive into deep conversations right away. Start with small talk and gradually move to more meaningful topics as you get more comfortable. Think of it like peeling an onion—layer by layer, without making anyone cry.
4. **Be Open to Unexpected Friendships:** Sometimes, the best friendships come from the most unexpected places. Maybe you strike up a conversation with the person sitting next to you at the dentist's office, or you bond with a colleague over a shared love of bad puns. Stay open to these opportunities—you never know where they might lead.

THE POWER OF BEING VULNERABLE (IN SMALL DOSES):

Okay, let's talk about something that makes most people squirm: **vulnerability**. I know, I know—just hearing the word might make you want to close this book and hide under a blanket. But hear me out. Vulnerability doesn't mean spilling your deepest, darkest secrets to every new person you meet. It means being open, honest, and real.

People are drawn to authenticity. When you're willing to share a bit about yourself—whether it's a funny story about your most embarrassing moment or a genuine comment about a challenge you're facing—it creates a space for others to open up too. It's like giving them permission to let their guard down. And that's where true connections are made.

Start small. Share a little, see how it feels, and gauge the other person's response. If they're receptive, share a bit more. If not, no worries—move on. The goal isn't to force vulnerability, but to create a space where it can naturally happen.

HOW TO AVOID THE TRAP OF "FRIENDSHIP FOMO":

Friendship FOMO (Fear of Missing Out) is real, and it can be a huge barrier to making friends. You see people on Instagram with their perfectly curated friendship circles, and you start thinking, "Why don't I have that?" or "Am I missing out on something?" But here's the thing—real friendships aren't Instagram-perfect. They're messy, they take time, and they don't always come with a hashtag.

Avoid the trap of comparing your social life to someone else's highlight reel. Focus on building genuine, meaningful connections, not on how it looks from the outside. Remember, quality always trumps quantity when it comes to friendships. One solid, reliable friend is worth more than a dozen superficial acquaintances.

SOCIAL ANXIETY EXERCISE #1: THE "FRIENDSHIP FROYO" APPROACH:

Here's a fun exercise to help you dip your toes into making new friends without feeling overwhelmed. I call it the **"Friendship Froyo" Approach**. Just like you would when choosing toppings for your frozen yoghurt, start small and add layers. Don't go for everything all at once; pick a few social opportunities that feel comfortable and see how they go.

For example, choose one event this month where you can meet new people—a class, a social gathering, or even an online meetup. Set a small goal for yourself, like talking to three new people or having one meaningful conversation. Keep it light, keep it fun, and most importantly, don't stress. You're just sampling, not committing.

EMBRACING THE "SLOW BURN" OF ADULT FRIENDSHIPS:

Finally, let's talk about the "slow burn" of adult friendships. Unlike childhood friendships that form quickly and intensely, adult friendships often take longer to develop. And that's okay! Don't rush the process. Let things unfold naturally, and remember that it's perfectly normal for friendships to grow slowly over time. Keep showing up, keep engaging, and let the connections build organically.

The goal isn't to fill your life with people; it's to fill it with **the right people**—those who make you feel good, who support you, and who you can genuinely connect with. And when you find those people, hold on to them. They're worth their weight in free pizza.

So, here we are at the beginning of your friendship-building journey. Remember, this isn't about transforming yourself into a social butterfly; it's about finding ways to connect with others that feel authentic and meaningful to you. Start small, be open, and most importantly, be yourself. Because at the end of the day, the best friendships are built on honesty, vulnerability, and a little bit of fun.

You've got this. Now go out there and find your people—one slice of pizza at a time.

Alright, friendship explorer, let's continue our journey into the art of building meaningful connections. Now that we've discussed the importance of friendship and how to dip your toes into new social waters without feeling like you're about to drown, let's focus on the next steps: **nurturing those budding friendships and turning them into something lasting**.

HOW TO NURTURE NEW FRIENDSHIPS WITHOUT FEELING LIKE A STALKER:

So, you've met someone new, had a good conversation, and maybe even bonded over a shared interest in true crime podcasts or a mutual disdain for pineapple on pizza. Congrats! Now comes the tricky part: How do you take this initial connection and turn it into a real friendship without coming across like you're auditioning for a role in a stalker film?

The key here is to **pace yourself and follow the flow**. Remember, friendships are like plants. You don't dump a bucket of water on them and expect them to flourish overnight. You nurture them slowly, a little bit at a time. Here's how to do it:

1. **Follow Up Casually:** After your initial meeting, don't be afraid to follow up with a casual message or comment. Something like, "Hey, I really enjoyed our chat the other day! Would love to continue it sometime—maybe over coffee?" Keep it light, keep it casual, and avoid putting any pressure on them to respond right away.
2. **Find Common Ground for Future Hangouts:** If you bonded over a shared interest, use that as a launching pad for future plans. "I saw there's a trivia night coming up next week—want to team up and see how much random knowledge we actually have?" This way, you're not just suggesting another hangout; you're giving it a purpose.
3. **Gauge Their Interest Level:** Pay attention to how they respond to your follow-up. Are they enthusiastic? Polite but noncommittal? If they seem genuinely interested, great! If they're lukewarm, don't take it personally. Not everyone is looking for new friends at the same time or at the same pace. Move on and keep the door open without pushing.
4. **Use Social Media Wisely:** Social media can be a great way to stay connected and get to know someone better without being too intrusive. If you're already connected online, comment on their posts occasionally or share something relevant to a past conversation. Just don't overdo it—no one wants a constant notification from someone they've only just met.

THE ART OF BEING A "LOW-MAINTENANCE" FRIEND:

In the adult world, where everyone's juggling careers, relationships, and Netflix binges, there's one thing that most people appreciate: a **low-maintenance friend**. A low-maintenance friend is someone who doesn't require constant attention or daily check-ins but is still there when it counts. They don't guilt-trip you for not texting back immediately or make you feel bad for needing space. They understand that life happens.

Becoming a low-maintenance friend doesn't mean being distant or uninterested; it means respecting boundaries, understanding that people have their own lives, and not taking it personally when someone needs time to themselves. Here's how to master the art:

1. **Keep It Light:** Not every conversation needs to be deep or profound. It's okay to keep things light and easy. A quick meme share or a "Hey, I thought of you when I saw this" text can keep the friendship warm without requiring a lengthy back-and-forth.
2. **Be Flexible:** Be open to rescheduling or changing plans without making a fuss. Life is unpredictable, and sometimes things come up. A simple, "No worries, let's catch up another time!" shows that you're understanding and easygoing.
3. **Reach Out Periodically:** Every now and then, check in with a friendly message. It doesn't have to be anything major—just a "Hey, how have you been?" to show you're thinking of them. This keeps the connection alive without being overwhelming.
4. **Be There When It Matters:** While being low-maintenance means not needing constant contact, it also means showing up when it counts. If your friend is going through a tough time or needs support, be there. That's when true friendships are forged.

NAVIGATING THE "FRIEND ZONE" (THE GOOD KIND):

Let's clarify something here: The "friend zone" isn't a bad thing. In fact, it's exactly where you want to be when building platonic friendships. But navigating the dynamics of friendship, especially when you're not sure where the boundaries lie, can feel like walking a tightrope. Here's how to keep things clear and comfortable:

1. **Be Honest and Open:** If you're worried about mixed signals or unclear intentions, be upfront about what you're looking for. A

simple "Hey, I'm really enjoying getting to know you as a friend" can set the tone without making things weird.

2. **Avoid Overthinking Every Interaction:** Not every message or hangout is loaded with hidden meaning. Trust the flow of the friendship and take things at face value. If something feels off, address it directly rather than letting it fester.
3. **Respect Boundaries:** Everyone has different comfort levels when it comes to friendship. Some people are more touchy-feely; others are more reserved. Pay attention to these cues and respect them. Friendships thrive on mutual respect.

HOW TO KEEP FRIENDSHIPS FRESH AND FUN:

Once you've established a new friendship, the challenge becomes keeping it fresh and fun. Nobody wants to fall into the trap of "same old, same old" where every interaction feels like a repeat of the last one. Here's how to keep things interesting:

1. **Try New Activities Together:** Whether it's a cooking class, a hike, or even just checking out a new restaurant, shared experiences are what create lasting memories. Don't be afraid to mix it up and suggest something neither of you has done before.
2. **Celebrate the Small Stuff:** Don't wait for birthdays or major life events to celebrate. Celebrate the small wins—the new job, the first successful DIY project, or even just surviving a rough week. It's these small celebrations that add colour to the friendship.
3. **Share Your Weird Side:** Everyone has a weird side. Maybe you have an obscure hobby or a collection of cat-themed socks. Sharing these quirks can deepen the friendship and lead to inside jokes that only the two of you understand. Embrace the weird!
4. **Create a Tradition:** Establishing a tradition, like a monthly movie night or a Saturday morning coffee run, gives you both

something to look forward to and builds a sense of continuity in the friendship.

THE REALITY OF FRIEND BREAKUPS (AND WHY THEY'RE OKAY):

Here's a hard truth: Not all friendships last forever. Sometimes, people grow apart, interests change, or life simply takes you in different directions. And that's okay. Friend breakups can be tough, but they're a natural part of life. The key is to handle them with grace and without drama.

If you sense that a friendship is fizzling out, don't force it. Let things drift naturally, and if the time comes to part ways, do so with kindness. It's not about burning bridges; it's about recognizing that sometimes, people are only meant to be in our lives for a certain chapter, and that's perfectly fine.

SOCIAL ANXIETY EXERCISE #2: THE "FRIENDSHIP INVENTORY" CHALLENGE:

Here's another exercise to keep you moving forward in your friendship-building journey: **The "Friendship Inventory" Challenge**. Take some time to think about your current friendships. Are there any that feel like they've run their course? Are there new ones you'd like to nurture more? Make a list of three friends you'd like to reconnect with or spend more time with, and reach out to them. Set a small goal—like meeting up for coffee or sending a thoughtful message—and see how it goes.

BUILDING FRIENDSHIPS THAT LAST:

And there you have it—some practical tips for nurturing new friendships, keeping them fresh, and knowing when to let go. Remember, friendships aren't about quantity; they're about quality. It's better to have a few meaningful, supportive connections than a dozen acquaintances who barely know you.

So, keep nurturing those friendships. Be open, be real, and don't be afraid to let things unfold naturally. Because the best friendships are the ones that feel effortless—like two puzzle pieces that just fit.

You're doing great, and the best is yet to come. Keep going, and soon you'll find yourself surrounded by the right people who make life a little brighter, one slice of pizza at a time.

Now that you're navigating the tricky waters of making and nurturing new friendships, it's time to address one of the biggest barriers to building those meaningful connections: **your own inner monologue**. Yes, that little voice in your head that loves to remind you of how awkward you are, how you're "not good at this," or how everyone is probably judging you. Spoiler alert: They're not. Most people are too busy worrying about their own awkwardness to notice yours.

MASTERING THE ART OF BEING YOURSELF WITHOUT OVERTHINKING IT:

We've all been there—replaying a conversation in our heads over and over, wondering if we said the wrong thing or if we came off as weird. But here's the thing: **the more you try to control how you're perceived, the less authentic you become**. And authenticity is what real friendships are built on. So, how do you master the art of being yourself without driving yourself crazy with overthinking?

1. **Embrace Your Awkwardness:** We're all awkward. The truth is, there's no such thing as a "perfect" person who never says the wrong thing or never has an awkward moment. Instead of trying to hide your quirks, own them. They're what make you, you. Next time you feel like you've said something awkward, laugh it off. Self-deprecating humour can be a powerful tool for disarming tension and showing others that you're comfortable with who you are.
2. **Stop Apologising for Your Existence:** One of the most common mistakes introverts make in social situations is apologis-

ing—constantly. "Sorry for talking too much," "Sorry for being late," "Sorry for... breathing?" Enough already! Unless you've genuinely done something wrong, there's no need to apologise for simply being yourself. Confidence comes from within, and it starts with recognizing that you have as much right to take up space and be heard as anyone else.

3. **Shift the Focus:** Instead of focusing on yourself and how you're being perceived, shift your focus to the other person. Ask questions, be genuinely curious, and engage in active listening. Not only does this take the pressure off you, but it also makes the other person feel valued and understood. And guess what? People love talking to someone who actually listens.
4. **Practise "Mindful Socialising":** Mindful socialising is about being present in the moment rather than lost in your own head. If you find yourself spiralling into overthinking, take a deep breath, ground yourself in the present, and remind yourself that most conversations aren't life-or-death situations. Give yourself permission to be imperfect.

GETTING COMFORTABLE WITH SILENCE: THE POWER OF THE PAUSE:

One of the greatest fears of introverts in social situations is **the dreaded awkward silence**. You're having a great conversation, and then suddenly... crickets. What do you do? Panic? Fill the silence with nonsensical chatter? Laugh nervously? None of the above!

Here's a radical idea: **Silence is okay**. In fact, it can be powerful. When you're comfortable with silence, it shows confidence. It means you're not afraid of pauses and don't feel the need to fill every moment with words. This, in turn, allows the conversation to flow more naturally. Here's how to get comfortable with silence:

1. **Pause for Effect:** Before rushing to fill a silence, take a moment to pause and gather your thoughts. This not only gives

you a chance to consider your response but also signals to the other person that you're actually thinking about what they've said. It's a subtle but effective way to show that you're engaged and thoughtful.

2. **Give Space for Reflection:** Sometimes, silence is a good thing. It gives both you and the other person time to reflect on what's been said and consider how to respond. Instead of seeing silence as a problem, see it as an opportunity for deeper connection.
3. **Practise Active Listening:** When you're truly listening to someone, rather than thinking about what you're going to say next, you'll find that silences feel less awkward. They're simply a natural part of the conversation, like a breath in a dance.
4. **Let Go of the Need to Impress:** Silence often feels awkward when you're trying too hard to impress the other person. But here's the secret: People aren't looking for perfection; they're looking for real. Letting go of the need to constantly impress allows you to relax and be yourself, awkward pauses and all.

HOW TO "READ THE ROOM" LIKE A PRO:

One of the most underrated social skills is the ability to "read the room"—that is, to pick up on the energy, mood, and dynamics of a social situation. It's the difference between knowing when to tell a joke and when to stay silent, when to share a personal story and when to listen. Reading the room is like social navigation; it helps you steer the conversation in the right direction. Here's how to do it:

1. **Observe Body Language:** People's body language often speaks louder than their words. Are they leaning in or away? Do they seem engaged or distracted? Are they crossing their arms or maintaining open posture? By observing these subtle cues, you can gauge whether it's a good time to dive deeper into a topic or change the subject.

2. **Pay Attention to Tone:** The tone of a conversation can change in an instant. If you notice the mood getting tense or someone becoming uncomfortable, it might be time to steer the conversation to safer waters. On the flip side, if people are laughing and smiling, it's a sign that they're open and receptive.
3. **Test the Waters with Small Comments:** If you're unsure how to proceed in a conversation, try making a small comment or observation and see how it's received. If the other person responds positively, you know you're on the right track. If not, it's a sign to pivot.
4. **Know When to Exit Gracefully:** Sometimes, the best thing you can do is recognize when a conversation has run its course. Rather than dragging things out or forcing more interaction, it's okay to exit gracefully. A simple, "This has been great, but I should probably get going—let's catch up again soon!" leaves things on a positive note.

THE INTROVERT'S GUIDE TO HANDLING SMALL TALK LIKE A PRO:

Small talk: two words that strike fear into the heart of many an introvert. But here's the truth—**small talk doesn't have to suck**. In fact, it's a crucial part of building new connections and transitioning into deeper conversations. Think of small talk as the appetiser before the main course. Here's how to make it work for you:

1. **Prepare a Few Go-To Topics:** Having a few go-to topics in your back pocket can ease the pressure of coming up with conversation starters on the fly. These could be anything from "Have you watched any good shows lately?" to "What's the most interesting thing you've read recently?" Keep it light and easy.
2. **Ask Open-Ended Questions:** Avoid questions that can be answered with a simple "yes" or "no." Instead, opt for open-ended questions that invite more than one-word responses. For ex-

ample, "What do you do for work?" can lead to a dead end, but "What do you enjoy most about what you do?" invites more depth.

3. **Find Common Ground:** Pay attention to what the other person seems enthusiastic about, and latch onto that. If they mention a hobby, interest, or recent experience, use it as a springboard for further conversation. Shared interests are the gateway to deeper connections.
4. **Don't Fear the Awkward Moments:** Small talk can sometimes feel awkward, and that's okay. Everyone experiences it. Rather than trying to avoid it, embrace it with humour. A well-timed "Well, that's not awkward at all" can lighten the mood and put both you and the other person at ease.

SOCIAL ANXIETY EXERCISE #3: THE "SMALL TALK MARATHON" CHALLENGE:

Here's another exercise to push you out of your comfort zone: **The "Small Talk Marathon" Challenge**. The next time you're in a social setting—whether it's a coffee shop, a networking event, or even a grocery store—set a goal to engage in small talk with at least three different people. It could be as simple as complimenting someone's outfit, asking for a recommendation, or making an observation about your surroundings. The goal is to practise and get more comfortable with spontaneous interactions.

OVERCOMING OVERTHINKING AND EMBRACING YOUR AUTHENTIC SELF:

So there you have it—tools for overcoming the crippling curse of overthinking, getting comfortable with silence, reading social cues like a pro, and mastering the art of small talk. Remember, the key to becoming a social ninja isn't to become someone you're not; it's to become the most confident, authentic version of yourself. Keep practising, keep pushing yourself out of your comfort zone, and most importantly, keep laughing through the awkward moments.

Your journey to becoming a socially savvy extrovert is well underway, and the best is yet to come. You're doing amazing—now let's keep going and conquer the world, one conversation at a time!

Alright, friend-builder, you've got this far and are diving deep into mastering the art of friendship. By now, you know how to make those initial connections, how to nurture them without overthinking, and how to handle the small talk marathon without breaking a sweat. Now, let's talk about a critical aspect of building meaningful friendships: **setting boundaries**.

THE POWER OF SETTING BOUNDARIES (WITHOUT BEING A JERK):

"Boundaries? Aren't those for relationships and work?" you might be wondering. Well, here's the reality: **Boundaries are the foundation of any healthy relationship, including friendships**. They're not about shutting people out; they're about ensuring you keep your sanity intact and protect your energy. As an introvert, you know how precious your alone time is. The key is learning how to communicate your needs without coming off as aloof or uninterested.

Think of boundaries as the rules of your personal playground. If you don't set them, people might end up running wild, unknowingly stepping on your toes. But when you communicate your boundaries clearly, you create a space where everyone knows how to play nicely together. So, how do you set boundaries without sounding like you're putting up walls? Here are some tips:

1. **Be Clear and Direct (But Kind):** When setting a boundary, clarity is key. Be straightforward but gentle. Instead of saying, "I don't want to hang out all the time," try, "I love hanging out, but I also need some time to recharge. How about we plan for

next week?" This communicates your needs without making it sound like you're pushing them away.

2. **Offer Alternatives:** If you're not up for a night out, suggest something more low-key that aligns with your energy level. "I'm not feeling up for a big night, but I'd love to grab a coffee and chat this weekend." This shows you still value friendship while honouring your limits.
3. **Use "I" Statements:** Avoid making it about the other person. Instead of "You're always texting me too much," try, "I need to take some time to unplug and recharge every now and then." This keeps the focus on your needs rather than making it feel like an accusation.
4. **Stick to Your Boundaries:** Setting a boundary is one thing; sticking to it is another. If you've communicated that you need a quiet weekend, don't let guilt or pressure change your mind. Respecting your own boundaries teaches others to respect them too.

HOW TO DEAL WITH "FRIENDSHIP GUILT":

One of the biggest challenges when setting boundaries is dealing with the inevitable **friendship guilt**. You know the feeling: "Am I being too harsh?" "What if they think I don't like them?" "What if I hurt their feelings?" Relax. Boundaries are a sign of a healthy, mature relationship. If someone can't respect your boundaries, that says more about them than it does about you.

Here's how to deal with friendship guilt:

1. **Remember Your "Why":** Remind yourself why you're setting this boundary in the first place. Whether it's to protect your energy, focus on personal growth, or simply recharge, keep in mind that your well-being is important.
2. **Be Empathetic, Not Apologetic:** It's okay to acknowledge that the boundary might be disappointing for the other person, but

don't apologise for it. "I get that it might be a bummer, but I really need some downtime this weekend. I hope you understand."

3. **Reframe the Narrative:** Instead of thinking, "I'm letting them down," think, "I'm setting a standard for how I want to be treated." Healthy boundaries are about mutual respect and understanding, not about feeling bad for prioritising yourself.
4. **Trust Your Gut:** If something doesn't feel right, it probably isn't. Trust yourself to know when and where to draw the line. Good friends will understand, and those who don't? Maybe they weren't the right fit in the first place.

THE IMPORTANCE OF RECIPROCAL FRIENDSHIPS:

Now, let's talk about something crucial: **reciprocity**. A healthy friendship is a two-way street. It's about giving and receiving, supporting and being supported. If you find yourself constantly giving—whether it's your time, energy, or emotional support—and not getting much in return, it's time to evaluate the balance of the friendship.

Here's how to spot and build reciprocal friendships:

1. **Notice the Balance:** Do you feel like the friendship is balanced, or do you often feel drained after hanging out? A good friendship leaves you feeling fulfilled, not exhausted. Pay attention to whether your needs are being met too.
2. **Communicate Your Needs:** If you feel the balance is off, don't be afraid to speak up. "I've noticed I'm always the one reaching out. I'd love it if you could initiate our next hangout!" is a great way to nudge things toward reciprocity without sounding accusatory.
3. **Give What You'd Like to Receive:** Want more meaningful conversations? Start one. Want more support? Offer it. Healthy friendships are mirrors—they reflect what you put into them.

4. **Know When to Walk Away:** If you've tried to balance the scales and it's still not working, it's okay to step back. Some friendships are seasonal, and that's alright. Focus on those that bring value and joy to your life.

HOW TO MAKE FRIENDS IN A DIGITAL AGE:

In today's world, making friends isn't limited to in-person interactions. In fact, some of the strongest friendships are built in the digital space. But online friendships come with their own set of rules. Here's how to navigate them:

1. **Join Online Communities:** Whether it's a Facebook group, a subreddit, or a Discord server, online communities are a great way to meet like-minded people. Look for groups that align with your interests—books, gaming, fitness, whatever makes you tick.
2. **Engage Genuinely:** Don't just lurk—participate! Comment on posts, share your thoughts, and engage in conversations. The more active you are, the more you'll stand out and start building connections.
3. **Move Beyond Text:** If you've built a good rapport with someone online, don't be afraid to suggest a video chat or even an in-person meetup (when safe and appropriate). Taking things beyond text helps solidify the friendship.
4. **Be Cautious and Safe:** While online friendships can be incredibly fulfilling, it's also important to be mindful of your safety. Trust your instincts, don't share personal information too soon, and meet in public spaces if you decide to meet in person.

MANAGING FRIENDSHIP DYNAMICS IN GROUP SETTINGS:

Group friendships can be a lot of fun—until they're not. Sometimes dynamics shift, cliques form, or drama arises. Here's how to navigate group friendships like a pro:

1. **Be Inclusive:** If you're in a group setting, make sure everyone feels included. Use open body language, direct questions to quieter members, and avoid inside jokes that exclude others.
2. **Stay Neutral in Conflicts:** Group dynamics can get messy, especially when conflicts arise. If you find yourself caught in the middle, try to stay neutral and avoid taking sides. Encourage open communication and be a peacemaker without inserting yourself too deeply.
3. **Respect Individual Relationships:** Just because you're part of a group doesn't mean you can't have individual friendships within it. It's okay to have closer bonds with some members than others, as long as you respect the group dynamic.
4. **Know When to Step Back:** If a group friendship becomes toxic or starts to drain you, it's okay to step back. Your well-being comes first, and sometimes that means removing yourself from a situation that no longer serves you.

SOCIAL ANXIETY EXERCISE #4: THE "DIGITAL FRIENDLINESS" CHALLENGE:

Here's a challenge to help you build more connections online: **The "Digital Friendliness" Challenge**. Over the next week, commit to engaging more in an online community or group that interests you. Start conversations, respond to comments, and even message someone whose posts you enjoy. The goal is to practise initiating digital friendships and see where they lead.

THE JOURNEY TO BALANCED, HEALTHY FRIENDSHIPS:

Building meaningful friendships isn't just about finding the right people—it's about being the right person, too. It's about setting boundaries, managing dynamics, and being authentic, whether online or offline. Remember, the best friendships are built on mutual respect, understanding, and a little bit of fun.

You're well on your way to creating a circle of friends who lift you up, challenge you, and share life's ups and downs with you. Keep going, keep growing, and remember—you're not just building friendships. You're building a community that feels like home.

Here we are, ready to wrap up Chapter 3 with a bang. You've come a long way in understanding the ins and outs of friendship—how to make new friends, nurture them without overthinking, set healthy boundaries, and even manage the wild west of online and group dynamics. Now, it's time to address one last piece of the puzzle: **keeping friendships strong over time**.

Friendships, like any relationship, require maintenance. You can't just set them on autopilot and expect them to thrive. But here's the good news: the "maintenance" doesn't have to feel like work. In fact, it can be one of the most rewarding parts of having friends. Let's explore some practical, fun ways to keep your friendships healthy, happy, and full of life.

THE MYTH OF EFFORTLESS FRIENDSHIPS:

Let's bust a myth right off the bat: **No friendship is truly effortless**. Even those friendships that seem "meant to be" require some level of care and attention. The idea that friendships should just magically sustain themselves without any effort is not only unrealistic but can lead to disappointment. The reality is, like any relationship, friendships need a bit of nurturing.

But here's the kicker: nurturing friendships doesn't have to be some grand gesture or time-consuming task. It's often the small, consistent efforts that make the biggest difference—like sending a funny meme, checking in after a tough week, or simply being present. The goal isn't to exhaust yourself trying to be the "perfect friend"; it's about showing up, being real, and being there when it counts.

HOW TO KEEP FRIENDSHIPS FRESH (EVEN WHEN LIFE GETS BUSY):

Life gets busy. We get it. Between work, family, personal growth, and, you know, sleeping, it can be hard to find time to keep up with friends. But the key is to find small, sustainable ways to stay connected. Here's how:

1. **Schedule Regular Check-Ins:** You don't need to be in constant contact to have a strong friendship, but regular check-ins can help keep the bond strong. Whether it's a monthly coffee date, a bi-weekly phone call, or a quick text here and there, set a rhythm that works for both of you. Make it a point to catch up, even if it's just a quick "How's life treating you?" message.
2. **Embrace "Micro-Moments" of Connection:** Not every interaction has to be a long, deep conversation. Sometimes, it's the little moments that matter most—a quick voice memo, a funny gif, or a "Saw this and thought of you" text. These micro-moments of connection help maintain the friendship without requiring a big time commitment.
3. **Celebrate Their Wins:** Whether it's a new job, a promotion, or simply making it through a tough week, take time to celebrate your friend's wins. It doesn't have to be elaborate; a simple "Congrats! I'm proud of you!" goes a long way. This not only shows you're paying attention but that you genuinely care about their happiness.
4. **Be Understanding When Things Get Busy:** Life happens. People get busy, overwhelmed, or caught up in their own stuff. When a friend isn't as available as usual, don't take it personally.

Instead, offer understanding and let them know you're there when they're ready to reconnect.

THE POWER OF "FRIEND DATES":

Yes, "friend dates" are a thing—and they're awesome. Just like you'd plan a date with a romantic partner, setting aside time for a "friend date" can do wonders for your friendship. Here's why:

1. **It's a Dedicated Time to Connect:** Unlike casual hangouts or random texts, a friend date is intentional. It's a dedicated time to connect, catch up, and focus on each other without distractions. Whether it's trying a new restaurant, hiking, or just chilling at home with Netflix, it's the quality time that counts.
2. **It Keeps Things Fresh:** Trying new activities together can keep the friendship feeling fresh and exciting. It could be something as simple as cooking together or as adventurous as skydiving (if that's your thing). The key is to create shared memories that strengthen the bond.
3. **It Shows You Value Friendship:** When you make an effort to plan a friend's date, it sends a message that you value the friendship and are willing to invest time in it. It's a simple gesture that can have a big impact.

HOW TO NAVIGATE CHANGES IN FRIENDSHIPS:

As we grow and evolve, so do our friendships. And sometimes, that means friendships change—whether it's due to moving to a new city, life changes like marriage or kids, or simply growing in different directions. Navigating these changes can be tricky, but it's all part of the journey. Here's how to handle it with grace:

1. **Acknowledge the Change:** If you notice a shift in your friendship, don't ignore it. Acknowledge it and talk about it openly. "I've noticed we haven't been hanging out as much

lately—everything okay?" This shows you care and are open to adapting.

2. **Adapt to New Dynamics:** Sometimes, friendships don't end; they just shift. Maybe you're not seeing each other every weekend like you used to, but you're still keeping in touch through calls or texts. Adapting to new dynamics doesn't mean the friendship is less meaningful—it's just evolving.
3. **Let Go of Resentment:** If a friend's life is pulling them in a different direction, don't take it as a personal rejection. People change, and that's okay. Instead of holding onto resentment, focus on the good memories and remain open to reconnecting in the future.
4. **Know When to Let Go:** Occasionally, a friendship may naturally come to an end. If a friendship feels one-sided, toxic, or no longer adds value to your life, it's okay to let go. Wish them well, cherish the memories, and make space for new friendships that better align with where you are now.

KEEPING FRIENDSHIPS STRONG ACROSS DISTANCES:

Thanks to technology, staying in touch with friends across distances is easier than ever. But it still requires some effort. Here's how to keep those long-distance friendships strong:

1. **Schedule Virtual Hangouts:** Virtual hangouts are a great way to keep the connection alive, whether it's a Zoom call, a FaceTime chat, or even a virtual game night. Make it a regular thing and stick to it.
2. **Send Snail Mail Surprises:** Everyone loves getting something in the mail that isn't a bill. Send a handwritten letter, a postcard, or a small care package. It's a thoughtful gesture that can brighten their day and show you're thinking of them.
3. **Stay in the Loop:** Make an effort to stay updated on what's happening in each other's lives. Whether it's through social

media, a shared photo album, or a quick text update, it helps you feel involved even when you're miles apart.

4. **Be Honest About the Challenges:** Long-distance friendships aren't easy, and it's okay to acknowledge that. Be honest about the challenges and work together to find ways to keep the friendship strong.

SOCIAL ANXIETY EXERCISE #5: THE "FRIENDSHIP FOLLOW-UP" CHALLENGE:

For your final exercise of this chapter, try the **"Friendship Follow-Up" Challenge**. Over the next month, pick three friends—old or new—that you'd like to reconnect with or strengthen your bond with. Reach out to them with a thoughtful message, a fun plan, or just a genuine check-in. See how they respond and use this as a way to practise maintaining friendships with intention.

THE ART OF LASTING FRIENDSHIPS:

And that brings us to the end of Chapter 3! By now, you've got a solid grasp of how to make, nurture, and maintain meaningful friendships that add value to your life. Remember, friendships aren't about perfection—they're about connection, effort, and mutual respect. Keep putting yourself out there, keep being authentic, and most importantly, keep enjoying the ride. Because the best friendships aren't just about having someone to share a pizza with; they're about having someone who makes life a little brighter, one laugh at a time.

You've got all the tools you need. Now go out there and build those lasting connections!

4

How to Be the Life of the Party

(Without Dreading Every Second)

Welcome to Chapter 4, my socially ambitious introvert! By now, you've mastered the art of conversation, built some solid friendships, and learned how to navigate the social world with confidence and authenticity. But now, it's time to tackle a beast that's been haunting introverts since the dawn of time: **parties.**

Yes, parties—the bustling gatherings full of people, noise, and endless small talk. The kind of events that make you secretly wish you could teleport back to the comfort of your own home with a cup of tea and a good book. But hear me out: you don't have to dread parties. In fact, with a few tricks up your sleeve, you can learn to enjoy them—or at least not hate them. So, let's dive in and learn how to be the life of the party without losing your sanity.

REFRAMING THE PARTY NARRATIVE:

First things first: Let's reframe how we think about parties. Most introverts approach parties with a sense of impending doom, picturing themselves trapped in a sea of extroverts who all seem to know each other. But here's the truth: **a party is just a series of smaller**

interactions happening in the same space. And you're already great at handling those smaller interactions.

Instead of thinking of a party as a big, overwhelming event, think of it as a collection of potential opportunities—opportunities to meet new people, deepen existing friendships, and maybe even surprise yourself by having fun. The key is to manage it on your terms.

PRE-PARTY PREP: SETTING YOURSELF UP FOR SUCCESS:

Like any great adventure, a successful party experience starts with preparation. And no, I'm not talking about planning your escape route (though it's good to have one just in case). I'm talking about **mental and physical preparation** to set yourself up for a good time.

1. **Set a Positive Intention:** Before heading out, take a moment to set a positive intention for the night. Instead of thinking, "Ugh, I just want to survive this," try, "I'm going to have at least one interesting conversation tonight" or "I'm going to focus on enjoying myself, not on impressing anyone." This shifts your mindset from survival mode to opportunity mode.
2. **Dress for Confidence:** Wear something that makes you feel comfortable and confident. It doesn't have to be flashy or super stylish—just something that makes you feel like the best version of yourself. When you feel good in your skin, it's easier to relax and engage.
3. **Have a Social Toolkit Ready:** Come armed with a few conversation starters, interesting anecdotes, or fun facts. This way, you're not caught off guard when someone asks, "So, what have you been up to?" It's like having a cheat sheet for social interactions.
4. **Decide on Your "Party Energy Level":** Be honest with yourself about how much energy you have to give. If you're feeling low on social energy, set a goal to engage meaningfully with a

few people rather than trying to meet everyone. If you're feeling more energetic, maybe challenge yourself to start a group conversation or join in a game.

NAVIGATING THE PARTY LIKE A PRO:

Once you've arrived at the party, it's game time. But don't worry—you've got this. Here's how to navigate the party like a pro without feeling like you're out of your element:

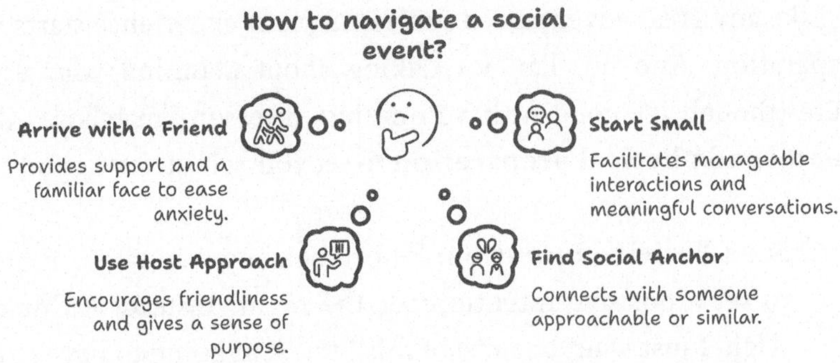

THE POWER OF THE "PARTY BUDDY" SYSTEM:

If you're nervous about attending a party, consider using the **"Party Buddy" system**. A party buddy is someone you attend the event with who knows your social style and can help you navigate interactions. Here's how to make it work:

1. **Agree on Signals:** Establish a few discrete signals for "help me out" or "let's move on." This way, you can support each other without needing to say anything awkward out loud.
2. **Divide and Conquer:** Don't just stick together the whole time. Split up occasionally and mingle separately, then reconvene to share stories or regroup if needed.
3. **Introduce Each Other to New People:** Use each other to branch out and meet new people. "Hey, have you met my friend? They have the best story about..." This way, you're both

expanding your social circles without feeling like you're alone in the crowd.

HOW TO TURN SMALL TALK INTO MEANINGFUL CONVERSATIONS:

We've covered the basics of small talk, but parties offer a unique opportunity to turn those surface-level interactions into something deeper. Here's how:

1. **Use the "Two-Step" Approach:** Start with a simple small talk question, and then follow up with a more open-ended, thought-provoking question. For example, start with, "How do you know the host?" then follow up with, "What's the most memorable party you've ever been to?"
2. **Share Personal Insights:** Don't be afraid to share a little bit about yourself in conversations. "I'm always curious about what draws people to events like this—I'm here trying to step out of my comfort zone a bit." This opens up the floor for others to share their experiences and creates a more personal dialogue.
3. **Look for "Conversation Sparkers":** Pay attention to what people get excited about when they talk. Is it their recent trip? A new hobby? Their weird obsession with collecting vintage board games? Use these sparks to dive deeper and explore those topics further.
4. **Stay Open and Curious:** The best conversations happen when you're genuinely interested in the other person. Ask follow-up questions, show genuine enthusiasm, and listen more than you speak. People love talking to those who make them feel heard.

HOW TO RECHARGE YOUR SOCIAL BATTERY WITHOUT LEAVING:

Even if you're having a good time, you may find your social battery running low. That's completely normal, especially for introverts. Here's how to recharge without leaving the party:

1. **Take a Bathroom Break (Even If You Don't Need One):** The bathroom is the universal safe haven at parties. Take a few minutes to breathe, regroup, and recharge before diving back in.
2. **Step Outside for Fresh Air:** If possible, step outside for a breath of fresh air. The change of environment can help reset your energy and prepare you to re-engage.
3. **Find a "Quiet Corner":** Every party has a quieter corner where you can retreat and take a breather. Grab a drink, people-watch, and enjoy a few moments of calm.
4. **Engage in Low-Energy Activities:** If the party has low-energy options, like a game or a quiet area to sit and chat, take advantage of them. This allows you to keep engaging without draining yourself too much.

SOCIAL ANXIETY EXERCISE #1: THE "PARTY PRACTICE" PLAN:

Here's your first exercise for Chapter 4: **The "Party Practice" Plan**. The next time you're invited to a party or social gathering, make a plan using the tips above. Set a specific goal, like "I will start a conversation with three new people" or "I will use the 'Host Approach' technique at least once." Write down your intention, visualise yourself doing it successfully, and then put it into action. The goal is to build confidence and see parties as opportunities rather than obstacles.

FINDING YOUR FUN AT PARTIES:

Congratulations! You've just armed yourself with a toolkit for navigating parties like a seasoned pro. Remember, the goal isn't to become the loudest person in the room or to force yourself into uncomfortable situations. It's about finding your own way to enjoy these social experiences, one conversation at a time. So, the next time you get invited to a party, go in with an open mind, a positive attitude, and maybe a friend or two for backup. Who knows? You might just find that parties aren't so bad after all.

You've got this—one party at a time!

Now that you've learned how to prepare for a party and navigate the social scene like a pro, it's time to explore how to **engage more deeply** and become someone people genuinely enjoy being around. Let's talk about how to develop that magnetic quality that draws people in without feeling like you're trying too hard or stepping outside of who you really are.

HOW TO MAKE AN IMPACT WITHOUT BEING THE LOUDEST IN THE ROOM:

The myth that you need to be the loudest, most outgoing person to make an impact at a party is just that—a myth. You don't need to dominate conversations or be the centre of attention to be memorable. In fact, many of the most engaging people are those who know how to make others feel seen, heard, and valued. Here's how you can do that:

1. **Be Genuinely Interested in Others:** The most magnetic people aren't the ones who talk about themselves nonstop—they're the ones who ask great questions and really listen to the answers. Make the conversation about the other person. Ask about their passions, their opinions, and their stories. "What's something you're passionate about that most people don't

know?" is a question that can lead to some unexpectedly meaningful conversations.

2. **Bring Positive Energy:** You don't need to be the life of the party, but bringing a positive attitude goes a long way. Smile, make eye contact, and show enthusiasm when you're talking to someone. People are naturally drawn to positive energy—it makes them feel good, and it makes you more approachable.
3. **Share a Good Story or Two:** We've talked about the art of storytelling in previous chapters, and parties are the perfect place to put that into practice. Have a couple of engaging, funny, or thought-provoking stories ready to share when the moment feels right. Remember to keep them concise and interactive—leave room for others to jump in and share their own experiences.
4. **Use Names and Remember Details:** People love hearing their names and knowing that you remember little details about them. If you've met someone before, try to recall something specific about your last conversation and mention it. "Hey, Sarah! Last time we talked, you mentioned you were starting a new job. How's that going?" This small gesture shows that you were genuinely paying attention and that you value the connection.

MASTERING GROUP CONVERSATIONS WITHOUT GETTING LOST IN THE MIX:

Group conversations at parties can be tricky—especially when there's a lot of energy and multiple people vying for attention. It's easy to get lost in the mix or feel like you're not contributing enough. But here's how you can stay engaged and make an impact without feeling overwhelmed:

1. **Lean in with Body Language:** Nonverbal cues are powerful in group settings. Leaning in slightly, nodding, and maintain-

ing eye contact with whoever is speaking shows that you're engaged and interested. It's a subtle way to participate even if you're not the one talking.

2. **Use the "Echo and Expand" Technique:** When someone shares a point, "echo" it by briefly summarise what they said, then "expand" on it by adding your own thought or question. For example, "I totally agree with what John said about travel—it really opens your mind. I'm curious, though, what's the most surprising place you've visited?" This keeps the conversation flowing and shows that you're actively listening.
3. **Don't Be Afraid to Jump In (Respectfully):** Group conversations can be fast-paced, and sometimes, waiting for the perfect pause means you'll never get a word in. If you have something to contribute, jump in when there's a natural gap. Just be mindful not to interrupt someone mid-sentence.
4. **Ask Questions to Pull Others In:** If you notice someone in the group hasn't spoken much, pull them into the conversation with a direct, open-ended question. "What do you think about this, Alex?" or "Has anyone else had a similar experience?" This makes you a facilitator of the discussion and shows you're considerate of everyone's voice.

HOW TO HANDLE PARTY ANXIETY IN REAL-TIME:

Even with all the prep and positive intentions, anxiety can still creep up on you mid-party. Maybe you start feeling overwhelmed by the noise, the crowd, or the sheer number of interactions. The key is to have a few **real-time anxiety management strategies** up your sleeve:

1. **Practice Grounding Techniques:** If you feel your anxiety rising, try a simple grounding technique. Focus on your senses—identify five things you can see, four things you can touch, three things you can hear, two things you can smell, and

one thing you can taste. This helps bring you back to the present moment and calm your mind.

2. **Take "Mini Breaks" as Needed:** You're not obligated to stay in the thick of things the entire time. Excuse yourself to grab a drink, use the bathroom, or step outside for some fresh air. These mini breaks give you a chance to reset and recharge before diving back in.
3. **Redirect Your Focus:** Shift your focus from "What are people thinking of me?" to "How can I make someone else feel comfortable?" This simple shift can help reduce self-consciousness and anxiety by giving you a new purpose—being a positive force for others.
4. **Have a "Party Buddy" Check-In:** If you're attending with a friend, agree to check in with each other periodically throughout the party. It's a nice way to reset, share a laugh, and keep each other grounded.

WHEN AND HOW TO MAKE A GRACEFUL EXIT:

Let's face it—sometimes, you've just had enough. You've socialised, mingled, and now your social battery is flashing red. There's no shame in recognizing when it's time to go. But how do you exit without it being awkward or coming off as rude? Here's how to make a **graceful exit**:

1. **Wait for a Natural Lull:** Look for a natural break in the conversation or a moment when things start to wind down. This is the perfect time to excuse yourself without interrupting the flow.
2. **Keep It Short and Sweet:** You don't need to make a grand announcement or give a long-winded explanation. A simple, "Hey, I'm going to head out—thanks for a great time!" works perfectly. You can add a personal touch by saying goodbye individually to those you've connected with.

3. **Express Genuine Gratitude:** If you're leaving early, especially if the host is a friend, be sure to thank them for inviting you. A quick, "Thanks for having me—I really enjoyed it!" leaves things on a positive note.
4. **Leave the Door Open for Future Plans:** If you've had a good time or met someone interesting, leave the door open for future plans. "We should definitely grab coffee sometime and continue this conversation!" is a great way to signal that you're interested in staying connected.

WHY YOUR PARTY PRESENCE MATTERS (EVEN IF YOU'RE NOT THE STAR):

You might still be wondering, "Why bother? I'm not going to be the star of the party anyway." But here's the thing—**your presence matters more than you think**. Being at a party isn't about outshining everyone else; it's about contributing to the atmosphere, building connections, and being part of the experience. You never know who you might meet, what conversations you might have, or what fun you might stumble upon when you're open to the possibilities.

Your unique style—whether it's calm and composed or quietly humorous—adds value to the mix. And when you show up with an open mind and a genuine interest in others, you become the kind of person people want to be around. You don't need to be the loudest to make an impact; sometimes, the most memorable people are the ones who simply bring their authentic selves to the table.

SOCIAL ANXIETY EXERCISE #2: THE "SILENT STAR" CHALLENGE:

This exercise is all about making an impact without being the centre of attention: **The "Silent Star" Challenge**. At the next party or social event you attend, challenge yourself to focus less on what you say and more on how you listen and engage. Set a goal to ask at least five open-ended questions, be the most attentive listener in the room, and see how people respond. You might be surprised at how much presence you can have by simply being genuinely interested in others.

MAKING YOUR PRESENCE FELT WITHOUT THE SPOTLIGHT:

And there you have it—tools and strategies to help you make your mark at any party without needing to be the loudest or most extroverted person in the room. Remember, it's not about changing who you are; it's about embracing your unique style and finding ways to connect that feel true to you. So, go out there, be present, be real, and most importantly—have fun. You might just find that parties have more to offer than you ever imagined.

You're doing amazing. Let's keep the momentum going and see where this journey takes us next!

courageous social explorer! You're now armed with the tools to dive into conversations and navigate the chaos of group dynamics like a seasoned extrovert. Today, we're stepping it up a notch—we're talking about how to **build a magnetic presence** that makes people think, "Who is this delightful, low-key interesting human, and where have they been all my life?"

No, you don't need to transform into a 24/7 dance machine or a cocktail-concocting stand-up comedian. Let's get into how to find the balance between being memorable and maintaining your sanity.

1. THE ART OF BECOMING MEMORABLE WITHOUT BECOMING A MEME:

Alright, let's get one thing straight. Being memorable at a party isn't about pulling outrageous stunts or becoming "that guy" who does something wild and regrettable (we've all seen that episode). It's about **making authentic connections** and bringing a unique twist to the social mix. Here's how you do it without feeling like you're losing yourself:

- **Share Your Quirks, Don't Hide Them:** One of the greatest myths is that you need to conform to some "social norm" to fit in. Wrong! Your quirks—those little things that make you, well, you—are what set you apart. Maybe you have an odd fascination with conspiracy theories or you can talk about bird-watching like it's an Olympic sport. Whatever it is, bring it into your conversations. People love to learn new things and hear different perspectives, and it makes you more memorable.
- **The Power of the Callback Joke:** This is one of the oldest tricks in the book, but it works like a charm. If someone says something funny or memorable early in the night, "call back" to it later. For instance, if someone mentions they have a fear of ducks, later on, you might say, "Well, at least there aren't any ducks here, right?" It's a lighthearted way to show you were paying attention, and it keeps the fun alive.
- **Be the "Connector":** Be the person who introduces people to each other. "Hey, Sam, meet Lisa—she's also a huge Game of Thrones fan!" or "Alex, this is Jake—he's been to Japan like you!" This not only makes you memorable as the social glue of the evening but also spreads the attention around and takes the pressure off you.

2. NAVIGATING THE FOOD AND DRINK TABLE LIKE A PRO:

Alright, we need to talk about the food and drink situation at parties. This might seem trivial, but think about it: the kitchen or snack area is where a lot of social magic happens. Here's your guide to **making the most of these spaces**:

- **The Food Table is Your Friend:** It's the perfect place to engage in small talk without feeling awkward. "Have you tried these? They're amazing!" or "I think I could eat a whole tray of these mini quiches" are simple conversation starters that work surprisingly well. Plus, people naturally gravitate towards food, so you're in a prime spot to meet new folks.

- **Offer to Help Refill or Set Up:** If you're at a house party, offering to help out is a great way to engage with people in a low-pressure way. "Need a hand with those drinks?" or "I can help refill the chips!" gets you involved without needing to force a conversation. It's a small gesture that shows you're approachable and considerate.
- **Balance Your Drink in One Hand:** Ever notice how people with a drink in one hand seem more comfortable at parties? It's because it gives you something to do with your hands. Keep your other hand free for handshakes or gestures—this creates a more open and inviting body language.

3. MASTERING THE "LEAVE THEM WANTING MORE" PRINCIPLE:

One of the greatest secrets of becoming someone people remember fondly is to **leave the party on a high note**. When you exit a party while people are still enjoying your company, you become a positive memory rather than "that person who stayed way too long." Here's how to apply this principle:

- **The "Irish Exit" (With a Twist):** The Irish Exit—leaving without saying goodbye—is a controversial move. But there's a way to do it with finesse. If you've made a good connection, a quick text after you leave like, "Hey, had a great time chatting! Let's catch up soon!" maintains the vibe without awkward goodbyes.
- **Make It a Quick Goodbye Tour:** If you're not into stealthy exits, keep your goodbyes short and sincere. Don't make it a big production. "Had a blast—see you all soon!" or "Thanks for a fun night, catch you next time!" does the job just fine.

- **Leave a Lasting Impression:** Give the host or someone you had a meaningful conversation with a specific compliment. "Thanks for hosting, Anna. I really enjoyed our chat about travel—let's keep in touch!" leaves a more personal touch.

4. BUILDING A REPUTATION AS "THE FUN INTROVERT":

Now, if there's one thing I want you to take away from this chapter, it's this: **Introverts can be the most fun people at a party**. Yes, I said it. I'm not just saying this to make you feel better; it's true. Introverts bring depth, thoughtfulness, and often a wickedly good sense of humour that flies under the radar. Here's how to build this reputation:

- **Be the "Occasional Wildcard":** Every so often, do something unexpected. It doesn't have to be grand—maybe you lead a game of charades, suggest a fun drinking game, or drop an unexpectedly funny comment that catches everyone off guard. It's about surprising people who might underestimate you.
- **Be the "Calm in the Chaos":** Parties can get wild, and not everyone enjoys that. Be the person others can retreat to for a more chill conversation. This balance of being approachable but also interesting is a unique strength.
- **Curate Your Own Party Moments:** Rather than waiting for the "right moment" to happen, create it. Start a small group activity—whether it's a guessing game, a "two truths and a lie" circle, or even suggesting a change of scenery like moving to a quieter spot for deep chats.

5. POST-PARTY SOCIAL STRATEGY: KEEPING THE MOMENTUM GOING:

Congratulations, you made it through the party and maybe even had a good time! But the fun doesn't have to stop there. Here's how to **follow up and keep the connections going**:

- **Send a Simple Follow-Up Message:** After the party, send a quick message to anyone you genuinely connected with. "Hey, it was great meeting you last night! Let's grab coffee sometime" or "Loved chatting with you about [insert topic]—let's keep in touch!" keeps the momentum alive.
- **Add People on Social Media (Strategically):** If you meet someone you'd like to know better, adding them on social media is a low-pressure way to stay connected. Don't be the person who adds everyone at the party, though. Focus on quality over quantity.
- **Host Your Own Event:** Consider hosting a small get-together yourself, even if it's just inviting a couple of new acquaintances for a board game night or a low-key dinner. It gives you more control over the environment and deepens connections in a setting you're comfortable with.

SOCIAL ANXIETY EXERCISE #3: THE "HOST WITH THE MOST" EXPERIMENT:

Here's an exercise for you, if you're feeling particularly daring: **The "Host with the Most" Experiment**. Start small—host a small gathering of friends and maybe one or two new people you've met. Keep it low-key and relaxed, something you'd enjoy. Observe how it feels to be in control of the social dynamics and build connections in a setting that suits you. It's a great way to practise your social skills in a more controlled, comfortable environment.

BUILDING YOUR MAGNETIC PRESENCE (YOUR WAY):

And there you have it—more tools to help you not just survive, but thrive, in the party scene. You're not trying to become someone else; you're simply leveraging your natural strengths and adding a bit of flair to the mix. You're learning that being memorable isn't about volume or showmanship—it's about authenticity, engagement, and knowing how to play the social game on your terms.

Keep showing up, keep experimenting, and keep finding joy in the unexpected. You're doing better than you think, and there's still so much more to discover.

You're cruising now, party master! You've learned how to bring your unique brand of fun to the mix, balance your energy, and make a lasting impression—all without having to fake extroverted theatrics. Now let's move on to another crucial aspect of thriving in social situations: **knowing when to shift gears** and **finding joy in the party's quieter moments.**

While high-energy parties are great for some, not every part of the night needs to be filled with loud laughter and dancing. The truth is, some of the best connections happen in those quieter, in-between moments—the ones introverts are often more naturally inclined to enjoy. Let's get into how to **make the most of these calmer times** and **connect deeply, even in a party environment**.

1. HOW TO THRIVE IN THE "CHILL ZONES" OF THE PARTY:

Every party has its "chill zones"—those quieter corners of the room where people sit down for a break, chat one-on-one, or engage in more relaxed activities. These areas are your goldmine for more meaningful connections. If high-energy activities aren't your thing, these spaces can be where you shine.

- **Find Your Corner:** Scan the room and identify a quieter spot—maybe it's near the snacks, on a patio, or a cosy corner of the living room. These spaces often attract people who, like you, want a break from the noise and small talk. Positioning yourself here increases the chance of having more engaging, thoughtful conversations.

- **Create Your Own Calm:** If the whole party feels a bit chaotic, don't be afraid to **create your own calm space**. Grab a drink, find a place to sit, and let others come to you. You'd be surprised how many people will follow your lead if they see someone who looks relaxed and approachable. It's almost like setting up an unofficial "Introverts' Lounge."
- **Use the Power of One-on-One Chats:** One of the best things about quieter zones is that they're perfect for one-on-one conversations. Parties tend to scatter attention, but these moments are where you can truly connect with someone. Ask deeper questions, share stories, and dive into topics that matter. These are the conversations that stick with people long after the party ends.

2. NAVIGATING AWKWARD SILENCES LIKE A CHAMP:

Ah, the awkward silence. It's the moment when you're mid-conversation, and suddenly... nothing. Crickets. For many, this is panic-inducing, but it doesn't have to be. In fact, introverts often excel at handling silences with grace because we're not always in a rush to fill them.

- **Embrace the Pause:** Awkward silences aren't awkward unless you make them awkward. Instead of rushing to fill the gap, take a breath and let it be. Silence can give the other person space to think or even redirect the conversation. Often, these pauses allow for more meaningful dialogue to emerge.
- **Ask a New, Thoughtful Question:** When the silence lingers a bit too long, have a few thoughtful questions ready to shift gears. Try something unexpected but still light, like, "What's

something you're really passionate about that most people wouldn't know?" or "What's one thing you've always wanted to try but haven't yet?" These questions spark interesting conversations and shift the mood naturally.

- **Acknowledge the Silence with Humor:** If the pause starts to feel awkward, call it out with a bit of humour. "Well, we nailed that awkward silence, didn't we?" Acknowledging it with a smile helps ease the tension and shows you're comfortable with the natural ebb and flow of conversation.

3. HOW TO BUILD DEEPER CONNECTIONS IN A PARTY ATMOSPHERE:

Parties are often seen as light, breezy events meant for mingling and fun, but that doesn't mean you can't build **deeper connections** in the process. It just takes a little intention and some well-timed conversation pivots.

- **Look for Moments to Go Beyond Small Talk:** Not every conversation needs to stay on the surface. If you're chatting with someone and they mention something that sparks your curiosity, don't be afraid to dig a little deeper. "You mentioned you love photography—what got you into it?" or "You said you just moved here. How are you finding the transition so far?" Going beyond the usual "What do you do?" questions can turn a simple chat into a memorable exchange.
- **Be Open About Your Own Interests:** It can be tempting to play it cool at parties and keep things light, but don't be afraid to share your own interests, especially if the conversation opens up naturally. Whether it's your love of hiking, your latest creative project, or even something nerdy (hey, nerdy is awesome!), being genuine about your passions is one of the best ways to build rapport.

- **Find Common Ground:** People connect most deeply over shared experiences and values. If you find common ground—whether it's a love for a certain type of music, a shared career path, or even mutual feelings about the party scene—capitalise on it. You don't need to force it, but highlighting those shared experiences builds a foundation for future interactions.

4. KNOWING WHEN IT'S TIME TO "RECHARGE" (AND HOW TO DO IT GRACEFULLY):

You're killing it at the party, but then it hits you—that familiar feeling of social exhaustion. As an introvert, knowing when to step back and recharge is critical to enjoying a social event without burning out. Here's how to recognize when it's time for a break and how to do it without disappearing altogether:

- **Listen to Your Energy Levels:** The first sign that it's time to recharge is when you start to feel overstimulated, tired, or just a bit "off." Don't ignore these feelings. Instead, listen to them and take action before you hit full burnout mode.
- **Step Away Without Disappearing:** You don't have to make a grand exit or hide in the bathroom for the rest of the night. Simply excuse yourself for a bit—grab some air outside, find a quiet spot, or take a long route to the kitchen for a water refill. These mini-breaks can help you reset without leaving the party entirely.
- **Give Yourself Permission to Leave Early (If You Need To):** If you've hit your limit and staying any longer would drain you completely, it's okay to leave. Be kind to yourself. Simply say a few quick goodbyes, thank the host, and head home. Remember, it's better to leave while you're still enjoying yourself than to stay too long and leave feeling exhausted.

5. MAKING A LASTING IMPRESSION (EVEN IN A SHORT INTERACTION):

You don't need to dominate the entire party to make a lasting impression. Sometimes, the smallest interactions can be the most impactful. Here's how to leave a mark, even if you're only having a few short conversations:

- **Be Present in Every Interaction:** Whether you're talking to someone for five minutes or thirty, be fully present. Listen attentively, ask thoughtful questions, and engage with what the person is saying. When people feel heard, they remember you fondly.
- **End Conversations on a High Note:** If you're wrapping up a conversation, leave it on a positive note. Compliment the person on something specific or mention something you genuinely appreciated about the interaction. "It was really great talking to you about [topic]—I learned something new!" leaves them feeling good about the exchange.
- **Follow Up Later:** If you connected with someone at the party, don't let the connection fade. Send a follow-up text or message afterward to solidify the bond. It can be something as simple as, "Hey, it was great meeting you at the party! Let's catch up again soon." These small actions go a long way in turning a one-time chat into a potential friendship.

SOCIAL ANXIETY EXERCISE #4: THE "ONE MEANINGFUL CONVERSATION" CHALLENGE:

For this exercise, your goal is to focus on **having one meaningful conversation** at the next party you attend. Rather than trying to meet everyone or be in the middle of every group, focus on connecting deeply with just one person. Ask thoughtful questions, share something personal, and see where the conversation goes. Afterward, reflect on how it felt to prioritise quality over quantity in your social interactions.

FINDING YOUR CALM IN THE CHAOS:

Parties don't always have to be high-energy or overwhelming. In fact, some of the best moments come from the quieter corners, the one-on-one conversations, and the moments where you can just be yourself. As an introvert, these are the moments where you can truly thrive and leave a lasting impact, all without needing to be the loudest voice in the room.

Remember, it's not about pushing yourself to fit into the party scene—it's about finding your way to enjoy it. Whether that's connecting with one person deeply or enjoying a few quiet moments to recharge, you've got the tools you need to make any social situation your own.

You're doing amazing—one meaningful connection at a time.

Alright, you've mastered the art of balancing your energy, diving into deeper conversations, and creating meaningful connections even in the chaos of a party. Now, for the final touch, let's focus on one of the most critical aspects of socialising: **leaving a positive, lasting impression**—not by being the loudest, but by being the person people want to keep around.

This page is all about taking what we've learned and turning it into sustainable, real-world practices that help you build your social reputation as someone who's always fun to have around—on your own terms. It's not about being the centre of attention but about being the person who makes others feel good just by being there.

1. HOW TO BE THE "EASYGOING" FRIEND EVERYONE WANTS TO INVITE:

You don't have to be a party animal to get invited to every social event—trust me. Being the "easygoing" person is often even better because people love hanging out with someone who brings a calm, positive vibe to the mix. Here's how to become that friend:

- **Be Low-Maintenance:** Nobody wants to feel like they have to entertain you all night or worry about whether you're having fun. One of the best things you can do is bring an easygoing attitude to every event. Even if the party isn't exactly your vibe, make the most of it. Have a couple of fun conversations, try the food, and engage with whoever's nearby. When you're adaptable and chill, people notice—and they'll want you around more often.
- **Say Yes (When You Can):** This doesn't mean you should say yes to every single invitation, but try to push yourself to accept social invites even when your instinct is to stay home. Show up when you can, and people will see you as someone who's engaged and part of the group—even if you only stay for a little while.
- **Contribute Something (Even if It's Small):** Offering to bring something to the party, whether it's a bottle of wine, snacks, or even helping the host with setup or clean-up, goes a long way in making you the kind of guest people appreciate. It's a simple gesture, but it shows that you're thoughtful and considerate.

2. BECOMING THE MASTER OF FOLLOW-UP:

One of the most underrated social superpowers is the ability to **follow up** after an event. It doesn't have to be elaborate, but a little message or action after a party can strengthen bonds and keep connections alive. Here's how you can master the art of following up:

- **Send a Quick Message to the Host:** If you've had a good time at a party, don't underestimate the power of sending a quick thank-you message to the host afterward. "Hey, thanks for having me—had a great time!" is simple but shows appreciation.

Hosts remember who makes the effort to thank them, and it'll make them more likely to invite you to future events.

- **Reconnect with New People:** If you've met someone new at a party and had a good conversation, don't let that connection fade. Reach out within a couple of days with something personal. "Hey, great meeting you at the party! I'd love to grab coffee sometime and chat more about [shared topic]." This cements the connection and opens the door for more meaningful friendships.
- **Follow Up on Conversations:** If someone mentioned an interest or project they're working on, follow up later. "Hey, you mentioned you were working on that art project—how's it going?" or "I just listened to that podcast you recommended—it was awesome!" It shows that you were genuinely engaged and that you care about continuing the conversation.

3. THE ART OF GIVING GENUINE COMPLIMENTS:

Here's a little secret: people **love** people who make them feel good. One of the easiest ways to leave a lasting positive impression is to master the art of giving **genuine compliments**. I'm not talking about over-the-top flattery—just simple, sincere observations that brighten someone's day. Here's how to do it:

- **Be Specific:** Instead of vague compliments like "You're so nice" or "That's cool," focus on something specific. "I love your energy—you really brought a lot of life to the conversation" or "You have great taste in music. I'm adding that band to my playlist tonight!" Specific compliments feel more personal and thoughtful.
- **Focus on Qualities, Not Just Looks:** Complimenting someone's physical appearance is fine, but it's even more impactful when you acknowledge qualities, talents, or efforts. "You have such a great way of making everyone feel included" or "I really

admire how passionate you are about [insert topic]" shows that you're paying attention to who they are, not just how they look.

- **Don't Overdo It:** A genuine compliment here and there goes a long way, but if you're constantly showering people with compliments, it can start to feel insincere. Make it natural—offer them when they genuinely come to mind, and they'll have a greater impact.

4. HOW TO KEEP FRIENDSHIPS ALIVE BETWEEN SOCIAL EVENTS:

One of the challenges of socialising as an introvert is keeping friendships alive **between events**. You might enjoy the time spent at a party, but what about all the time in between? Here's how to maintain connections without feeling overwhelmed:

- **Stay in Touch (Without Being Overwhelmed):** You don't need to be in constant contact to maintain a friendship. A quick message every now and then to check in or share something interesting (an article, a meme, or a podcast) is enough to keep the connection going. It's about quality, not quantity.
- **Suggest Low-Key Hangouts:** If you'd like to spend more time with someone but don't want to jump into another big event, suggest something low-key like grabbing coffee, going for a walk, or watching a movie. These smaller, more intimate hangouts are often more manageable for introverts and allow for deeper connections.
- **Be Honest About Your Social Energy:** If you need time to recharge, it's okay to say so. You can let friends know that while you're not always available to hang out, you value the friendship and will catch up when you can. "I'm laying low for a bit, but let's catch up soon!" keeps the door open without making you feel pressured.

5. LEARNING TO ENJOY SOCIAL WINS (NO MATTER HOW SMALL):

One of the things we often forget to do is to **celebrate our social wins**. Whether it's making a new connection, starting a meaningful conversation, or just surviving a party without wanting to run for the door—it's worth celebrating! Here's how to acknowledge your own progress:

- **Acknowledge the Small Wins:** Even if you didn't talk to everyone at the party or stayed longer than you planned, celebrate the small victories. Maybe you had a great conversation with one person, or maybe you tried something new, like joining a group chat. These small steps add up and build your social confidence.
- **Reflect on Your Growth:** Take a moment after each social event to reflect on how you've grown. What went well? What did you enjoy? What could you improve on? Reflection helps you track your progress and makes socialising feel more rewarding.
- **Give Yourself Credit:** Socialising as an introvert takes effort. Don't be hard on yourself if things don't go perfectly. Celebrate the fact that you put yourself out there—that alone is worth acknowledging.

SOCIAL ANXIETY EXERCISE #5: THE "COMPLEMENT AND CONNECT" CHALLENGE:

Here's a fun, final challenge to wrap up Chapter 4: **The "Complement and Connect" Challenge**. At the next social event you attend, challenge yourself to give two genuine, specific compliments to people you meet. It could be something about their energy, their interests, or even something simple like their style. The goal is to make a connection through kindness and leave a lasting positive impression.

Afterward, reflect on how those compliments were received. Did it open up new conversations? Did it make you feel more confident in your social interactions? Practise this at future events and watch how it transforms the way people respond to you.

CELEBRATING YOUR SOCIAL JOURNEY:

You've done it! By now, you've gained the skills to not just survive social events, but to truly thrive in them. You've learned how to manage your energy, create meaningful connections, and leave a lasting positive impression—without ever needing to sacrifice your authentic self.

Remember, it's not about being the loudest, the most extroverted, or the life of the party in the traditional sense. It's about bringing your own strengths—your depth, your curiosity, your calm energy—into social situations and making them work for you.

So, as you continue on this journey, take pride in how far you've come. Each conversation, each new connection, and each party is a step toward becoming more confident in your social abilities. You're building a reputation as someone who's fun to have around, someone people trust, and someone who knows how to make the most out of any situation.

You've got this. Keep going, keep growing, and most importantly, keep enjoying the ride.

5

How to Handle Extroverts – A User Manual

Alright, let's face it—extroverts are everywhere. You probably have at least one in your life, and while their energy may sometimes feel like it's on a completely different frequency from yours, extroverts have a lot to offer. They're social butterflies who can effortlessly navigate any room, make friends in seconds, and somehow seem to thrive in situations that make you want to run for the hills. But here's the thing: you can learn to **handle** them—and dare I say, **even enjoy** them.

This chapter is your go-to guide for understanding these wild creatures known as extroverts and how you, the introverted marvel that you are, can survive (and even thrive) around them without losing your mind.

UNDERSTANDING THE MIND OF AN EXTROVERT:

To deal with extroverts effectively, it helps to understand what's going on in their minds. While you, dear introvert, recharge in the calm solitude of your own company, extroverts recharge through social interaction. To them, parties, meet-ups, and even random run-ins at the grocery store are energy-boosting, fun-filled experiences.

The key thing to remember? **It's not personal**. When your extroverted friend wants to hang out *again*, it's not that they're ignoring your need for downtime—they simply don't realise how different your energy system works. It's like they're solar-powered, and you run on quiet, well-placed battery charges.

1. STRATEGIES FOR SURVIVING THEIR BOUNDLESS ENERGY:

So, how do you deal with someone whose energy level rivals that of a five-year-old on a sugar high? Here's a breakdown:

- **Set Boundaries Early:** The most important tool in your survival kit is setting clear boundaries. Extroverts will invite you to every social event they hear about—and probably some they just make up on the spot. It's okay to say no. In fact, it's essential. You can set expectations early on by saying something like, "I'd love to hang out, but I need some alone time to recharge. How about we catch up next week instead?"
- **Embrace the "15-Minute Rule":** If you get roped into an event, give yourself permission to leave after 15 minutes if you're not feeling it. Sometimes, knowing you can exit whenever you need to makes it easier to stay longer. And often, once you're there, it's not as bad as you anticipated.
- **Tag Along, But on Your Terms:** If your extrovert friend insists on bringing you to their 8,000th social gathering of the month, try tagging along but with a personal limit. For example, tell yourself, "I'll go, but I'm only staying for an hour." You can engage for a little while, then gracefully retreat when your social battery hits red.

2. THE EXTROVERT'S "NEED TO SHARE" (EVERYTHING) – HOW TO MANAGE IT:

Extroverts love to talk—and I mean *love* to talk. They'll happily tell you about their latest project, their vacation plans, their new favourite restaurant, and that random person they met on the subway yesterday. It's not that they're self-centred; it's just how they process information—they talk it out. But, if you're not careful, it can feel like you're stuck in an endless monologue.

Here's how to manage it:

- **Practise Active Listening:** I know, this sounds like the opposite of what you want when someone is talking your ear off, but here's the trick—**active listening doesn't mean long listening**. It's about focusing on the key points, nodding, and showing you're engaged. You don't have to catch every single detail. This way, you can be present without feeling overwhelmed.
- **Redirect the Conversation (When Needed):** If your extrovert friend is dominating the conversation and you're feeling drained, politely shift the topic. "That's really interesting! Hey, what do you think about [insert new topic here]?" This keeps the conversation moving without letting it stay in one energy-draining place for too long.
- **Use the "Bathroom Escape Hatch":** Classic but effective. If things get too intense, you can always say, "Excuse me for a moment" and take a bathroom break to reset. No one will question a bathroom break, and it gives you a few precious minutes of silence to recharge.

3. LEARNING TO LOVE (OR AT LEAST TOLERATE) THEIR SOCIAL NATURE:

Now, for the part you're probably dreading: learning to appreciate the extrovert in your life. Believe it or not, extroverts can actually make life more fun for introverts—when managed correctly.

- **Let Them Be the Social Buffer:** One of the best things about having extroverted friends is that they can handle the social legwork for you. They'll introduce you to people, keep the conversation going, and carry the interaction when your energy is dipping. You can just sit back and let them do the heavy lifting.

- **Lean Into Their Positivity:** Extroverts are great at bringing up the energy in a room. If you're feeling down or anxious, spending a little time with an extrovert can help lift your spirits—just don't let it go on too long. It's like jumping into a pool of warm water; it's fun for a while, but eventually, you'll want to get out.
- **Pick Your Moments to Engage:** You don't need to match your extrovert friend's social energy all the time. Save your energy for moments when you really want to be social. For example, attend a fun dinner or party they're hosting, but skip the back-to-back bar hopping. Balance is key.

4. REAL-LIFE EXAMPLES OF EXTROVERT/INTROVERT FRIENDSHIPS:

It's not just theory—extrovert/introvert friendships work, and they work well. Here are a few real-life examples that show how these dynamics can create lasting, meaningful connections:

5. EMBRACING THE DIFFERENCES (AND NOT LETTING THEM DRIVE YOU CRAZY):

At the end of the day, extroverts and introverts just process the world differently. The more you understand and embrace these differences, the easier it becomes to enjoy their company without getting overwhelmed.

- **Let Them Be Themselves:** Trying to change an extrovert is like trying to stop a train with your bare hands—it's not going to happen. Instead of wishing they'd be quieter or less intense, appreciate their energy for what it is. It doesn't mean you need to match it, but accepting it makes the relationship smoother.
- **Accept Your Own Needs:** Just as extroverts thrive on social interaction, you thrive on solitude. Own it. There's nothing wrong with needing alone time after a hangout. Make it clear to your extroverted friends that you'll be back once you've recharged. They'll appreciate your honesty, and you'll avoid burnout.

Now, I understand that being around extroverts can feel like navigating a theme park where the rides are just too fast, too loud, and somehow... never-ending. But here's the thing — extroverts aren't trying to exhaust you on purpose. They're just wired differently. Imagine that, for them, social interaction is like a phone charger, and every conversation, every group gathering, is like a boost to their battery. Meanwhile, you're sitting there, watching your own social battery drain faster than you can say, "I'm going to the bathroom," and considering not coming back.

But here's the kicker: you don't have to become an extrovert to handle one. Nope, the goal is to understand them, maybe even admire their *boundless* energy (at least in small doses), and learn a few tricks to survive their social tornado.

STRATEGY 1: THE ART OF SELECTIVE ENGAGEMENT

Extroverts thrive on engagement. They throw out ideas, ask questions, and they *really* want to hear from you. Now, the introvert's knee-jerk reaction might be to retreat — to listen passively or to just nod while mentally preparing an escape route. But here's a little secret: extroverts don't need you to talk non-stop, they just need to know you're there. It's about participating when it counts.

So how do you handle this? Engage selectively. Give them a solid contribution when the moment strikes. Say something like, "That's an interesting point," or ask a genuine question. They'll latch onto that nugget of conversation like it's gold. You can then sit back and enjoy watching them run with it.

Real-life example:

Picture this. You're at a friend's party, and your extroverted buddy is explaining his grand plan to become a YouTube sensation by reviewing... obscure types of cheese. You're not exactly excited about it, but you know if you just humour him with one well-placed question—"What's the weirdest cheese you've tried?"—he'll happily monologue for the next ten minutes, leaving you free to sip your drink in peace. It's a win-win!

STRATEGY 2: SET BOUNDARIES LIKE A PRO

If you're an introvert, you probably have a "people limit." That's not a bad thing — in fact, knowing when you've hit your limit is a superpower. But here's the part that might make you uncomfortable: communicating that boundary to an extrovert. They're often so caught up in their whirlwind of plans and energy that they don't realise they're draining you. You have to let them know — gently but firmly.

Try phrases like:

- "I'm having a great time, but I think I need a break."

- "I'd love to catch up more, but I need some quiet time right now."
- "This was fun! I'm going to recharge for a bit."

Notice none of these say, "I hate you and I'm done with people." They're polite but direct, and most extroverts will totally understand. You'd be surprised how often they appreciate the clarity.

Real-life example:

Ever been invited to an extrovert's "chill night" only to find out it's a full-blown event with 20 people, loud music, and games you've never heard of? Yeah, that's not chill. If you sense this happening, give yourself an out. You can say something like, "Hey, this looks like fun, but I think I'm going to head out a little early tonight." Trust me, they'll respect it — and you'll leave before your social energy reaches critical levels.

STRATEGY 3: LEVERAGE THEIR STRENGTHS

Extroverts have a natural talent for making connections, which can be incredibly useful if you play it right. For example, if you need to get to know someone or network, but the idea of approaching strangers makes you want to hide behind a potted plant, enlist your extrovert friend. They'll practically jump at the chance to introduce you, because that's their jam.

You don't need to be the life of the party when you have a buddy who already is. Let them be your social wingman (or wingwoman) while you focus on the interactions that matter to you.

Real-life example:

Imagine you're at a work event. It's crowded, there's chatter everywhere, and the thought of introducing yourself to strangers is about as appealing as getting a root canal. Lucky for you, your extrovert coworker loves this stuff. Simply say, "Hey, can you introduce me to a few people?" Boom. They'll light up, drag you into conversations, and all you have to do is smile and nod.

STRATEGY 4: USE HUMOUR TO DEFLECT

One of the best ways to handle an extrovert who's pushing you a bit too hard is with humour. It diffuses the situation without making things awkward and lets you communicate that you're done without being confrontational.

Example: Your extroverted friend is trying to get you to join yet another group activity when you're already mentally checked out. You can say something like, "I'd love to, but my couch and I have a standing date tonight. Maybe next time?" It's light, it's funny, and it makes your point.

Real-life example:

Your chatty friend won't stop inviting you to every single social gathering in existence. You could say, "Listen, if I go to one more event this week, I'm going to need a nap the size of a small vacation." It'll get a laugh and, more importantly, get them off your back for a while.

Alright, let's dive deeper into our extrovert survival guide. Now that we've covered selective engagement, setting boundaries, leveraging their strengths, and using humour as a social shield, let's explore some practical **scientific exercises** you can use to boost your extrovert-handling skills. And hey, if all else fails, remember: you're not alone in this social jungle.

STRATEGY 5: THE "RECHARGE" TECHNIQUE — KNOW YOUR LIMITS (AND STICK TO THEM)

Let's be real here: hanging out with an extrovert can be like charging your phone on 1% battery with the world's slowest charger. You might get through some parts of the day fine, but soon enough, the battery dies, and all you're left with is social fatigue.

The solution? **Recharge proactively**. Don't wait until your social battery is completely drained before you take a step back. Think of it like scheduling rest stops on a road trip. Even if you think you can push through, having those little breaks will keep you going longer.

Exercise: The 10-10 Rule Here's a simple exercise: for every 10 minutes of intense social interaction (think high-energy conversations or large group settings), take 10 minutes to recharge. You can excuse yourself to go for a quick walk, find a quiet corner, or even just stand outside and enjoy the fresh air. This break doesn't have to be dramatic — no need to announce, "I'm off to recharge my introvert battery, goodbye!" Simply take a small mental timeout and return when you're ready.

Real-life example: At a work event or party, rather than feeling the need to engage non-stop, set small goals like, "I'll talk to two new people, then step outside for a breather." You'll find that those breaks help you come back feeling more refreshed and able to keep going without the exhaustion that normally hits after 30 minutes of forced chit-chat.

STRATEGY 6: TOLERATING THE "EXTROVERT VORTEX" — WHEN THEY WON'T STOP TALKING

It's not that extroverts talk too much (okay, maybe it is), but more so that sometimes you don't have the energy to listen to them ramble on about last week's trivia night for the seventh time. They love the back-and-forth exchange of ideas. You love silence.

The goal here isn't to change them but to **manage your response** to their chatter. You don't need to tune in to every word. In fact, **strategic zoning out** is a highly underrated skill. Politely nod, make eye contact, and insert small interjections like "Wow" or "That's interesting!" as needed. They'll be none the wiser.

Exercise: "Active Detachment" Here's a fun exercise: when an extrovert gets rolling on a topic, let yourself zone out (yes, you have permission). Instead of stressing over keeping up with their every word, focus on two things you can remember from their story — something you can repeat back later if needed. Meanwhile, relax and enjoy a brief mental escape. Trust me, this works wonders.

Real-life example: Say your extroverted coworker is telling you *again* about their weekend hiking trip. You can be present enough to say, "That sounds intense! How long did you hike?" and then quietly let your mind wander to that episode of your favourite show you've been meaning to catch up on.

STRATEGY 7: THE "SOCIAL CHAMELEON" TECHNIQUE — BORROWING A BIT OF EXTROVERT MAGIC

One of the perks of being around extroverts is that they have an almost contagious enthusiasm. You can actually **use this to your advantage** by stepping into their energy field when you need a social boost. No, you're not morphing into them (don't worry), but you are borrowing a little bit of that social charisma to blend in more easily.

Here's the trick: for a limited time, **mimic their body language and energy level**. Match their enthusiasm, even if it's just for a short while. You'll be surprised how much easier it is to navigate social situations when you're syncing with someone who's already running on high. Afterward, you can slip back into your comfort zone, knowing you've done your part.

Exercise: "Social Energy Matching" The next time you're with an extrovert in a group setting, try mimicking their body language. If they're leaning forward and gesturing a lot, subtly do the same. If they're speaking with high energy, raise your own tone a bit to match. You're not pretending to be extroverted — you're simply borrowing their social style for a brief moment. Try it in small doses and see how it feels.

Real-life example: At a friend's birthday party, you're cornered with a group of chatty people who are animatedly discussing their latest vacation. Instead of feeling out of place, mirror their energy for just a few minutes—lean in, ask a few questions, and participate. Then, when you've had enough, retreat with grace. You'll be remembered as engaged and friendly without overextending yourself.

WHY EXTROVERTS ARE ACTUALLY GOOD FOR YOU (YES, REALLY)

Alright, introverts, time for some tough love: despite how exhausting extroverts can be, there's a reason why they're good for you. Yes, you heard that right. Extroverts push you out of your comfort zone, and sometimes that's exactly what you need. You can't live inside your cosy introverted bubble forever (trust me, I've tried).

Reason #1: They Make Networking Easier We've already talked about how extroverts can help you network without feeling like a sleazy car salesman. But here's the deeper truth: extroverts naturally connect with people, and being around them opens doors for you. They'll introduce you to people, start conversations, and take the pressure off of making the first move.

Reason #2: They Give You a Social Break Ironically, having an extrovert in your circle often gives you a social break. You don't have to worry about filling awkward silences or carrying a conversation. Extroverts are more than happy to do all that heavy lifting while you nod, smile, and quietly sip your drink.

Reason #3: They Expand Your World Let's be honest — introverts are great at creating a safe, comfortable world, but extroverts pull you into new experiences. You'll end up going places and trying things you'd never attempt alone, and though it might be scary at first, it often leads to memorable experiences and personal growth.

EXERCISE: THE "SAY YES" CHALLENGE

Here's your final exercise: the next time your extrovert friend invites you somewhere (and you know they will), say yes. Even if it's not your usual scene, give it a shot. Set a time limit for yourself, and if you don't like it, leave. But I challenge you to push yourself to try something new. You never know — you might actually enjoy it.

You've now got a full arsenal of strategies for handling your extroverted friends, coworkers, and family members. Whether you're using humour to deflect their energy, setting firm boundaries, or even borrowing a bit of their enthusiasm when needed, you're officially prepared to deal with extroverts like a pro.

Remember, extroverts aren't your enemies — they're just different. And once you know how to manage that difference, you'll find that their energy and social prowess can actually benefit you. So, next time you find yourself stuck in a whirlwind of conversation, you'll be ready. You've got this.

6

Networking for People Who Would Rather Not

Ah, networking—the word alone is enough to make most introverts break out in a cold sweat. It conjures images of rooms filled with strangers, awkward small talk, and the overwhelming pressure to make a good impression. But before you throw your hands up in defeat, hear me out. **Networking doesn't have to suck**. In fact, it can even be... dare I say... enjoyable?

You see, networking isn't just about business cards and sales pitches. It's about building genuine connections, and spoiler alert: **introverts are actually really good at that**. You don't need to work the room like a politician or be the loudest voice at the event. Instead, you can bring your thoughtful, quiet strengths into play and still walk away with meaningful contacts. Let's break this down in a way that doesn't make you want to crawl under a table.

THE MYTH OF THE SCHMOOZE: WHY NETWORKING ISN'T JUST FOR EXTROVERTS

First, let's dispel a big myth: **networking isn't just for extroverts**. Sure, extroverts seem to thrive in these settings with their endless charm and knack for mingling, but that doesn't mean introverts are left in the dust. In fact, introverts often build stronger, more genuine connections because they don't focus on working the room—they focus on **quality over quantity**.

Networking isn't about how many people you can meet in an hour. It's about finding **real connections**—people who you can have a good conversation with, who you might want to work with or learn from. And that, dear introvert, is something you can absolutely master.

1. START SMALL: THE ONE-ON-ONE CONNECTION

One of the biggest mistakes people make when they approach networking is thinking they need to meet everyone in the room. But here's the truth: **you don't**. You only need to make a connection with one or two people to have a successful networking experience.

Start by focusing on a one-on-one conversation. Pick someone who seems approachable, maybe someone standing off to the side like you, and strike up a casual chat. You don't need to make it formal or business-focused right away—just see where the conversation goes naturally. Most people at networking events are just as nervous as you are, so you're likely to find someone who's relieved to have a real conversation instead of superficial small talk.

Exercise: "The One Connection Challenge" The next time you're at a networking event, challenge yourself to make just one meaningful connection. Forget about everyone else in the room—just focus on having a good conversation with one person. You can even make this your **exit goal**: once you've made one connection, you're free to leave guilt-free.

Real-life example: At a conference, you notice someone standing by the coffee table, looking a little lost in the sea of people. You approach them with a simple, "Hey, have you been to one of these events before?" Boom, instant connection. You're now chatting with someone who feels just as out of place as you, and suddenly, the whole thing feels a lot more manageable.

2. THE ART OF ASKING GOOD QUESTIONS

Introverts have a secret weapon when it comes to networking: **we're natural listeners**. We don't need to fill every silence with chatter; instead, we can use questions to guide the conversation. The key to being a great networker is not how much you say, but how well you listen. People love talking about themselves (especially extroverts), so use this to your advantage.

Ask thoughtful, open-ended questions that allow the other person to share their experiences, ideas, or goals. Questions like, "What brought you to this event?" or "What projects are you excited about right now?" give the other person the chance to open up, and you'll be remembered as someone who actually cared about the conversation.

Exercise: "The Three-Question Strategy" Before your next networking event, come up with three go-to questions that you can use to start or continue a conversation. Keep them open-ended and focused on the other person's experiences. These questions are your safety net for when the conversation lulls or you're not sure what to say next.

Real-life example: You're at a business mixer, and you meet someone who works in marketing. Instead of giving them your elevator pitch right away, you ask, "What's the most exciting project you've worked on this year?" This allows them to dive into their favourite topic while you sit back and listen. Bonus: you'll learn something interesting and might find a point of connection.

3. THE POWER OF THE FOLLOW-UP

The real magic of networking doesn't happen at the event itself—it happens **afterward**. This is where introverts have a huge advantage. While extroverts are out meeting as many people as possible, you can focus on a few key connections and build on them after the fact.

A simple follow-up email or message can turn a casual conversation into a lasting professional relationship. After the event, reach out to the person you connected with, mention something specific from your conversation, and suggest staying in touch. You don't have to push for a business deal or a job offer right away. Just focus on keeping the door open for future opportunities.

Exercise: "The 48-Hour Follow-Up" After any networking event, challenge yourself to follow up with the people you connected with within 48 hours. A quick, polite message like, "Hey, I really enjoyed our conversation about [topic]—would love to stay in touch!" is all it takes to keep the connection alive.

Real-life example: You've just had a great conversation with someone at a conference. Two days later, you send them a brief message: "It was great chatting with you at the event! I really enjoyed hearing about your work in [industry]—let's keep in touch!" Now you're on their radar, and the next time there's an opportunity for collaboration, they'll remember you.

4. USING YOUR STRENGTHS AS AN INTROVERT

You might think that because you're not a natural schmoozer, you're at a disadvantage in networking situations. Not true. **Introverts have unique strengths** that make them great at building meaningful connections, especially when you play to those strengths.

- **Quality over quantity:** As mentioned earlier, introverts excel at focusing on depth rather than breadth. While others are trying to collect as many business cards as possible, you're having real conversations. People remember that.
- **Thoughtful follow-up:** Introverts are naturally reflective, which means we're good at remembering details. Use this to your advantage by referencing specific parts of your conversation when you follow up. This level of thoughtfulness is rare and makes you stand out.
- **Listening more than talking:** Listening is one of the most valuable skills in networking. It makes people feel valued and

heard, and it allows you to gather useful information. Don't underestimate the power of being a great listener.

Real-life example: You're at a networking lunch, and while others are bouncing from person to person, you take your time with one or two meaningful conversations. Later, when you follow up, you reference a specific story they told or a mutual interest. You'll stand out because you took the time to genuinely connect, rather than rushing through the motions

You've got this, introvert. Networking doesn't have to be a nightmare, and you don't need to transform into an extroverted powerhouse to succeed. By focusing on building genuine connections, asking good questions, and following up thoughtfully, you can turn even the most intimidating networking event into a series of manageable, meaningful interactions.

Remember, it's not about quantity. You don't need to meet everyone—you just need to meet the right people, and that's something you can do in your own introverted style.

Now that you've learned how to navigate networking by focusing on **quality over quantity** and using your introverted superpowers, it's time to go deeper. Let's face it: sometimes, even the most well-prepared introvert needs a little extra push to get through those events. Whether it's a professional conference, a friend's launch party, or that dreaded office mixer, you can't always avoid networking situations. But here's the good news: you can handle them like a pro—without feeling like you're selling your soul to the networking gods.

Let's dive into more strategies to help you thrive in these environments, even if you'd rather be at home binge-watching your favourite show.

5. REFRAME NETWORKING AS "LEARNING"

One of the biggest reasons introverts dread networking is because it feels fake—like you're supposed to be selling yourself or schmoozing just for the sake of it. But here's a different way to think about it: **what if you saw networking as a learning opportunity instead?** What if, instead of thinking, "I have to impress these people," you told yourself, "I'm here to learn something new?"

Approaching networking with a mindset of curiosity can take a lot of the pressure off. You don't need to be the most outgoing person in the room—you just need to be interested. Ask questions, listen to people's stories, and treat the whole experience like you're there to gain knowledge, not to perform.

Exercise: "The Learner's Mindset" At your next networking event, challenge yourself to approach it with a learner's mindset. Instead of trying to "network," focus on learning from the people you meet. Ask questions like, "What's been your biggest takeaway from working in this industry?" or "What's the most interesting thing you've learned recently?" You'll find that conversations flow more naturally, and the pressure to be impressive fades away.

Real-life example: You're at a company mixer, and instead of nervously trying to sell yourself, you approach a colleague with, "I've been hearing about your work in [field]—what got you interested in that?" Suddenly, the conversation is no longer about making an impression; it's about learning something new. You relax, and so do they, making the interaction much more enjoyable for both of you.

6. THE POWER OF THE "TWO-MINUTE CONVERSATION"

Sometimes, the thought of having a long, drawn-out conversation at a networking event can feel overwhelming. You might worry about what to say, how to keep things going, or when to gracefully exit. But here's a secret: **you don't need to have long conversations to network effectively**. In fact, some of the best networking happens in short, two-minute bursts.

The key is to **get in, make an impact, and get out**—all within a couple of minutes. This approach works especially well in larger events where people are moving around a lot. A quick introduction, a relevant comment, and an exchange of contact details can be just as effective as a 20-minute chat.

Exercise: "The Two-Minute Rule" At your next networking event, practise the Two-Minute Rule. Aim to have short, focused conversations with a few people rather than long, drawn-out exchanges. Start with a friendly introduction, ask a question or share something relevant, and then wrap up with something like, "It's been great chatting—let's stay in touch!" This allows you to meet more people without feeling drained.

Real-life example: You're at a tech conference, and after introducing yourself to someone at the coffee station, you ask them about their work. They respond with a quick summary, and you follow up with a brief comment on something you've read or seen in the industry. After a couple of minutes, you wrap up with, "I'd love to continue this conversation sometime—let me grab your contact info." Boom, you've made a connection without feeling stuck in a long conversation.

7. PRACTISE THE "BUDDY SYSTEM"

Here's a hack that will save you at every networking event: the **buddy system**. If you're attending an event with a friend or colleague, you don't have to navigate the room alone. Team up, and use each other to make introductions, get out of awkward conversations, and generally support each other through the process.

Your networking buddy can act as a social buffer, helping to break the ice when you're feeling unsure or offering a way out when you need a break. You can take turns leading the conversation or introducing each other to new people. It's a great way to reduce the pressure on yourself while still making connections.

Exercise: "The Networking Wingman" Next time you attend a networking event, pair up with a friend or coworker and agree to be each other's wingman. Your job is to introduce each other to new people, offer support during conversations, and help each other find the right moments to exit when things get awkward. This makes the whole experience feel more like a team effort than a solo mission.

Real-life example: You and a colleague are at an industry dinner. They introduce you to someone they know, and you do the same for them. When the conversation lags, you step in with a new topic or suggest grabbing drinks together to keep things moving. When you're feeling overwhelmed, your buddy takes the lead, allowing you to recharge.

8. LEVERAGE TECHNOLOGY: LINKEDIN AND SOCIAL MEDIA

Who said networking has to be done face-to-face? In today's digital world, you can network just as effectively (sometimes more so) through platforms like **LinkedIn** and **social media**. These platforms allow you to connect with people on your own terms, in your own time, without the pressure of in-person interactions.

After a networking event, don't be afraid to follow up with a message on LinkedIn. Mention something specific from your conversation and send a connection request. The great thing about networking online is that you can take your time to craft thoughtful messages and build relationships without the immediate pressure of a live conversation.

Exercise: "The Post-Event Follow-Up" After your next networking event, follow up with at least three people you met by sending them a LinkedIn message or email. Reference something specific from your chat, and suggest connecting further. Keep the message light and professional, and don't worry about pushing for anything concrete—just focus on staying in touch.

Real-life example: You've met a couple of interesting people at a panel discussion. The next day, you send them a LinkedIn message: "Hey, it was great meeting you at the event yesterday! I really enjoyed our conversation about [topic]—would love to stay in touch." Now, you've taken the conversation from a short in-person interaction to an ongoing professional relationship.

9. HOW TO "QUIETLY" STAND OUT

One of the best parts about being an introvert at a networking event is that **you don't need to be loud to stand out**. In fact, some of the most memorable people are those who make a quiet, thoughtful impression. Instead of trying to work the room like an extrovert, focus on a few key things that can help you leave a lasting impact:

- **Be memorable in your follow-up:** As we mentioned before, sending a thoughtful follow-up message can make a huge difference. Reference something specific from your conversation, show genuine interest, and suggest a future interaction. This level of care and attention sets you apart.
- **Offer value:** If you can offer something of value in your conversation—whether it's a useful resource, a book recommendation, or an introduction to someone in your network—you immediately become memorable. People appreciate connections that give them something concrete to walk away with.
- **Focus on being genuine, not flashy:** You don't need to be the person with the loudest voice or the most eye-catching business card. Instead, focus on being genuine, thoughtful, and engaged. People remember authentic connections far more than they do superficial ones.

Exercise: "The Thoughtful Connector" At your next networking event, aim to make one connection where you offer something of value—whether it's a recommendation, a tip, or an introduction to someone in your network. This approach not only helps you stand out but also positions you as someone who adds value to your connections.

Real-life example: During a networking event, you meet someone who's new to your industry and looking for advice. You mention a great book or podcast that you've found helpful and offer to connect them with a colleague who's an expert in their area. You follow up with a message the next day, reinforcing the connection. You've now made a strong, memorable impression, all without needing to "work the room."

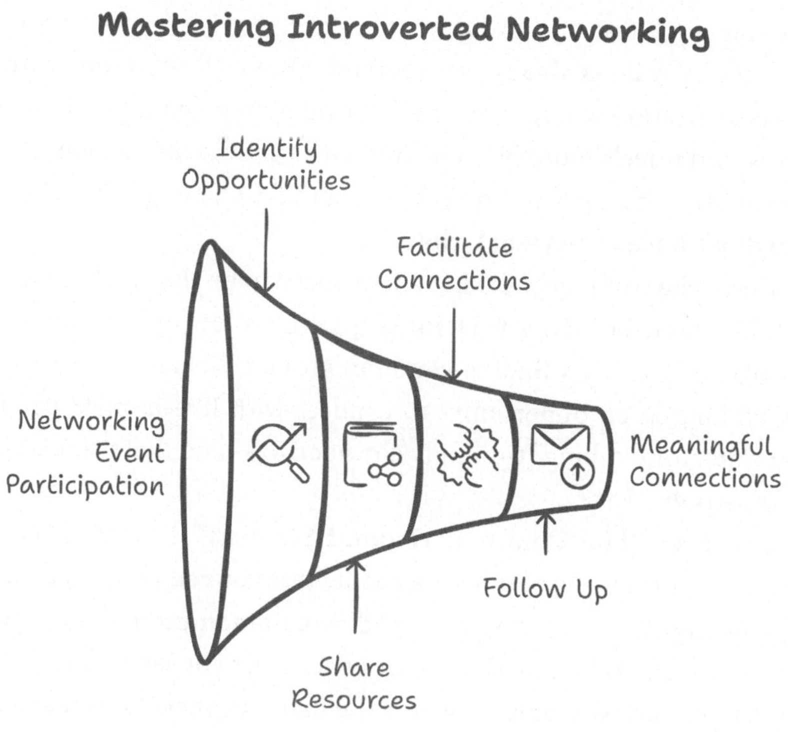

Now that you've picked up some powerful strategies like the "Two-Minute Rule" and the "Buddy System," and learned how to reframe networking as a learning experience, you're officially ready to take on any event. But let's not stop there—because there's more to mastering networking as an introvert than just surviving the experience. You can actually **thrive** in these situations and maybe even enjoy them (gasp, I know).

Let's dig deeper into **how you can turn your introverted traits into networking superpowers** and build long-term relationships that go beyond business cards and LinkedIn connections.

10. HOW TO NETWORK WITHOUT FEELING LIKE A SLEAZY SALESPERSON

One of the biggest turn-offs for introverts when it comes to networking is the fear of coming across as fake, overly self-promotional, or—let's be real—**a sleazy salesperson**. We've all been there: stuck in a conversation where someone is trying way too hard to sell themselves, and it feels more like a pitch than a genuine interaction. If the idea of being "that person" makes your skin crawl, I've got good news: **you don't have to network that way.**

Here's the truth: networking doesn't have to be about selling yourself. It's about **building relationships**. Focus less on pushing your agenda and more on finding common ground. When you approach networking as an opportunity to connect with like-minded people, you shift from "selling" to simply **connecting**—and that's something introverts excel at.

Exercise: "The Common Ground Strategy" Instead of going into a networking event thinking about what you can *get* from people, try flipping the script. Focus on finding common ground—whether it's shared interests, experiences, or goals. Start conversations with a mindset of curiosity, and see where the natural connections take you. This not only makes networking feel more genuine but also leads to more meaningful, lasting relationships.

Real-life example: At an industry happy hour, you meet someone who works in a field similar to yours. Instead of launching into your own work experience, you start by asking, "What's something about your job that you find really exciting right now?" This opens the door to a deeper conversation about shared professional challenges and successes, rather than a shallow exchange of business cards.

11. THE "SOFT SELL" APPROACH TO NETWORKING

Even if you're not trying to be a sleazy salesperson, there are still moments where you need to share your work or your goals with others in a networking setting. The key is to do it in a way that feels **natural and low-pressure**—something I like to call the "**soft sell**".

Instead of giving a polished elevator pitch, introduce what you do in a more casual, conversational way. Share what excites you about your work or projects, and let your passion speak for itself. People are more likely to engage with you if they sense you're genuinely enthusiastic about what you do, rather than feeling like you're trying to close a deal.

Exercise: "The Soft Sell in Action" The next time someone asks, "So, what do you do?" try responding with a short, authentic description of what excites you about your work. Focus on sharing a project you're passionate about or a challenge you've been working on, rather than reciting your job title and a rehearsed pitch. Keep it light, and let the conversation flow naturally from there.

Real-life example: Someone asks you what you do at a networking event, and instead of jumping into a formal pitch, you respond with, "I'm working on a really cool project right now that involves [insert interesting project detail]. It's been a great challenge—what about you? What are you working on?" This not only introduces what you do in a natural way but also invites them to share, keeping the conversation balanced.

12. AVOIDING "NETWORK BURNOUT" – HOW TO PACE YOURSELF

We've all experienced it—the slow, creeping exhaustion that comes from too much social interaction in too short a time. **Network burnout** is real, especially for introverts. If you're not careful, a single networking event can leave you feeling drained for days. But it doesn't have to be that way.

The trick is to **pace yourself**. Just like running a marathon, you need to conserve your energy so you don't burn out halfway through. Networking doesn't have to be an all-or-nothing experience. You can set small, manageable goals for yourself, take breaks when needed, and give yourself permission to leave early if you've made meaningful connections.

Exercise: "The Networking Marathon Strategy" When you attend your next networking event, set small, realistic goals for yourself. For example, aim to have three meaningful conversations and take two breaks. You can even give yourself permission to leave early if you've hit your goals and feel like your social battery is running low. It's about pacing yourself, not pushing yourself to the limit.

Real-life example: You're at a day-long industry conference. Instead of trying to meet everyone and attend every session, you set a goal to have three solid conversations and take a break between each one. After meeting your goals, you find a quiet spot to recharge for a bit before deciding whether you want to continue networking or head home. This way, you avoid the dreaded social burnout while still being productive.

13. THE POWER OF NETWORKING WITH OTHER INTROVERTS

Here's a little-known secret: **networking with other introverts** can be one of the most rewarding experiences you'll have. While extroverts are bouncing around the room, introverts tend to gravitate towards quieter, more meaningful conversations—and that's where you shine. Connecting with fellow introverts can lead to deeper, longer-lasting relationships because you both value quality over quantity.

So, how do you find these elusive introverts at a networking event? Look for people who seem like they're taking a break from the chaos. Whether it's someone quietly sipping their drink in the corner or a small group chatting on the sidelines, these are your people. Approach them with a simple introduction, and you'll likely find that they're relieved to have a calmer, more thoughtful conversation.

Exercise: "The Introvert Radar" At your next networking event, try using your **introvert radar** to find others who are hanging back. Approach them with a casual, friendly introduction like, "Mind if I join you over here? It's a bit quieter than the rest of the room." You'll often find that fellow introverts are just as eager to have a meaningful conversation as you are.

Real-life example: You're at a networking event where the energy is high, but you notice someone standing near the snacks, looking just as overwhelmed as you feel. You walk over and say, "Looks like we found the quietest spot in the room." Instantly, they smile, and you're both relieved to be having a more low-key conversation. By connecting with someone who values calm interactions like you, you're able to network without the usual pressure.

14. NETWORKING WITHOUT THE EVENT: BUILDING RELATIONSHIPS ORGANICALLY

Here's a radical idea: **you don't have to attend official networking events to network.** In fact, some of the best networking happens outside the typical conference room or cocktail party. You can build relationships organically through **shared interests**, hobbies, and even online communities.

If the idea of going to a big networking event still feels like too much, start small. Join a local group related to your industry, attend workshops, or participate in online forums. These spaces offer the same opportunities to connect with like-minded people but in a more relaxed, less formal setting. Plus, you'll already have something in common with the people you meet, which makes starting conversations so much easier.

Exercise: "Organic Networking" Think of one area of interest, whether it's related to your work or a personal hobby, and find a group, club, or online community where you can meet like-minded people. The goal isn't to go in with a networking agenda but to **build relationships naturally**. Over time, you'll find that these connections often lead to professional opportunities without the pressure of traditional networking.

Real-life example: You love photography and join a local photography group. Over time, you build friendships with people who share your passion. One day, someone in the group mentions they're looking for a photographer for a project, and suddenly, your hobby leads to a professional opportunity—all without attending a single "networking" event.

You're now armed with the tools to network without feeling like a pushy salesperson, to avoid social burnout, and to even find meaningful connections with other introverts. By pacing yourself, using the "soft sell" approach, and focusing on organic relationship-building, you'll find that networking doesn't have to be a chore. In fact, it can even become an enjoyable part of your personal and professional growth.

Remember, networking is about **quality over quantity**, and your introverted strengths—thoughtfulness, listening, and depth—are your biggest assets in building real connections. Keep showing up, keep practising, and most importantly, keep being yourself.

7

The Art of Saying Yes (and Knowing When to Say No)

Here's the thing about being an introvert: while we excel at a lot of things (like thoughtful reflection and deep conversations), we often struggle with **saying yes**. And not because we're lazy or uninterested—it's because saying yes typically means entering a world of social interactions, which, let's face it, can be **draining**.

But what if I told you that learning to say yes—strategically—could open doors to incredible opportunities, friendships, and even personal growth? And that knowing **when to say no** could protect your energy and make you feel more in control? Welcome to the delicate balancing act of knowing when to push your boundaries and when to assert your limits. In this chapter, we'll explore how to master this art with real-life examples and a little humour along the way.

WHY SAYING "YES" IS HARD FOR INTROVERTS

Let's be honest—saying yes to things like social events, networking opportunities, or even a quick coffee meetup can feel like agreeing to run a marathon when you're already running on empty. You instinctively want to **protect your energy**, and saying yes to too many things often leads to burnout.

For introverts, saying yes can sometimes feel like gambling with your energy. What if it's too loud? What if the people aren't your vibe? What if you have to make small talk for two hours straight? (Shudder.) But here's the thing: **saying yes doesn't mean losing yourself**. It's about choosing when to step out of your comfort zone to let new experiences into your life—experiences that might surprise you in a good way.

1. THE POWER OF SAYING YES (EVEN WHEN YOU DON'T WANT TO)

Let's start with why saying yes more often could be one of the best things you can do for yourself. Think of it this way: every time you say yes to something, you're **inviting possibility**. You're giving yourself a chance to meet new people, discover new interests, and grow in ways you never would've expected.

Now, I'm not saying you should become a yes-man (or woman) who never turns down an invitation. But what if, instead of immediately saying no to things that seem outside your comfort zone, you paused and asked yourself, "Could this lead to something positive? Could I get something out of this?" The answer is often yes.

Exercise: The "Yes Challenge" For the next week, challenge yourself to say yes to one thing you would normally turn down. Maybe it's a friend's invite to a game night, a work happy hour, or even trying a new hobby with a group of people. The goal is to step out of your comfort zone and see what happens. Even if it's not the greatest time of your life, you'll walk away with more confidence for having tried.

Real-life example: Your coworker invites you to a casual after-work gathering. Normally, you'd decline, but this time, you say yes. You show up, and while the event isn't exactly your scene, you end up having a great one-on-one conversation with a colleague you hadn't connected with before. Suddenly, you've built a relationship that might benefit you at work—and it all started with saying yes to something you'd usually avoid.

2. SAYING YES STRATEGICALLY – THE "ENERGY BANK" APPROACH

Okay, here's where it gets interesting. You don't need to say yes to **everything**. That's a surefire way to deplete your energy and leave yourself feeling burned out. Instead, think of your social energy like a bank account—let's call it your "Energy Bank."

Every time you say yes to a social event or a new opportunity, you're making a withdrawal from your Energy Bank. When you stay in, read a book, or spend time alone recharging, you're making a deposit. The goal is to balance your deposits and withdrawals so that you're not left in the red, exhausted, and wondering why you agreed to go to that loud concert on a Thursday night.

Exercise: The "Energy Bank Ledger" Take a moment to write down the last five things you said yes to. Did they energise you or drain you? Were any of them opportunities you're glad you took? Going forward, keep a mental ledger of your Energy Bank—if you've made a lot of withdrawals recently, give yourself permission to say no and make some deposits by recharging. But if your Energy Bank is full, try saying yes to an event or opportunity that could stretch your comfort zone.

Real-life example: You've had a few quiet weekends, and your energy levels are feeling solid. So when a friend invites you to a social gathering, you say yes, knowing that you've got enough in your Energy Bank to handle it. The next week, after a string of meetings and social events, you say no to an invite because you need to recharge. The result? A perfect balance between socialising and solitude.

3. THE ART OF SAYING NO (WITHOUT FEELING GUILTY)

Now let's talk about **saying no**. As much as it's important to say yes to things that push your boundaries, it's equally important to know when to say no. And here's the kicker: **you don't need an elaborate excuse**. Saying no can be as simple as, "Thanks, but I'm going to pass this time."

The key is to **say no without guilt**. You don't owe anyone a detailed explanation for why you're not attending their event or meeting for drinks. No one expects you to be available all the time, and most people will respect your boundaries as long as you set them clearly and politely.

Exercise: The "Graceful No" Practice saying no to a few things this week without feeling like you need to explain yourself. Use a phrase like, "I'd love to, but I'm going to take it easy this time," or "Thanks for the invite, but I'm not available." Remember, it's better to say no up front than to commit to something you'll dread and regret later.

Real-life example: Your friend invites you to a weekend getaway with a big group. Normally, you'd feel pressured to go, but this time, you're feeling drained and know it's not the right time for a trip. You say, "Thanks for thinking of me, but I'm going to skip this one." No guilt, no pressure, and most importantly, you get to recharge on your own terms.

4. LEARNING TO LOVE THE WORD "MAYBE"

Here's a little trick: if you're not sure whether you want to say yes or no, **say maybe**. It's perfectly fine to give yourself a little more time to think about it, especially if you're unsure how you'll feel closer to the event.

Saying maybe gives you a buffer—it allows you to assess your energy levels closer to the time and decide what's best for you. Just be careful not to use maybe as a way to avoid making a decision. At some point, you'll have to commit one way or the other, but giving yourself a window of flexibility can reduce the pressure.

Exercise: The "Maybe Buffer" Next time someone invites you to an event or activity, and you're not sure whether you want to go, say, "I'm not sure yet, but I'll let you know closer to the time." This gives you the chance to check in with your Energy Bank later and make a decision that feels right for you.

Real-life example: A friend invites you to a movie night, but after a long week, you're not sure if you'll have the energy to attend. Instead of committing on the spot, you say, "That sounds fun! Let me see how my week goes, and I'll confirm closer to the time." When the day comes, you assess your energy and decide whether you're up for it. You've left yourself room to make the best decision for your well-being.

Learning the art of saying yes and knowing when to say no is all about balance. Saying yes more often can open doors to new experiences and relationships, while saying no protects your energy and ensures you're not overextending yourself. The key is to approach both with intention and mindfulness—knowing when to step out of your comfort zone and when to protect it.

Remember, your social energy is valuable, and it's up to you to decide when to invest it. By mastering this balance, you'll find that you can engage with the world in a way that's fulfilling, without feeling overwhelmed or drained.

Now that we've tackled the basics of saying yes and no, let's dive a little deeper into the art of making choices that respect your boundaries without shutting off opportunities. The challenge for introverts often lies in figuring out which situations are worth stepping out of your comfort zone for, and which ones will leave you feeling like you've just run a marathon on one hour of sleep. In this part, we'll talk about **real-life strategies** for making these decisions and how to avoid the dreaded "yes regret."

5. THE "OPPORTUNITY FILTER" – HOW TO DECIDE WHAT'S WORTH A YES

It's easy to say yes to things out of obligation or guilt, but how do you make sure you're saying yes to the **right things**? That's where the **Opportunity Filter** comes in. This little mental exercise helps you weigh the potential benefits of saying yes against the costs (hello, social exhaustion).

Whenever you're invited to something, ask yourself these questions:

1. **Will this event/meeting help me grow or learn something new?**
2. **Is there a chance I'll meet people who inspire or interest me?**
3. **Does this align with my goals or values?**
4. **Will attending leave me drained or energised?**
5. **Is this something I might actually enjoy, or am I just saying yes out of obligation?**

By running invitations through this filter, you'll have a clearer sense of whether the opportunity is worth a yes. It's not about being selfish—it's about protecting your time and energy while still pushing yourself to try new things.

Exercise: The "Opportunity Filter" in Action The next time you're faced with an invitation or opportunity, mentally run it through the Opportunity Filter. If it checks at least three of the boxes (growth, meeting people, alignment with goals, etc.), it's worth considering a yes. If it doesn't, give yourself permission to decline without guilt.

Real-life example: You're invited to a weekend workshop on public speaking—a subject that both excites and terrifies you. Running it through the Opportunity Filter, you realise that attending could help you grow, meet like-minded people, and align with your goal of becoming more confident in communication. So, you say yes, knowing it might be uncomfortable but valuable in the long run.

6. KNOWING WHEN TO BAIL – THE ART OF THE STRATEGIC EXIT

Let's be honest: sometimes, even when you've said yes to an event, you realise halfway through that it was a mistake. Maybe the crowd's too loud, the conversations aren't flowing, or your social battery just hits zero out of nowhere. This is where the **Strategic Exit** comes in handy.

The key to a successful exit is to **plan it in advance**. When you say yes to something, give yourself an out—a polite, non-awkward reason to leave if the event isn't serving you. This could be anything from "I have an early morning tomorrow" to "I promised myself I'd leave by 9." The goal is to make sure you don't feel trapped.

Exercise: The "Exit Plan" Next time you say yes to a social event, mentally prepare your exit plan in advance. You don't need to broadcast it to anyone, but having an exit strategy in place will give you peace of mind and the freedom to leave if you need to. If you're having a great time, you can always stay longer, but if not, your exit is already mapped out.

Real-life example: You agree to go to a party your friend is throwing, but you know large gatherings can be hit or miss for you. Before you even arrive, you set a personal rule: if you're not enjoying yourself after an hour, you'll leave. You show up, give it a solid try, but after an hour, you feel your energy fading. With your exit plan in place, you casually thank your friend and head out without any awkwardness.

7. SAYING NO WITHOUT THE GUILT – THE KEY TO SELF-PRESERVATION

Saying no can feel uncomfortable—especially if you're turning down friends, family, or colleagues. But here's a liberating truth:

you're allowed to say no without explaining yourself to anyone. You're not required to provide a detailed account of why you're skipping the group dinner or why you're not available for drinks after work.

One of the best ways to say no without guilt is by using **soft yet firm language**. Phrases like, "Thanks for thinking of me, but I'm going to pass this time," or "That sounds great, but I'll have to take a rain check," allow you to decline without sounding abrupt or rude.

Exercise: The "Polite No" Challenge For one week, practice saying no to things that don't align with your energy or goals. Whether it's declining an invitation or setting a boundary at work, use polite but firm language. Notice how people respond—more often than not, you'll find that people respect your no and move on without any drama.

Real-life example: A coworker invites you to yet another after-hours work dinner, but you're feeling burnt out from a busy week. Instead of making up an excuse, you simply say, "Thanks for the invite, but I'm going to pass tonight and recharge. Let's catch up soon, though!" No guilt, no over-explaining—just a firm but friendly no.

8. USING "YES" AS A TOOL FOR GROWTH

Here's a surprising twist: **sometimes, saying yes is the key to breaking out of a rut**. When you feel stuck in a routine or overwhelmed by your usual patterns, saying yes to new experiences can spark growth and lead to exciting changes. The trick is to say yes intentionally—to things that stretch you just a little, without pushing you over the edge.

Think of your yes as a tool for **personal expansion**. It's not about saying yes to everything, but about recognizing when a yes could lead to a breakthrough, a new friendship, or an unexpected opportunity. This doesn't mean you'll love every experience, but you'll definitely learn something from each one.

Exercise: The "Growth Yes" Challenge Identify one area of your life where you've been playing it safe or staying in your comfort zone. Maybe it's public speaking, dating, or trying a new hobby. For the next month, challenge yourself to say yes to at least one opportunity that scares you a little but excites you a lot. The goal isn't to say yes to everything, but to push your boundaries just enough to grow.

Real-life example: You've always been nervous about public speaking, but when you're invited to speak on a small panel about your work, you decide to say yes—even though it scares you. You prepare, push through the discomfort, and end up having a great experience. Not only do you gain confidence, but you also meet people who are impressed with your insights and want to collaborate with you in the future.

9. HOW TO BALANCE "YES" AND "NO" IN RELATIONSHIPS

One of the trickiest parts of saying yes or no is navigating relationships—whether it's with friends, family, or coworkers. We all want to be supportive and helpful, but constantly saying yes to others can leave us feeling resentful or overwhelmed. On the other hand, saying no too often can make us feel disconnected from the people we care about.

The key to balance is **knowing your priorities**. Ask yourself: does saying yes to this request or event support my personal or professional goals? Will saying no help me protect my energy or maintain my boundaries? By keeping your priorities in mind, you can say yes or no without feeling torn between your needs and other people's expectations.

Exercise: The "Priority Check" The next time someone asks for your time or invites you to something, do a quick check-in with your priorities. Will saying yes support those priorities, or will it pull you away from them? Make your decision based on what matters most to you—not on the fear of disappointing others.

Real-life example: A friend invites you to a weekend trip, but you've been working on a personal project that's important to you. After doing a priority check, you realise that the project needs your attention more than a weekend getaway. You politely decline, explaining that you're focusing on your work, and your friend understands. You've said no without feeling guilty because you're staying true to your priorities.

Saying yes and no is an art—one that requires balance, intention, and a good understanding of your personal boundaries. By using tools like the Opportunity Filter, the Strategic Exit, and the Priority Check, you'll be able to make decisions that not only protect your energy but also help you grow in ways that matter.

Remember, saying yes can open doors to new experiences, while saying no helps preserve your well-being. Both are essential, and mastering the balance between the two will allow you to engage with the world on your terms, without feeling overwhelmed.

The Strategic No: Saving Your Sanity

Imagine this: You've been invited to a back-to-back series of weekend activities—Saturday brunch, followed by a game night, and Sunday's hiking trip. Sounds exhausting just reading it, right? Yet somehow, the word "sure" slips out every time you're asked to join. Why do we do this to ourselves?

Here's the thing: saying "yes" feels easier at the moment. The real discomfort comes later when you're staring at your calendar, horrified by the relentless social events you've signed up for. It's like knowing you've ordered way too much food at a restaurant but not wanting to cancel the extra side of fries because, well, they sound good right now. But when they arrive, you're stuffed, and that last bite just isn't as satisfying.

Real Life Example: The Time I Became a Yes-Bot

True story—I once agreed to attend three birthday parties in one weekend. By Sunday afternoon, I was desperately practising my fake cough in the bathroom to get out of party number three. It didn't work, but I did discover that committing to too many things is the quickest way to burn out your social energy faster than a low-battery iPhone.

The lesson here? It's okay to say no sometimes, especially when you know it's for your own well-being. That doesn't make you a bad friend or antisocial; it makes you human. Or at least a version of humans that prefers Netflix marathons to actual marathons.

How to Say No Without Guilt

Let's talk about tactics. Saying no is an art form, and much like painting a masterpiece, it requires a delicate touch. You don't want to crush anyone's spirits (unless you do, but let's save that for another chapter), so here are a few ways to politely decline without spiralling into an apology fest.

- **The Classic Excuse**: "I'd love to, but I've already got plans." Plans can mean anything—self-care, catching up on a book, or just sitting in silence because that's what you need.

- **The Deflector**: If you're not ready for a full-blown "no," try "Let me check my schedule and get back to you." It buys you time to gather the courage to decline without feeling pressured.
- **The Honest Approach**: This one's for the brave. Just be upfront: "I really need some downtime." You'll be surprised how much people respect honesty, even if they don't fully get it.

When Saying Yes Is Worth It

Now, let's not completely vilify "yes." There are times when saying yes can lead to amazing opportunities—both socially and personally. Like when you reluctantly agree to go to a random concert and end up discovering your new favourite band or meeting people who unexpectedly become friends for life.

Learning when to push yourself out of your comfort zone is key. Remember, personal growth often happens in those moments when you say "yes" to something that scares you a little bit. The trick is knowing which "yes" will give you a rush of excitement and which will leave you drained.

Exercise: The "Yes Test"

Here's a quick test you can try next time you're stuck between saying yes or no to an invitation. Ask yourself two questions:

1. **How do I feel when I think about going?** If you're dreading it, that's a clear sign it might be better to say no.
2. **How will I feel after it's over?** If you know you'll feel proud of yourself for going, then maybe it's worth the social discomfort.

It's like running: no one loves the process (okay, some people do), but afterward, you usually feel like a champion, ready to take on the world—or at least ready for brunch.

Great! Now that you've explored the balancing act between yes and no, let's talk about the **long-term impact** of mastering this art—especially on your relationships, your energy, and your personal growth. Saying yes and no isn't just about social engagements; it's about shaping the kind of life you want to live. After all, the choices you make define how you spend your time and, more importantly, how you feel about the time spent.

In this final page, we'll dive into how saying "yes" and "no" strategically can influence your overall well-being and help you build stronger, more fulfilling connections with others—without compromising your need for downtime.

1. Strengthening Relationships Through Boundaries

Here's a little-known fact: **saying no can actually strengthen your relationships**. Wait, what? Yes, you read that right. By setting boundaries, you're showing people what your limits are and giving them permission to respect those limits. When you say no to a social invitation, you're not rejecting the person—you're protecting your energy so that when you do say yes, you're showing up as your best, fully-charged self.

Think about it: would you rather hang out with someone who's reluctantly there, checking their watch every five minutes, or someone who genuinely wants to be present and engaged? The latter, right? By saying no when you need to recharge, you're ensuring that when you do say yes, your energy and attention are fully available, which leads to **more meaningful interactions**.

Real-life example: Your close friend invites you to dinner after a long week, but you're completely drained. Instead of forcing yourself to go and be half-present, you say, "I'd love to catch up, but I'm really wiped out this week. How about we grab coffee next weekend instead?" Not only have you protected your energy, but you've also offered an alternative that shows you still value the relationship—just on a timeline that works better for you.

2. Why Your "Yes" Should Be Authentic

There's nothing worse than feeling obligated to say yes when you're really screaming "no" on the inside. But here's a truth that will free you: **people can tell when your yes isn't authentic**. It comes through in your body language, your tone, and your overall vibe. And trust me, no one enjoys being around someone who doesn't actually want to be there.

That's why it's so important to **own your yes**. When you agree to something, make sure it's coming from a place of genuine enthusiasm (or at least curiosity). If you're saying yes just because you feel guilty, take a step back and reassess. Authentic yeezy leads to authentic experiences, which are ultimately more fulfilling.

Exercise: The "Authentic Yes" Inventory The next time you say yes to something, check in with yourself. Are you excited about it? Does it feel like a real yes, or are you agreeing out of obligation? If you find yourself saying yes when you don't really want to, practise a pause. It's okay to say, "Let me think about it" before giving an answer.

Real-life example: You're invited to a networking event that you're on the fence about. Instead of automatically saying yes (because you feel like you *should*), you take a moment to think about it. Will this event help you grow? Is there a part of you that's excited about it? If the answer is yes, go for it! If not, gracefully decline and save your energy for something that aligns better with your current needs.

3. The Ripple Effect of No

Saying no doesn't just protect your energy—it can also inspire others to respect their own boundaries. When you confidently decline an invitation or set a limit, you're modelling healthy behaviour for those around you. It might even encourage your friends, family, or colleagues to rethink their own yes/no habits.

This ripple effect can lead to deeper connections where people feel empowered to be honest about what they need. Suddenly, you're not just saying no to protect yourself—you're part of a movement that values **well-being and balance** over constant availability.

Exercise: "The Ripple of No" Challenge For the next week, practice saying no to things that don't align with your energy or priorities. Notice how others respond. You might be surprised to find that people respect your boundaries and, in some cases, even appreciate your honesty. Pay attention to whether this inspires others to set their own boundaries as well.

Real-life example: At work, you're asked to take on an extra project, but your plate is already full. Instead of piling more onto your workload, you say, "I'd love to help, but I'm at capacity right now. Could we revisit this next month?" Your colleague is initially surprised but ends up appreciating your honesty—and a few days later, they start delegating more of their own tasks instead of saying yes to everything.

4. Using "Yes" as a Tool for Growth and Connection

While no can be empowering, **strategic yeses** can lead to some of the most rewarding experiences of your life. Every time you say yes to something that pushes you out of your comfort zone, you're creating an opportunity for growth. This is especially important for introverts, who might naturally lean toward the safety of routine and solitude.

But growth doesn't happen in a vacuum—it happens when you're willing to step into new situations, meet new people, and embrace the unknown. By saying yes to the right opportunities, you're expanding your world, even if it's just one small step at a time.

Exercise: The "Growth Yes" For one month, challenge yourself to say yes to something that scares you a little but excites you a lot. This could be a new hobby, a social event, or even a professional opportunity. The goal is to use yes as a tool for growth, not as a way to overwhelm yourself.

Real-life example: You've always wanted to learn how to paint, but you've been too nervous to join an art class. After weeks of thinking about it, you finally say yes and sign up for a beginner's class. Not only do you discover a new creative outlet, but you also meet a group of people who share your passion. What started as a hesitant yes turns into a meaningful part of your life.

WRAPPING UP CHAPTER 7

By now, you've mastered the art of saying yes and no with intention. You've learned how to protect your energy, strengthen relationships, and use both yes and no as tools for personal growth. Whether it's setting boundaries or stepping into new opportunities, the choices you make have a lasting impact on your well-being—and that's something worth celebrating.

Remember, it's not about saying yes to everything or no to everything—it's about **balance**. Your time and energy are precious, and learning how to manage them effectively will lead to a more fulfilling, less stressful life. You're in control of your yeses and nos, and that's a powerful thing.

8

Dating – The Ultimate Introvert's Challenge

Ah, dating. That magical, nerve-wracking, sometimes awkward journey of trying to get to know another human being while secretly hoping they don't ask you to a loud bar or suggest going on a spontaneous group outing with their equally loud friends. For introverts, dating can feel like walking a tightrope between wanting to connect with someone and desperately needing alone time to recharge after every social interaction.

But here's the thing—**dating as an introvert isn't a curse**. In fact, introverts bring something special to the dating game that extroverts sometimes miss: the ability to create deep, meaningful connections. You just have to learn how to navigate the process in a way that works for your energy, your boundaries, and your social battery.

In this chapter, we'll break down everything from first dates (shudder) to online dating, all while keeping things light, funny, and totally manageable for your introverted soul. Let's dive in.

1. The Introvert's First Date Survival Guide

First dates are notorious for making introverts want to fake an emergency call just so they can leave early. Why? Because they often involve small talk, which is basically the arch-nemesis of any introvert. But here's the good news: **you don't have to endure a painful first date full of awkward pauses and surface-level chit-chat**. There are ways to make first dates less terrifying and more enjoyable.

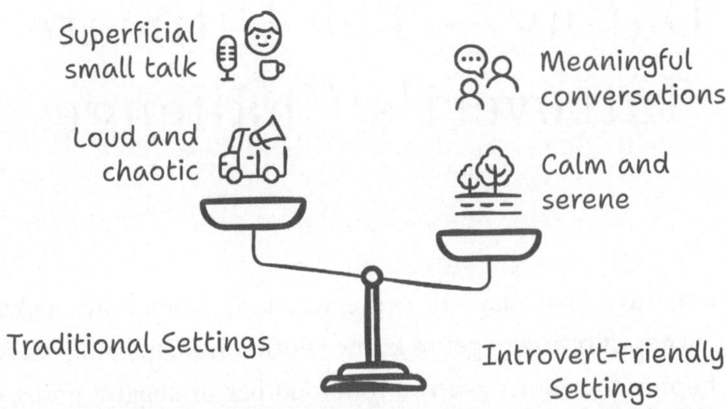

Choose the right setting for deeper connections.

Pro Tip #2: Have a Few Conversation Starters Ready We've all been there—that moment when the conversation lags, and suddenly, it feels like you're both stuck in an awkward staring contest. To avoid this, have a few conversation starters in your back pocket. Try asking about their favourite book, a hobby they're passionate about, or even their dream travel destination. These questions naturally lead to deeper conversations without feeling forced.

Exercise: The "First Date Prep" Challenge Before your next first date, pick a low-key location that aligns with your introverted energy. Then, prepare three conversation starters that go beyond small talk. If you're nervous, practice in front of the mirror or with a friend. This way, you'll feel more confident going into the date.

Real-life example: Instead of agreeing to drinks at a busy bar, you suggest a local park where you can walk and talk at your own pace. The conversation flows naturally as you ask, "What's something you're passionate about but most people don't know?" Suddenly, you're both discussing your favourite hobbies instead of awkwardly trying to talk about the weather.

2. Navigating Online Dating Without Losing Your Mind

Let's face it: **online dating can be overwhelming** for anyone, but especially for introverts. The endless swiping, the constant notifications, the pressure to craft the perfect message—it's enough to make you want to throw your phone into the nearest river. But with the right approach, online dating can actually be a great way for introverts to meet people without the anxiety of real-time conversations.

Pro Tip #1: Curate Your Dating Profile Your profile is the first impression potential matches will have of you, so make it count. Instead of writing something generic like "I love to laugh," try to showcase your personality in a way that's authentic to who you are. Mention the things you're passionate about, whether it's photography, cooking, or binge-watching documentaries. This will attract people who share similar interests and make it easier to start conversations.

Pro Tip #2: Take Your Time with Responses One of the best things about online dating is that it doesn't require an immediate response. Take advantage of that! If you receive a message, give yourself time to think about your reply. You don't have to rush into a conversation just because someone messaged you first.

Exercise: "The Profile Refresh" If you're already on a dating app, take a look at your profile and ask yourself: does this reflect the real me? If not, spend some time updating it with a few key details about your interests and hobbies. For those new to online dating, create a profile that feels true to your personality—don't try to be someone you're not.

Real-life example: Your dating profile previously said, "I like hanging out with friends," but that doesn't quite capture who you are. You update it to say, "Introvert who loves rainy days, good books, and low-key movie nights." Now, you're more likely to attract people who appreciate your quieter lifestyle, and the conversations that follow are more aligned with your interests.

3. How to Handle "Dating Energy" (Without Burning Out)

Here's a dilemma: you want to put yourself out there and meet new people, but you also know that too much dating can drain your energy faster than a dead phone battery. So, how do you balance your desire to date with your need for solitude?

Pro Tip #1: Set Boundaries with Your Time You don't have to accept every date invitation or stay out for hours on end. It's okay to set time limits for yourself. For example, you might tell your date ahead of time, "I can stay for about an hour, but then I need to head out." This lets you control the duration of the date without feeling trapped.

Pro Tip #2: Space Out Your Dates There's no rule that says you need to go on multiple dates in a single week. If you're someone who needs time to recharge after social interactions, space out your dates accordingly. Allow yourself a few days (or even a week) between dates to recover.

Exercise: The "Dating Energy Meter" For one month, track how much energy you have before and after each date. Afterward, ask yourself: Was this date worth the energy I spent? Did I feel drained, or did I leave feeling positive? By being more aware of your energy levels, you can better manage how often you go on dates and who you choose to spend time with.

Real-life example: You schedule a coffee date for Saturday afternoon but set a time limit of one hour because you know that any longer will leave you feeling exhausted. After the date, you reflect on how you feel—energised and happy because you connected with someone interesting, and you didn't stay too long. You're more likely to want to see them again because you didn't burn yourself out trying to impress them.

4. The Awkwardness of Small Talk – And How to Get Past It

Let's be honest: **small talk is painful**, especially on a date. But the reality is that most dates start with some level of small talk before diving into deeper conversations. The good news is that you don't have to get stuck in the small talk phase forever—you just need a strategy to move past it quickly.

Pro Tip #1: Use Small Talk as a Springboard Instead of seeing small talk as a necessary evil, try using it as a springboard to more meaningful conversations. For example, if your date asks, "How was your weekend?" don't just give a short answer—expand on it. "It was good! I spent a lot of time working on my photography. Do you have any creative hobbies?"

Pro Tip #2: Ask Open-Ended Questions One of the best ways to avoid awkward silences is by asking open-ended questions that encourage your date to share more about themselves. Instead of asking yes/no questions like, "Do you like your job?" try, "What's the most interesting part of your job?" This opens the door to a more engaging conversation.

Exercise: The "Small Talk Escape" Next time you're on a date, practice turning small talk into something deeper. If the conversation feels like it's stuck in a loop of mundane topics, steer it toward something more meaningful by sharing a personal experience or asking a thought-provoking question.

Real-life example: Your date starts with the typical, "So, what do you do?" Instead of giving a brief answer, you expand on it: "I'm a graphic designer, but I'm really passionate about photography in my spare time. Do you have any creative outlets?" Suddenly, you're discussing creativity, hobbies, and interests instead of just exchanging job descriptions.

You're doing great so far, introverted dating warrior! Now that we've talked about surviving first dates and navigating online dating without pulling your hair out, let's move on to some **advanced strategies** for dating as an introvert. These are the tips that'll take you from surviving dates to thriving in them—without feeling like you're pretending to be someone you're not.

Remember, the key to dating as an introvert is to embrace who you are while still pushing yourself (gently) out of your comfort zone. Let's dive deeper into how you can **balance your introverted tendencies** with the excitement and unpredictability of dating.

5. The Power of Solo Time in Between Dates

One of the best-kept secrets for introverts is the **importance of alone time between dates**. As an introvert, your energy doesn't automatically replenish after social interactions. You need time to **recharge**, reflect, and get back to your normal levels of zen before jumping into the next social situation.

Here's why it matters: when you allow yourself to recharge between dates, you show up to the next one as your best self—**engaged, relaxed, and present**. But if you try to squeeze too many social interactions into a short period, you risk burnout and end up dreading the very thing you're supposed to be enjoying.

Pro Tip #1: Schedule Downtime After each date, block off some time for yourself—whether it's a few hours or a full day—to do something that helps you recharge. Read a book, take a walk, or simply enjoy some quiet time at home. Giving yourself this space will ensure that you don't feel overwhelmed by the dating process.

Pro Tip #2: Don't Feel Guilty About Needing Space. It's easy to feel guilty about needing alone time—especially if your date wants to see you again soon. But remember, it's perfectly okay to say, "I had a great time, but I need a little downtime before we hang out again." Most people will appreciate your honesty and understand your need to recharge.

Exercise: The "Recharge Ritual" Create a personal recharge ritual that you can use after dates. This could be as simple as watching your favourite TV show, journaling about the experience, or indulging in some self-care. The goal is to reset your energy so that you're excited (not exhausted) when it's time for the next date.

Real-life example: After a fun but socially draining dinner date, you spend the next day unwinding with a good book and a cup of tea. You avoid scheduling another date until you've fully recharged. When your date texts you later asking to hang out again, you reply with, "I'd love to! How about next weekend?"—giving yourself plenty of time to restore your energy before meeting again.

6. How to Stay True to Your Introverted Self While Dating

There's a common misconception that dating requires you to **act extroverted** to be successful. This couldn't be further from the truth. In reality, some of the best dates happen when you lean into who you really are—introverted tendencies and all. After all, the goal of dating isn't to pretend you're someone you're not. It's to find someone who appreciates you for who you are.

Pro Tip #1: Be Honest About Your Needs Early On If you're someone who values quiet time, dislikes loud environments, or prefers deeper one-on-one conversations, it's important to communicate this to your date. Don't feel pressured to go along with activities that don't suit your personality just because you're trying to make a good impression. Chances are, your date will respect you more for being upfront about your needs.

Pro Tip #2: Plan Dates That Align with Your Personality Instead of forcing yourself into high-energy social situations, plan dates that align with your introverted nature. Think nature walks, quiet coffee dates, museum visits, or even a cosy evening at a bookstore. These settings allow for meaningful conversations without overwhelming your senses.

Exercise: The "True You" Date For your next date, suggest an activity that genuinely excites you as an introvert. Whether it's a walk in the park, a visit to a local art gallery, or a casual brunch, make sure it's something you'll enjoy and feel comfortable doing. Pay attention to how much more relaxed and present you feel when the setting aligns with your preferences.

Real-life example: You're planning a second date and suggest a visit to a local bookstore, followed by coffee. The setting is calm and quiet, which suits your introverted energy, and the conversation flows naturally as you browse through books and share recommendations. By choosing a date that fits your personality, you feel more like yourself and enjoy the experience without feeling drained.

7. Managing the Follow-Up: How Often Should You Text or Call?

Let's talk about **communication**—the great dating dilemma. One of the most stressful parts of dating for introverts can be figuring out how often to text, call, or keep in touch between dates. Too much communication can feel suffocating, while too little can leave you wondering if the connection is fizzling out.

So, how do you find the sweet spot? The key is to **strike a balance** between staying in touch and maintaining your own space.

Pro Tip #1: Set Communication Boundaries If you're not someone who enjoys constant texting or phone calls, it's okay to set boundaries around how often you communicate. You don't need to reply to every message immediately or engage in long text conversations every day. Let your date know you prefer quality communication over quantity, and suggest that you both check in when it feels natural.

Pro Tip #2: Mix It Up To keep things interesting, mix up your communication style. Instead of texting all the time, send a voice note, share an interesting article, or plan your next date over the phone. This keeps communication engaging without overwhelming you with constant back-and-forth messages.

Exercise: The "Text Check-In" For the next week, pay attention to how texting or calling your date makes you feel. Do you enjoy it, or does it feel like a chore? If it's the latter, consider adjusting the frequency or style of communication to something that feels more natural and comfortable for you.

Real-life example: You're texting someone new, but after a few days of constant back-and-forth messages, you feel like it's too much. Instead of ghosting them or forcing yourself to keep up, you send a quick message saying, "Hey, I love our conversations, but I'm more of a 'meet in person' kind of person. Let's chat more at our next date this weekend!" This takes the pressure off daily texting while still showing interest.

8. What to Do When You're Not Feeling It

We've all been there—you're a few dates in, and something just isn't clicking. Maybe the person is nice, but there's no spark. Or maybe they're an extrovert who's planning weekend parties, and the thought of attending makes you want to hide under a blanket. So, what do you do?

First off, it's important to **trust your gut**. If you're not feeling a connection, it's better to be honest than to keep forcing something that's not working. Being introverted doesn't mean you have to endure situations that drain your energy or make you uncomfortable.

Pro Tip #1: Be Honest (But Kind) If you realise that a relationship isn't what you're looking for, have a conversation about it early on. You don't need to over-explain or make excuses—just let them know that while you enjoyed getting to know them, you don't think it's a match. Most people appreciate honesty, even if it's not the outcome they were hoping for.

Pro Tip #2: Know When to Walk Away It's easy to fall into the trap of staying in a situation longer than necessary because you don't want to hurt someone's feelings. But remember, your energy is valuable, and staying in a situation that isn't right for you only prolongs the inevitable. Walking away when it's clear that things aren't working is the best way to respect both your time and theirs.

Exercise: The "Gut Check" If you're unsure whether to continue seeing someone, take a few moments to check in with your gut feelings. Do you look forward to seeing them, or does the idea fill you with dread? Pay attention to how you feel both before and after your interactions. If the negative outweighs the positive, it's probably time to move on.

Real-life example: You've gone on three dates with someone who's fun but much more extroverted than you. You like them, but their constant invitations to group activities are starting to feel overwhelming. After your latest date, you decide to have an honest conversation and say, "I've had a great time getting to know you, but I think we're looking for different things." They appreciate your honesty, and you part ways on good terms.

Alright, let's keep the momentum going as we continue navigating the world of dating as an introvert. By now, you've learned how to handle first dates, embrace your need for space, and even master the art of communication without feeling overwhelmed. Now, it's time to take things a step further: **long-term relationships** and **the realities of dating extroverts**. You know, those whirlwind socialites who seem to never run out of energy? Yup, we're going there.

Long-term dating can feel like an even bigger challenge for introverts because it requires consistent social interaction and compromise. But don't worry—just because you're introverted doesn't mean you're doomed to a life of exhausting relationships. With the right strategies, you can create a relationship that's fulfilling, balanced, and perfectly tailored to your introverted needs.

9. How to Date an Extrovert Without Losing Your Mind

So, you've met someone who ticks all the boxes—smart, kind, funny—but they're also an extrovert. They thrive in crowds, love spontaneous social events, and somehow manage to text you 57 times in one day. As an introvert, this can feel like you've landed on an alien planet. But here's the good news: **introvert-extrovert relationships can work beautifully**, as long as both parties understand each other's needs and are willing to compromise.

Here's how you can date an extrovert without sacrificing your sanity:

Pro Tip #1: Communicate Your Needs Clearly The biggest challenge in introvert-extrovert relationships is that extroverts often don't realise how draining constant social interaction can be for introverts. That's why it's so important to **communicate your need for alone time** early on. Don't wait until you're completely overwhelmed to mention that you need a break. Instead, set clear expectations about your social limits from the start.

For example, let your extroverted partner know that while you love spending time with them, you also need downtime to recharge. This doesn't mean you're avoiding them—it's just how you manage your energy.

Pro Tip #2: Find the Middle Ground Extroverts recharge through social interactions, while introverts recharge through solitude. But that doesn't mean you can't find a middle ground. The key is to **mix social events with quiet, one-on-one time**. You don't have to attend every party or group outing, but it's important to support your extroverted partner's need for socialising.

Compromise by agreeing to go to certain events, but also suggest more low-key activities like movie nights, dinner at home, or quiet walks. This way, both of your needs are met.

Exercise: The "Balance Builder" Next time your extroverted partner invites you to a big social event, offer a compromise. Say something like, "I'd love to go, but can we plan a quiet night the next day?" This lets your partner know you're willing to join in on the social fun, but you'll need some downtime afterward to recover.

Real-life example: Your extroverted partner invites you to a large weekend party, but you're not feeling up to it. Instead of immediately declining, you offer a compromise: "How about we go for an hour, and then grab a quiet dinner afterward?" This way, you're participating in the social event without overextending yourself, and you both get some quality one-on-one time afterward.

10. Avoiding Social Overload in Relationships

When you're dating someone, especially an extrovert, it's easy to fall into the trap of **over-committing** to social events. Suddenly, you're attending every family gathering, work party, and spontaneous hangout session, and before you know it, you're feeling completely burned out.

The key to avoiding social overload is to **set boundaries** early on and stick to them. Just because your partner enjoys back-to-back social engagements doesn't mean you have to say yes to every invitation.

Pro Tip #1: Pick and Choose Your Events It's okay to say no to some social invitations, especially if you've already had a busy week. Be selective about the events you attend. If there's a big gathering coming up, try to space out your social activities so that you have time to recharge before the event.

Pro Tip #2: Be Honest About Your Social Capacity If your partner invites you to multiple social events in a short time, it's okay to say, "I'm feeling a little burned out. Can we skip this one and do something more low-key instead?" This shows that you're not avoiding socialising altogether—you're just managing your energy.

Exercise: The "Social Capacity Metre" For one month, track how much socialising you're doing in your relationship. If you find that you're feeling constantly drained, take a step back and adjust your boundaries. Let your partner know that you'll need to space out your social commitments so that you don't feel overwhelmed.

Real-life example: Your partner invites you to two back-to-back events over the weekend. After a busy week, you feel your social battery running low, so you say, "I can do one of the events, but I'll need some downtime for the rest of the weekend." By managing your social capacity, you avoid burnout and still get to enjoy the event you choose to attend.

11. The Art of Recharging Together

Believe it or not, introverts and extroverts can **recharge together**—you just have to find activities that allow both of you to enjoy each other's company without feeling overstimulated. While your extroverted partner might love the buzz of social events, they can also appreciate the calm and relaxation of quiet moments with you.

The trick is to find activities that offer **low-key connection**, where you can spend time together without draining your social energy.

Pro Tip #1: Create "Quiet Time" Together Suggest activities that allow both of you to relax and enjoy each other's presence without needing to constantly engage in conversation. This could be reading together, watching a movie, or even going for a walk in nature. These moments offer a chance to connect without the pressure of socialising.

Pro Tip #2: Take Breaks During Social Events If you're at a social gathering and starting to feel overwhelmed, it's okay to take a break. Step outside for a few minutes or find a quieter corner where you can recharge. Your partner can join you for these mini-breaks, which can give both of you a moment to reset before diving back into the social scene.

Exercise: The "Low-Key Date" Plan a date that's centred around quiet, low-energy activities. This could be a picnic in the park, a lazy Sunday morning at a café, or even just cooking dinner together at home. Notice how much more relaxed and connected you feel when the pressure to be social is removed.

Real-life example: You and your partner spend a Saturday evening cooking dinner together at home, followed by a movie. The atmosphere is relaxed, and there's no pressure to entertain each other. By the end of the night, you both feel recharged and connected—without the need for a loud, overstimulating night out.

12. Handling Different Social Needs in Long-Term Relationships

One of the biggest challenges in introvert-extrovert relationships is handling the **different social needs** of both partners. While your extroverted partner might thrive on frequent social interactions, you might need more alone time to feel balanced. This can lead to tension if not addressed early on.

The key to making it work is to create a rhythm that honours both of your needs. You don't need to force yourself to socialise constantly, and your partner doesn't need to give up their social life. It's all about finding a balance that works for both of you.

Pro Tip #1: Create a "Social Calendar" If you're in a long-term relationship, it can help to create a social calendar where you plan your social activities in advance. This allows you to prepare mentally for upcoming events and gives you time to recharge in between. Your partner can still enjoy their social life, but you have more control over how much you participate.

Pro Tip #2: Alternate Between Social and Quiet Time Another way to balance social needs is by alternating between high-energy and low-energy activities. For example, if you attend a party one weekend, plan a quiet weekend at home the next. This keeps both of you happy without overextending yourself.

Exercise: The "Social Rhythm" Plan Sit down with your partner and create a plan for how you'll balance social activities and quiet time in your relationship. Decide which events you'll attend together, which you'll skip, and how you'll recharge afterward. This ensures that both of you feel supported and understood.

Real-life example: You and your partner create a social calendar where you alternate between attending social events and spending quiet weekends together. This gives your partner the social engagement they need while giving you the space to recharge. Over time, this rhythm becomes second nature, and you both feel more connected and balanced.

You've made it this far, and by now, you're equipped with a toolkit for navigating the sometimes overwhelming world of dating as an introvert. Whether you're dating a fellow introvert or someone with extroverted tendencies, you've learned how to protect your energy, communicate your needs, and balance social engagements with solo time.

But what about the **deeper emotional side** of relationships? While boundaries, alone time, and social capacity are critical, building a lasting relationship also requires emotional openness—something that can be tricky for introverts, who often keep their inner world to themselves.

In this final part of the chapter, we'll explore how to cultivate deeper emotional intimacy in your relationship, while still honouring your introverted need for space and reflection.

13. Cultivating Emotional Intimacy Without Overwhelm

For introverts, emotional intimacy can sometimes feel as daunting as socialising. The idea of opening up and sharing your innermost thoughts, feelings, and vulnerabilities can feel like you're handing someone the keys to your internal fortress. But here's the thing: **emotional intimacy is the foundation of a lasting, meaningful relationship**.

The good news? You don't have to dive into the deep end of emotional vulnerability right away. Just like social interactions, emotional intimacy can be built slowly, at a pace that feels comfortable for you. It's about finding moments to connect deeply with your partner, rather than constantly being emotionally "on."

Pro Tip #1: Share in Small Doses Emotional intimacy doesn't have to mean spilling your heart out all at once. Start by sharing small, personal details about yourself—your hobbies, dreams, or memories from childhood. These little windows into your inner world will help your partner understand you better and build a foundation of trust.

Pro Tip #2: Create Safe Spaces for Sharing Introverts often need a safe, quiet environment to open up emotionally. If you're trying to have a deep conversation in a busy restaurant or during a loud party, it's unlikely you'll feel comfortable enough to be vulnerable. Instead, choose moments where you both feel relaxed and connected—like during a quiet evening at home or while taking a walk together.

Exercise: The "Small Share" Challenge Start by sharing something small but meaningful with your partner—something you wouldn't normally bring up in casual conversation. It could be a childhood story, a book that had a big impact on you, or a personal goal you're working toward. Pay attention to how your partner responds and notice how these small moments of sharing bring you closer together.

Real-life example: You're having a quiet evening with your partner, and as you're chatting, you share a memory from your childhood that shaped who you are today. Your partner listens attentively, and this moment of vulnerability brings you closer together. It's not a grand, dramatic gesture—it's a small, genuine connection that deepens your emotional bond.

14. Setting Boundaries Around Alone Time (Without Hurting Feelings)

Here's a common challenge in relationships: you love your partner, but sometimes, you just **need space**. As an introvert, alone time is essential for recharging, but in a relationship, especially a new one, it can feel awkward to ask for that space. You might worry about hurting your partner's feelings or making them think you're not interested.

The key is to set clear boundaries around your need for alone time **without making your partner feel rejected**. It's not about pulling away from them—it's about taking care of yourself so that you can show up more fully when you're together.

Pro Tip #1: Frame Alone Time as Self-Care When asking for alone time, make it clear that it's about **self-care**, not avoidance. You're not withdrawing from the relationship; you're simply taking time to recharge so you can be more present and engaged. Let your partner know that alone time is something you need to maintain balance in your life.

Pro Tip #2: Reassure Them With a Plan If your partner feels uncertain about your need for space, reassure them by offering a plan for when you'll reconnect. For example, if you need a quiet night to yourself, suggest planning a fun activity together the next day. This shows your partner that while you need space now, you're still invested in the relationship.

Exercise: The "Recharge Schedule" For one week, create a schedule that balances alone time with quality time with your partner. Communicate this schedule clearly to your partner so that they understand when you'll be taking time for yourself and when you'll be reconnecting. Notice how much more relaxed and energised you feel when you have space to recharge.

Real-life example: You've had a busy week filled with social events, and by the weekend, you're craving some alone time. You tell your partner, "I've had a really draining week, so I'm going to take tonight to relax on my own. How about we plan a fun brunch tomorrow morning?" By offering a plan to reconnect, you protect your need for space without making your partner feel left out.

15. Managing Conflict as an Introvert

Here's a scenario that most introverts dread: **conflict**. Whether it's a small disagreement or a larger issue in the relationship, the thought of dealing with conflict can make you want to retreat to the nearest quiet corner and avoid the whole thing. But here's the deal—**conflict is a natural part of any relationship**, and learning how to handle it effectively is crucial for long-term success.

As an introvert, your first instinct might be to avoid confrontation or minimise the issue to keep the peace. But this approach can lead to resentment and unspoken frustrations that eventually bubble over. Instead, the goal is to **address conflict calmly and directly**—in a way that respects both your emotional needs and your partner's.

Pro Tip #1: Take Time to Reflect Before Responding Introverts often process emotions internally before they're ready to discuss them. If you're feeling upset or frustrated, it's okay to take time to reflect before responding. Let your partner know that you need a moment to gather your thoughts and that you'll come back to the conversation when you're ready.

Pro Tip #2: Use "I" Statements When addressing conflict, try to avoid sounding accusatory or defensive. Instead of saying, "You never listen to me," try framing it with an "I" statement, like, "I feel unheard when we're having conversations, and it's important to me that we work on communication." This approach helps keep the conversation constructive rather than confrontational.

Exercise: The "Pause and Reflect" Technique The next time a conflict arises, practice pausing before responding. Take a moment to reflect on your feelings and consider what you want to communicate. Once you're ready, approach the conversation calmly and use "I" statements to express your concerns.

Real-life example: You and your partner have a disagreement about how often you spend time together. Instead of reacting immediately, you tell your partner, "I'm feeling a little overwhelmed right now. Can I take some time to think about this, and we can talk later?" After reflecting on your feelings, you come back to the conversation later and say, "I feel like I need more downtime during the week, but I also want to make sure we're spending quality time together. Can we work out a balance?"

16. The Importance of Recharging Together—Quiet Time as a Couple

Introverts and extroverts alike can benefit from **shared quiet time** in a relationship. While your partner might enjoy social events, they can also appreciate the peace and relaxation that comes with simply being in each other's company without the need for constant conversation or activity.

Shared quiet time allows both of you to recharge while still feeling connected. It's a way to enjoy each other's presence without draining your energy, and it's especially important for introverts who thrive in calm, low-stimulation environments.

Pro Tip #1: Plan Quiet Time as a Couple. Make it a regular habit to plan quiet, low-energy activities together—whether it's reading side by side, watching a movie, or going for a walk. These moments of calm can strengthen your relationship and give you both a chance to recharge without the pressure of socialising.

Pro Tip #2: Embrace Silence In a healthy relationship, silence doesn't have to be awkward. Embrace the moments of silence as an opportunity to relax and enjoy each other's presence. There's no need to fill every moment with conversation—sometimes, the most meaningful connections happen in the quiet moments.

Exercise: The "Silent Date" For your next date, plan an activity that doesn't require much talking, like a nature hike, a visit to a museum, or even just relaxing at home with a book or movie. Notice how you feel more connected after spending quiet time together, and appreciate the comfort of being with someone who doesn't require constant conversation.

Real-life example: You and your partner spend a Sunday afternoon lounging at home, reading your favourite books and enjoying the silence. There's no pressure to talk or entertain each other—it's simply a peaceful, shared moment that leaves you both feeling recharged and connected by the end of the day.

9

The Office–Surviving Meetings and Water Coolers

Welcome to the jungle—the office jungle, that is. For introverts, navigating the workplace can sometimes feel like being thrown into an endless reality show where extroverts thrive on small talk, networking, and (gasp) team-building exercises. While the office isn't exactly a natural habitat for introverts, it doesn't have to be a place of social anxiety and endless awkwardness either.

Let's face it: **workplaces are designed for collaboration**, which often means attending meetings, interacting with colleagues, and even making small talk over the coffee machine (deep breaths). But fear not, fellow introverts—this chapter is all about how you can **survive and thrive in an office environment** while staying true to your introverted self.

In this chapter, we'll explore how to handle the big three: meetings, water-cooler chats, and team-building exercises. You'll learn how to navigate office politics, communicate effectively, and even make work friends (yes, it's possible).

1. Meetings: How to Speak Up Without Draining Your Energy

Let's start with one of the biggest hurdles for introverts: **meetings.** For some reason, the workplace loves meetings—whether they're status updates, brainstorming sessions, or the dreaded "let's all get in a room and talk about this" kind of meetings. As an introvert, speaking up in front of a group of colleagues can feel overwhelming, but here's the thing: **meetings don't have to be exhausting or anxiety-inducing.**

You don't need to dominate the room or be the loudest voice to contribute meaningfully. Instead, focus on **strategic communication**—finding moments where your input is valuable and speaking up in a way that feels authentic to you.

Pro Tip #1: Prepare in Advance One of the best ways to reduce meeting anxiety is to prepare ahead of time. Review the meeting agenda (if there is one) and think about the points you'd like to contribute. If you're worried about being put on the spot, have a few notes ready that you can refer to during the discussion.

Pro Tip #2: Choose Your Moments to Speak. You don't need to jump into every part of the conversation. Instead, choose a few key moments where your input can add value. It's better to make one thoughtful comment than to try to contribute to every topic. Your colleagues will appreciate the quality of your insights, and you won't feel pressure to fill every silence.

Exercise: The "One Comment" Challenge For your next meeting, set a simple goal: make at least one meaningful contribution. This could be a question, a comment, or a suggestion. The goal isn't to dominate the meeting, but to find a moment where your voice can add value. After the meeting, reflect on how it felt to contribute without overextending yourself.

Real-life example: You're in a project status meeting, and the conversation turns to a topic you've been working on. Instead of waiting for someone to call on you, you jump in with, "I've been looking into that, and I think one solution might be..." You speak confidently but briefly, adding value without taking over the meeting. Your colleagues appreciate your input, and you feel accomplished for contributing without feeling drained.

2. The Water Cooler (AKA Small Talk): Making It Work for You

Ah, the classic **water cooler conversation**—those short, often awkward chats in the breakroom, hallways, or on the way to the printer. For introverts, small talk can feel pointless or exhausting, but here's the secret: **small talk is actually a powerful tool** for building relationships at work, and it doesn't have to be painful.

Instead of dreading these moments, think of them as an opportunity to make connections without diving into deep, draining conversations. The key is to **keep it light** and focus on common interests—whether it's the weather, weekend plans, or that TV show everyone's talking about.

Pro Tip #1: Have a Go-To Topic Having a go-to topic in your back pocket makes small talk much easier. Whether it's something you know is universally relatable (like the latest Netflix series) or a simple comment about the workday, it gives you something to fall back on when the conversation lags. Bonus points if your topic has a natural exit, like "Well, I'll let you get back to it!"

Pro Tip #2: Ask Open-Ended Questions If you find yourself stuck in an awkward conversation, ask an open-ended question to keep the other person talking. This takes the pressure off you to keep the conversation going and gives them a chance to share. Questions like "What are your plans for the weekend?" or "How was your last project going?" are great ways to engage without diving too deep.

Exercise: The "One Topic" Practice For the next week, practice using a go-to topic during casual interactions with colleagues. Keep the conversation light, and pay attention to how it feels to engage without overcommitting. Focus on making brief connections rather than feeling pressured to have long conversations.

Real-life example: You're refilling your coffee when a colleague walks up and asks, "How's your week going?" Instead of panicking, you use your go-to topic: "Pretty good! I'm catching up on that new series everyone's talking about—have you seen it yet?" The conversation stays light and easy, and you leave the break room without feeling drained or awkward.

3. Team-Building Exercises: Surviving (and Maybe Even Enjoying) Them

Here's a sentence no introvert wants to hear: **"We're doing a team-building exercise!"** Whether it's a trust fall, a group brainstorming session, or (worst of all) role-playing, team-building activities can feel like an introvert's worst nightmare. But here's the thing: team-building doesn't have to be terrible. In fact, when done right, it can actually help you build stronger relationships at work—without draining all your energy.

The key is to **reframe team-building** as an opportunity to observe, listen, and participate in a way that feels comfortable for you.

Pro Tip #1: Observe First, Participate Second You don't need to be the first person to jump into every team-building activity. If you're feeling unsure, hang back a little and observe how others are participating. This gives you time to figure out how you can contribute without feeling pressured to take centre stage.

Pro Tip #2: Find Roles That Suit You Not every part of a team-building exercise requires you to be the loud, outgoing leader. If there's a brainstorming session, for example, focus on listening to others and offering insights when you feel ready. Look for roles that align with your strengths, like being the one who helps organise ideas or provides thoughtful feedback.

Exercise: The "Observer's Role" At your next team-building exercise, practice being an active observer. Instead of jumping in right away, listen to the conversation and look for opportunities to contribute in a way that feels comfortable. You'll still be part of the activity without feeling the pressure to lead.

Real-life example: Your team is asked to do a brainstorming exercise where everyone takes turns sharing ideas. Instead of stressing out about what to say, you hang back and listen to the first few people. When your turn comes, you build off what someone else has said, offering a thoughtful suggestion without feeling like you're on the spot.

4. Networking Within the Office: Building Relationships at Your Own Pace

While networking often conjures up images of large conferences and cocktail mixers, **internal networking**—the relationships you build within your own office—can be just as important. Whether you're aiming for a promotion, a new project, or just trying to create a supportive work environment, networking within the office is key to your long-term success.

The good news? **You don't need to be the life of the office to build strong connections.** Introverts often excel at forming deeper, more meaningful relationships with a few key people, rather than trying to connect with everyone.

Pro Tip #1: Start Small Instead of trying to get to know everyone at once, focus on building relationships with a few key colleagues. This could be people you work with regularly, those in your department, or anyone whose work you admire. By starting small, you can create a network that feels manageable.

Pro Tip #2: Be Consistent Networking isn't just about making an impression once—it's about consistently showing up. This could be as simple as checking in with a colleague over coffee once a week, offering to help on a project, or sending a quick email to share something interesting related to their work. Consistency builds trust and connection over time.

Exercise: The "One Connection" Goal For the next month, set a goal to build or strengthen a connection with one colleague. This could mean having lunch together, offering to collaborate on a project, or simply chatting with them about something non-work-related. The goal is to create a deeper connection over time, rather than rushing to make as many connections as possible.

Real-life example: You work closely with a colleague on several projects, but you haven't had much time to get to know them outside of work. You suggest grabbing lunch one day to chat about a shared interest. Over time, this becomes a regular thing, and you build a strong, supportive relationship that helps both of you feel more connected in the office.

Awesome! Let's keep going and dive deeper into surviving and thriving in the office as an introvert. In this next section, we'll talk about **how to stand out without being the loudest person in the room**, managing office politics (yes, they exist), and how to balance your energy when the workday feels never-ending.

The key to all of this? **Playing to your strengths** as an introvert—using your ability to think deeply, observe carefully, and build meaningful connections to your advantage. You don't need to shout to be heard, and you don't need to be the social butterfly to make a strong impact.

5. How to Stand Out at Work Without Being Loud

One of the biggest myths about the workplace is that you have to be **outgoing and loud** to stand out or get ahead. As an introvert, the idea of constantly speaking up, promoting yourself, or being the centre of attention might feel exhausting. But here's the thing: **you don't need to be the loudest voice in the room** to make an impact. In fact, introverts often excel by offering thoughtful contributions and focusing on quality over quantity.

Here's how to stand out without exhausting yourself in the process:

Pro Tip #1: Let Your Work Speak for Itself As an introvert, you likely thrive in environments where you can focus, think deeply, and produce high-quality work. One of the best ways to stand out in the office is to let the results of your work do the talking. When you consistently deliver excellent work, people will notice—even if you're not constantly promoting yourself.

Pro Tip #2: Offer Thoughtful Insights (When It Counts) You don't need to speak up at every meeting or offer input on every single topic. Instead, focus on **strategic contributions**—offer insights or suggestions when you have something meaningful to add. People will remember your contributions because they're thoughtful and well-timed, rather than just filling space in the conversation.

Exercise: The "One Insight" Challenge At your next team meeting, focus on contributing just one thoughtful insight or suggestion. This could be a solution to a problem, a different perspective, or even a well-placed question. By limiting yourself to one key contribution, you'll reduce the pressure to speak constantly while still making an impact.

Real-life example: During a project brainstorming session, you listen carefully to your colleagues' ideas. After hearing a few suggestions, you speak up with a thoughtful question that challenges the group to think about a potential obstacle they hadn't considered. Your contribution shifts the conversation and helps the team come up with a stronger solution. You didn't have to dominate the discussion—just one strategic insight made a difference.

6. Navigating Office Politics (Without Losing Your Soul)

No one likes to talk about it, but **office politics** are a reality in most workplaces. While some people seem to navigate these waters with ease, it can feel more difficult for introverts, who might prefer to focus on their work rather than playing the social game. But here's the thing: you don't need to lose your integrity or compromise your values to **navigate office politics** effectively.

The key is to understand how the system works without getting sucked into the drama. You can build influence, manage relationships, and protect your reputation without turning into someone you're not.

Pro Tip #1: Build Relationships With Key People One of the best ways to navigate office politics is to build **genuine relationships** with key people in the office. This doesn't mean sucking up to your boss or joining in on gossip—rather, it's about forming connections with colleagues who can support you and help you achieve your goals. These relationships are built on trust and mutual respect, not manipulation.

Pro Tip #2: Avoid Gossip Like the Plague Office politics often come with gossip and drama, and getting involved in it can harm your reputation. As an introvert, it's easy to steer clear of the gossip mill by **staying focused on your work** and politely distancing yourself from conversations that feel negative or toxic. People will respect you more for staying above the fray.

Exercise: The "Genuine Connection" Plan For the next month, focus on building or strengthening relationships with a few key people in your office. This could include your direct supervisor, colleagues in other departments, or mentors who can offer guidance. Approach these relationships with authenticity—offer help, ask for advice, and focus on building trust.

Real-life example: You've noticed that a colleague from another department seems to have a lot of influence in meetings. Instead of trying to "win them over" in an obvious way, you approach them for advice on a project they've worked on before. Over time, you build a rapport based on mutual respect, and this relationship helps you gain more visibility in the office without having to play the political game.

7. Managing Your Energy Throughout the Workday

Let's be real: the typical office workday isn't exactly designed for introverts. Between meetings, collaborative projects, and casual conversations, it can feel like you're constantly "on"—and by the end of the day, your social battery might be completely drained. But don't worry: there are ways to **manage your energy** throughout the day so that you don't burn out before 5 p.m.

Pro Tip #1: Schedule Breaks to Recharge One of the most effective ways to manage your energy is to schedule **mini-breaks** throughout your workday. These breaks don't have to be long—just 5-10 minutes where you can step away from your desk, take a walk, or find a quiet spot to reset. These small moments of solitude can help you recharge before jumping back into the next meeting or task.

Pro Tip #2: Set Boundaries With Your Time If you're constantly being interrupted by colleagues or pulled into meetings, it's important to set **boundaries around your time**. Let your coworkers know when you're available for conversations and when you need focused work time. This can be as simple as blocking off time in your calendar or wearing headphones to signal that you're in "deep work" mode.

Exercise: The "Energy Tracker" For one week, track how your energy levels fluctuate throughout the day. Notice when you feel most energised and when your social battery starts to dip. Use this information to plan your workday around your natural energy patterns. For example, if you know you feel drained after lunchtime meetings, schedule a quiet solo task for the afternoon.

Real-life example: You've noticed that after the morning's back-to-back meetings, you always feel mentally drained by noon. To manage this, you start scheduling a 10-minute walk outside after your last meeting of the morning. This brief break helps you recharge and return to your desk feeling refreshed and ready to tackle the rest of the day. Over time, this small adjustment makes a big difference in how you manage your energy throughout the day.

8. Quiet Leadership: Leading as an Introvert

Leadership isn't reserved for extroverts who love to take charge in meetings or give big presentations. In fact, **introverted leaders** often bring unique strengths to the table—like deep listening, thoughtful decision-making, and the ability to empower others. If you're an introvert, you might not see yourself as a natural leader, but the truth is that **quiet leadership** can be just as effective (if not more so) than traditional leadership styles.

Here's how to embrace leadership in a way that feels authentic to your introverted nature:

Pro Tip #1: Lead Through Listening One of the greatest strengths of introverted leaders is their ability to listen deeply to others. In meetings or team settings, focus on **actively listening** to your colleagues, asking thoughtful questions, and gathering input before making decisions. This approach shows that you value other perspectives and can lead to better, more inclusive solutions.

Pro Tip #2: Empower Others Introverted leaders don't need to be the loudest voice in the room—instead, they excel at **empowering others** to shine. Focus on supporting your team members, giving them opportunities to take ownership of projects, and offering guidance when needed. By lifting others up, you build a strong, motivated team without needing to be the centre of attention.

Exercise: The "Lead by Listening" Challenge For the next month, focus on leading through listening in meetings or group settings. Instead of feeling the need to direct the conversation, practice asking open-ended questions, gathering input from your team, and offering support when needed. Notice how this approach builds trust and collaboration among your colleagues.

Real-life example: You're leading a team meeting, but instead of dominating the discussion, you start by asking your team members for their ideas and suggestions on a new project. You listen carefully to each person's input and then help the group come to a consensus. By empowering your team to contribute, you lead the project without needing to be the loudest voice in the room. Your colleagues appreciate the collaborative atmosphere, and you feel confident in your quiet leadership style.

You're doing great—navigating the workplace jungle like a pro, armed with strategies that allow you to preserve your energy while still making an impact. Now that we've covered how to stand out, handle office politics, and manage your energy throughout the day, it's time to dig into a few more crucial elements of office life. These include **handling feedback, remote work, and building your confidence** as an introvert in a work environment that may not always be designed with introverts in mind.

The modern workplace is changing, and with more opportunities for remote work and hybrid models, introverts are finding new ways to **excel** without the pressure of constant social interaction. Let's explore how you can take advantage of these trends while continuing to shine in a way that feels true to your introverted nature.

9. Handling Feedback: Taking It In Without Taking It Personally

Receiving feedback at work can be a tricky area for introverts, who might internalise criticism more deeply than extroverts. Feedback—whether positive or constructive—can sometimes feel overwhelming, especially if you're used to working quietly and not drawing too much attention to yourself. But here's the truth: **feedback is essential for growth**. Learning how to receive it gracefully and act on it will help you advance in your career.

The key to handling feedback as an introvert is to **stay open to the message** without letting it derail your confidence. It's all about knowing what to take in, what to leave behind, and how to turn feedback into an opportunity for personal and professional growth.

Pro Tip #1: Separate the Feedback From Your Identity When receiving constructive feedback, it's important to remember that feedback is about your work—not about you as a person. It can be easy to take feedback personally, especially if you've put a lot of effort into a project, but try to separate yourself from the critique. Ask yourself, "How can I use this feedback to improve my work?" rather than seeing it as a reflection of your worth.

Pro Tip #2: Ask for Clarification If feedback feels vague or unclear, don't be afraid to ask for more details. Sometimes, managers or colleagues may give feedback that's broad or nonspecific, which can leave you wondering what exactly you need to work on. Politely ask for clarification, like, "Could you give me a specific example of how I could improve in this area?" This helps you focus on actionable steps rather than feeling confused or overwhelmed.

Exercise: The "Feedback Filter" After receiving feedback, take a few moments to reflect on it. Use a simple filter: What's useful? What's not? Write down one or two specific actions you can take based on the feedback, and then let go of anything that feels overly critical or unhelpful.

Real-life example: During a performance review, your manager mentions that you need to work on being more vocal in team meetings. Instead of feeling deflated, you ask for clarification: "Can you give me an example of a situation where I could have contributed more?" Your manager explains that in a recent meeting, they were hoping for your input on a key decision. Armed with this information, you make a plan to contribute earlier in future meetings, turning the feedback into an opportunity for growth.

10. Thriving in Remote or Hybrid Work Environments

With the rise of remote and hybrid work models, **introverts are finding new ways to excel** without the constant pressure of in-office interactions. For many introverts, the opportunity to work from home (even part-time) is a game-changer, allowing them to manage their energy more effectively and focus on their work without the distractions of a busy office.

But remote work comes with its own set of challenges, including maintaining connections with your team and staying visible when you're not physically present. Here's how you can thrive in a remote or hybrid work environment as an introvert:

Pro Tip #1: Create a Structured Workday Remote work can sometimes blur the lines between work and personal life, making it harder to switch off at the end of the day. To avoid burnout, **structure your workday** by setting clear start and end times. Create a routine that includes regular breaks to recharge, just as you would in an office setting. This structure will help you stay focused and productive without feeling overwhelmed.

Pro Tip #2: Stay Connected Without Overdoing It One of the challenges of remote work is maintaining connections with your team. While introverts may prefer to work independently, it's still important to check in with colleagues and managers regularly. Schedule virtual coffee chats or short check-ins to stay connected without overloading your calendar with too many meetings.

Exercise: The "Connection Balance" For the next month, track how often you're connecting with colleagues and your manager. Aim to schedule one or two virtual check-ins per week to stay visible, but also make sure to block off time for focused, solo work. Notice how this balance helps you stay connected while protecting your energy.

Real-life example: You're working remotely three days a week and have noticed that while you enjoy the solitude, you've started feeling a bit disconnected from your team. To strike a balance, you schedule a 15-minute virtual coffee chat with a colleague once a week, and check in with your manager every other week. This helps you stay engaged without overwhelming yourself with constant video calls.

11. Building Confidence as an Introvert at Work

Let's talk about **confidence**. It's often assumed that confidence comes naturally to extroverts, but introverts can be just as confident—just in a quieter, more reflective way. The key to building confidence as an introvert in the workplace is to **trust in your unique strengths** and recognize the value you bring to the table.

Confidence isn't about being the loudest or the most outgoing person in the room. It's about feeling secure in your abilities, knowing your worth, and contributing in ways that feel authentic to you.

Pro Tip #1: Focus on Your Strengths Introverts often excel at deep thinking, problem-solving, and creating meaningful connections. Rather than trying to emulate the extroverts around you, focus on what you do best. Whether it's producing high-quality work, offering thoughtful feedback, or helping to create a calm, productive atmosphere, your strengths are valuable and shouldn't be overlooked.

Pro Tip #2: Celebrating Small Wins Building confidence is a gradual process, and it starts with recognizing your achievements—no matter how small. Each time you contribute to a meeting, solve a problem, or complete a project, take a moment to acknowledge the accomplishment. Over time, these small wins will build up and help you feel more confident in your role.

Exercise: The "Confidence Journal" Start a simple confidence journal where you write down one small win at the end of each workday. This could be anything from finishing a project to speaking up in a meeting. Reflect on how these daily wins are building your confidence over time.

Real-life example: After contributing a key idea in a team meeting, you feel proud of how you spoke up, even though it was outside your comfort zone. You jot down the moment in your confidence journal, noting how you felt after the meeting. Over time, these reflections help you see how your confidence is growing, one small step at a time.

12. The Long Game: Career Growth as an Introvert

Career growth doesn't always come in the form of loud, public victories or constant networking events. For introverts, career success often comes through **consistency, quality work, and strong relationships** built over time. While you may not be the person shouting from the rooftops about your achievements, your steady, thoughtful approach to work will naturally lead to opportunities for growth and advancement.

Here's how to play the long game and set yourself up for career success as an introvert:

Pro Tip #1: Seek Out Mentors Having a mentor—someone who can offer guidance, support, and career advice—is invaluable, especially for introverts who might not always be comfortable navigating office politics or advocating for themselves. Seek out a mentor within your company or industry who understands your strengths and can help you strategize your career growth.

Pro Tip #2: Advocate for Yourself (Even Quietly) While self-promotion might not come naturally, it's important to advocate for yourself—especially when it comes to raises, promotions, or new opportunities. You don't have to be boastful or over-the-top. Simply keep track of your achievements and contributions, and when the time comes, present them confidently to your manager.

Exercise: The "Career Tracker" Keep a simple career tracker where you document your accomplishments, projects, and feedback throughout the year. This will come in handy during performance reviews or when discussing career goals with your manager. By keeping a record of your contributions, you can confidently advocate for your career progression without needing to "sell" yourself.

Real-life example: After working on several successful projects over the past year, you meet with your manager to discuss a potential promotion. You bring your career tracker with you, outlining your achievements, the impact of your work, and how you've contributed to the team's success. Your manager appreciates the detailed approach, and the conversation leads to a well-deserved promotion.

Fantastic! Let's wrap up Chapter 9 by tackling a few more essential topics that will help you **thrive in the workplace as an introvert**. Now that we've covered standing out, managing feedback, remote work, and career growth, it's time to look at the subtle art of **collaboration**, **dealing with difficult colleagues**, and **handling group projects**—all of which can be a bit daunting for those of us who prefer solo work. But don't worry, I've got your back. There are ways to engage in group dynamics without draining your energy or losing your voice in the process.

13. The Subtle Art of Collaboration

Collaboration is a core part of almost every workplace, but for introverts, it can sometimes feel overwhelming. Whether it's working in small teams or jumping into brainstorming sessions, the fast-paced, often high-energy environment can clash with an introvert's natural preference for **quiet reflection**. But here's the good news: **collaboration doesn't mean losing your introverted strengths**. In fact, your ability to listen, think deeply, and offer thoughtful contributions is exactly what many teams need.

Here's how to approach collaboration in a way that works for you:

Pro Tip #1: Play to Your Strengths In collaborative settings, focus on what you do best. You might not be the person throwing out a dozen ideas in a brainstorming session, but you can offer a well-thought-out solution once the initial excitement has died down. Your team will appreciate your perspective, and you'll feel more comfortable contributing in a meaningful way.

Pro Tip #2: Use Written Communication If you're more comfortable articulating your thoughts in writing than in real-time discussions, use that to your advantage. Suggest following up brainstorming sessions with written summaries or proposals, where you can take your time to reflect and share your insights without the pressure of on-the-spot conversation.

Exercise: The "Post-Meeting Follow-Up" After your next collaborative meeting, follow up with an email that summarises your thoughts or contributions. This could be a list of key takeaways, a proposed solution, or even just a few ideas that you didn't have the chance to mention during the meeting. This way, you add value to the conversation without feeling like you have to jump in during the chaos.

Real-life example: You're in a brainstorming session with your team, but instead of feeling pressured to throw out ideas on the spot, you take notes and focus on listening. After the meeting, you send a follow-up email with a few additional suggestions that you've had time to reflect on. Your manager appreciates the thoughtfulness of your ideas, and you feel more confident contributing at your own pace.

14. Handling Difficult Colleagues Without Draining Your Energy

Every workplace has them—the difficult colleagues who seem to thrive on conflict, gossip, or just making life harder than it needs to be. As an introvert, dealing with these kinds of colleagues can be especially draining, as you likely prefer to avoid unnecessary drama and focus on your work. But here's the truth: **you don't need to engage with negativity** or let it sap your energy.

Here's how to handle difficult colleagues in a way that protects your peace of mind:

Pro Tip #1: Set Boundaries Early If you have a colleague who tends to dominate conversations, criticise others, or stir up drama, it's important to set **clear boundaries** early on. This doesn't mean being confrontational—it can be as simple as limiting your interactions with them or redirecting negative conversations back to work-related topics. Protecting your energy is your top priority.

Pro Tip #2: Don't Engage in Gossip When difficult colleagues try to pull you into office gossip or complaints, politely distance yourself. You don't need to engage in these conversations, and removing yourself from the gossip mill will help protect your reputation. Simply redirect the conversation to a neutral topic, or excuse yourself if the conversation becomes toxic.

Exercise: The "Polite Exit" Strategy For the next month, practice politely excusing yourself from negative conversations with difficult colleagues. This could be as simple as saying, "I've got to finish up this project, but let's catch up later," or redirecting the conversation with, "I've got to head to a meeting—let's talk about this another time." Notice how much more energy you have when you avoid getting pulled into office drama.

Real-life example: A colleague starts complaining about a coworker during your lunch break, but you don't want to get involved in the gossip. Instead of engaging, you say, "I've got to run and prepare for a meeting, but I'll see you later!" By leaving the conversation politely, you protect your energy and reputation while still maintaining a professional relationship with the colleague.

15. Thriving in Group Projects Without Feeling Overwhelmed

Group projects can be tricky for introverts. While collaboration can lead to great results, the constant communication and frequent meetings that often come with group projects can feel overwhelming—especially if the group dynamics are chaotic. But with the right strategies, you can thrive in group settings without feeling like you've lost control of your workload or your energy.

Here's how to handle group projects like a pro:

Pro Tip #1: Define Your Role Early One of the best ways to navigate group projects is to **define your role early on**. Be clear about what responsibilities you're taking on, and set expectations with your team about how you prefer to communicate. If you're more comfortable working independently on certain tasks, let the group know that you'll handle your part and provide updates at key checkpoints.

Pro Tip #2: Use Asynchronous Communication When Possible If your group project requires constant communication, suggest using asynchronous tools like email or project management software where everyone can share updates without needing to be in constant meetings. This gives you more control over your time and allows you to contribute thoughtfully without the pressure of real-time discussions.

Exercise: The "Role Clarifier" At the start of your next group project, be proactive about clarifying your role and how you'll contribute. Let your team know how you'll be handling your tasks and when they can expect updates from you. This will give you more control over your workload and help you avoid feeling overwhelmed by group dynamics.

Real-life example: You're assigned to a group project, and the first meeting is full of energetic brainstorming and rapid-fire ideas. Instead of getting swept up in the chaos, you offer to take on a specific task and update the group through your project management tool. You also suggest setting up one meeting per week to review progress, rather than meeting daily. This approach helps you manage your workload while still being a valuable team member.

16. The Power of Quiet Influence: Leading Without Loudness

As an introvert, you may not feel like the "obvious leader" in the office. You're not the person rallying the team with high-energy speeches or dominating meetings with bold ideas. But here's the thing: **quiet influence is just as powerful**—and sometimes, even more so.

Introverts have a unique ability to **lead by example**, offering thoughtful guidance, building trust, and creating a calm, focused work environment. Your influence doesn't need to come from being the loudest voice in the room. It comes from your consistency, your ability to listen, and your dedication to helping your team succeed.

Pro Tip #1: Lead Through Action One of the most effective ways to lead as an introvert is to **lead by example**. Focus on producing high-quality work, supporting your team members, and staying calm under pressure. Over time, your colleagues will come to respect your leadership style because it's based on action rather than words.

Pro Tip #2: Build Strong One-on-One Relationships Introverts often excel at building deep, meaningful connections with individuals. Use this strength to your advantage by cultivating strong one-on-one relationships with your team members. Offer support, mentorship, or just a listening ear when needed. These personal connections will strengthen your influence and build trust within your team.

Exercise: The "Action-Oriented Leadership" Plan For the next month, focus on leading through action. Rather than trying to be the loudest voice in meetings, focus on delivering high-quality work and supporting your team behind the scenes. Notice how your influence grows naturally as people come to rely on your consistency and dedication.

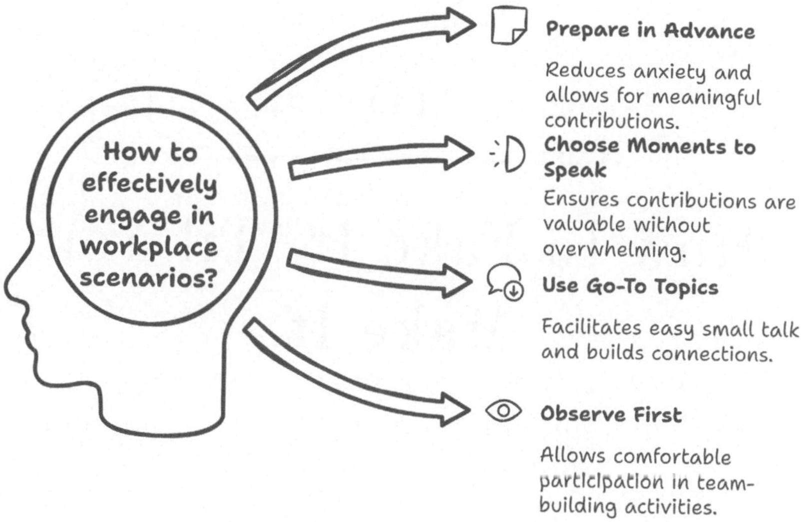

Wrapping Up Chapter 9:

By now, you've mastered the art of **surviving and thriving in the workplace as an introvert**. You've learned how to manage meetings, small talk, team-building exercises, and even difficult colleagues—all while staying true to your introverted nature. Whether you're navigating office politics, leading a project, or just trying to make it through the workday without feeling drained, you've got the tools you need to succeed.

Remember, your strengths as an introvert—thoughtfulness, deep listening, and quiet influence—are invaluable in any workplace. You don't need to change who you are to succeed. Instead, lean into your natural strengths, and you'll find that you can excel in ways that feel authentic and rewarding.

10

How to Fake It 'Til You Make It

(Because Everyone Else Is Doing It)

Okay, introvert friends, buckle up, because this chapter is all about **faking it 'til you make it**—and guess what? Pretty much everyone else is doing it too! Yup, even those super confident extroverts who seem like they were born to own every room they walk into. The truth is, most people are just winging it, whether they admit it or not. So, if you've ever felt like you're the only one who's pretending to have it all together, you're in good company.

This chapter is your guide to **faking confidence** when you don't feel it, **acting extroverted** when you'd rather crawl into a quiet corner, and using **strategic "faking it" tactics** to help you get through those awkward social moments. But don't worry—this isn't about becoming someone you're not. It's about embracing a little **extroverted theatre** until you start to feel more comfortable in situations that would normally make you want to run for the hills.

Let's get started!

1. The Myth of Confidence: Spoiler Alert, Nobody Has It All Figured Out

Before we dive into the strategies, let's debunk a myth: **confidence is not a fixed trait**. It's not something you either have or don't have. In fact, confidence is often more of a **performance** than anything else. The people who seem the most confident are usually just really good at **projecting confidence**, even if they're freaking out on the inside.

Pro Tip #1: Start Small You don't have to go from wallflower to spotlight in one giant leap. Start by practising small, manageable confidence-boosting behaviours. Make eye contact when you speak to someone, give a firm handshake, or offer a quick comment during a conversation. These little moments add up, and over time, you'll start to feel more at ease.

Pro Tip #2: Fake It Until It's Real Here's the trick: **the more you fake confidence**, the more you'll start to feel it. Your brain is wired to adapt, so if you keep practising confident behaviours, they'll eventually start to feel natural. Think of it as building a muscle—every time you flex your confidence, it gets a little stronger.

Real-life example: You've been dreading a presentation at work. Normally, you'd want to blend into the background, but instead, you decide to try faking it. You walk in with a confident stride, make eye contact with the audience, and speak with conviction. Sure, you might be sweating inside, but to everyone else, you look calm and collected. And guess what? By the end of the presentation, you actually start to believe in the confidence you're projecting.

2. Channelling Your Inner Extrovert Without Losing Yourself

Faking it 'til you make it doesn't mean you have to abandon your introverted nature. It's not about pretending to be someone you're not. Instead, it's about **strategically channelling certain extroverted traits** when the situation calls for it. Think of it like putting on a costume—sometimes you need to wear the "extrovert suit" to get through a social event or a work meeting, but underneath, you're still you.

Pro Tip #1: Create an Extrovert Persona One way to ease into faking extroversion is by creating a **persona**—a version of yourself that you can call on in social situations. This doesn't mean being fake, but rather amplifying certain aspects of your personality that help you navigate social settings more easily. Your extrovert persona might be more outgoing, more talkative, or more willing to take risks in conversation.

Pro Tip #2: Use "Extrovert Mode" in Small Doses You don't need to stay in extrovert mode all the time. It's perfectly fine to switch back to your introverted self when you need to recharge. Think of it as **using extrovert mode in bursts**—during a meeting, a social event, or any situation where being more outgoing helps. Once it's over, you can retreat to your introverted safe space and relax.

Exercise: The "Extrovert Alter Ego" Create an extrovert alter ego—someone who is confident, social, and outgoing. Give this persona a name, and practice stepping into their shoes in situations where you'd normally feel nervous. For example, you could channel your alter ego when meeting new people at a party or speaking up in a meeting. The more you practise, the easier it will become to switch into extrovert mode when needed.

Real-life example: You've got a networking event coming up, and the idea of making small talk with strangers is stressing you out. Instead of dreading it, you decide to create an extrovert alter ego named "Charismatic Chris." When you walk into the event, you imagine that you're Charismatic Chris—someone who loves meeting new people and strikes up conversations effortlessly. By stepping into this persona, you feel more at ease, and before you know it, you're chatting with people and actually enjoying yourself.

3. The Power of Acting Like You Belong

One of the most effective "fake it 'til you make it" strategies is acting like you belong in any situation, even if you feel out of place. This is called **imposter syndrome**, and guess what? Pretty much everyone experiences it at some point. The key to overcoming imposter syndrome is to **act as if you belong**, even when your brain is telling you that you don't.

Pro Tip #1: Walk into Every Room Like You Own It This doesn't mean being arrogant or overconfident—it's about **projecting a sense of belonging**. When you walk into a room, hold your head high, make eye contact, and act as though you're meant to be there.

People will take their cues from you, and if you act like you belong, they'll believe it too.

Pro Tip #2: Reframe Your Self-Talk When you start to feel like an imposter, remind yourself that everyone else is probably feeling the same way. Instead of thinking, "I don't belong here," try reframing it as, "I deserve to be here just as much as anyone else." This simple shift in mindset can help you project more confidence, even when you're feeling unsure.

Exercise: The "Power Walk" The next time you walk into a meeting, event, or social gathering, practise the power walk. Stand tall, make eye contact with the people around you, and walk with purpose as if you own the place. Notice how this simple change in body language makes you feel more confident and in control.

Real-life example: You're attending a big conference for work, and the thought of mingling with industry leaders is intimidating. But instead of shrinking into the background, you decide to walk into the room like you own it. You hold your head high, make eye contact with the people around you, and introduce yourself confidently. By the end of the day, you've made several new connections, and you no longer feel like an imposter.

4. Mastering the Art of Small Talk (Without Dying Inside)

Let's face it: small talk is the worst. For introverts, the idea of making idle chit-chat about the weather or weekend plans can feel like pure torture. But here's the thing—**small talk doesn't have to be painful**. In fact, it can be a great way to ease into social situations without the pressure of deep conversation. The key is to **approach small talk with a sense of humour** and see it as a stepping stone to more meaningful interactions.

Pro Tip #1: Use Small Talk as a Warm-Up. Think of small talk as a warm-up exercise for more meaningful conversations. You don't need to dive into deep discussions right away. Start with light, easy topics, and gradually build rapport with the people you're talking to. Once you're more comfortable, you can shift the conversation to something more interesting.

Pro Tip #2: Prepare a Few Go-To Topics If you dread small talk, it helps to have a few **go-to topics** ready to break the ice. These could be simple questions like, "What's been the highlight of your week?" or "Have you read any good books lately?" Having a few conversation starters in your back pocket can make small talk less awkward and more enjoyable.

Exercise: The "Small Talk Warm-Up" At your next social event or work gathering, use small talk as a warm-up. Start with easy, light topics like weekend plans or recent news, and gradually steer the conversation toward something more engaging. Pay attention to how the conversation evolves and how much easier it feels once you get past the initial small talk phase.

Real-life example: You're at a company holiday party, and small talk is inevitable. Instead of dreading it, you decide to use it as a warm-up. You ask a colleague about their weekend plans, and before you know it, you're talking about your shared love of hiking. The conversation naturally evolves into a deeper discussion, and you realise that small talk doesn't have to be painful—it's just the gateway to more meaningful interactions.

Great! Let's keep building on your arsenal of "fake it 'til you make it" strategies. We've already covered confidence, channelling your inner extrovert, and even surviving the dreaded small talk. Now, let's dive into a few more advanced techniques that will help you **not only survive** but **thrive in social settings** and professional environments. We'll explore how to **fake confidence in high-pressure situations**, **how to handle networking like a pro**, and even how to **use body language to project confidence**, even when you're feeling anything but.

Remember, this isn't about pretending to be someone you're not—it's about using specific tools to help you navigate situations that might otherwise feel overwhelming. Eventually, what starts as "faking it" will begin to feel more natural, and your introverted self will start to shine through in ways you never expected.

5. High-Pressure Situations: Faking Confidence When the Stakes Are High

Whether it's giving a presentation, attending a big event, or meeting someone important for the first time, high-pressure situations can trigger anxiety for anyone—especially introverts. But here's a secret: **nobody is born good at handling high-pressure situations**. The people who seem calm and collected in these moments have learned how to manage their nerves and project confidence, even when they don't feel it.

Here's how to **fake confidence** when the stakes are high:

Pro Tip #1: Control Your Breathing One of the easiest ways to calm your nerves and appear more confident is by **controlling your breathing.** Before stepping into a high-pressure situation, take a few deep breaths to centre yourself. Slow, deep breathing signals to your brain that you're in control, which helps reduce anxiety and makes you appear more composed.

Pro Tip #2: Practice Power Posing Yes, power posing is a real thing! Research shows that **body language affects your mood**, and standing in a confident, open posture (think hands on hips, shoulders back, head up) can actually help boost your confidence levels. Before a big meeting or presentation, take a minute to practise a power pose in private—trust me, it works.

Exercise: The "Pre-Event Power Pose" Before your next big event, presentation, or high-stakes situation, take a few minutes to practise power posing. Stand tall with your feet shoulder-width apart, place your hands on your hips or stretch your arms out wide, and hold the pose for two minutes. Notice how your body language affects your mindset and how much more confident you feel heading into the event.

Real-life example: You're about to give a presentation to a room full of colleagues and clients. Normally, you'd feel anxious and avoid making eye contact, but this time, you try something different. Before the presentation, you find a quiet spot, take a few deep breaths, and strike a power pose for two minutes. When it's time to present, you walk in with confidence, make eye contact, and speak with authority—faking confidence until it starts to feel real.

6. Networking: How to Fake Your Way Through It (and Actually Enjoy It)

Ah, **networking**—the ultimate test of faking it 'til you make it. For introverts, the idea of walking into a room full of strangers and striking up conversations might sound like pure torture, but here's the good news: **you don't have to be the life of the party to succeed at networking**. In fact, introverts often have an edge when it comes to networking because they tend to form deeper, more meaningful connections, rather than bouncing from person to person.

Here's how to fake your way through networking events without feeling completely drained:

Pro Tip #1: Set Small, Achievable Goals Don't overwhelm yourself by trying to meet everyone in the room. Instead, set a small, manageable goal—like having two meaningful conversations with new people. By focusing on quality over quantity, you'll feel less pressured and more in control of the situation.

Pro Tip #2: Have a Few Go-To Questions One of the hardest parts of networking is knowing how to start conversations. To make this easier, prepare a few **go-to questions** that you can use to break the ice. These could be simple, non-intimidating questions like, "How did you hear about this event?" or "What do you enjoy most about your work?" Having these in your back pocket can help you start conversations without overthinking it.

Exercise: The "Two Conversations" Rule At your next networking event, set a goal to have just two meaningful conversations with new people. Use your go-to questions to break the ice, and focus on listening more than talking. By setting this small, achievable goal, you'll feel more relaxed and less overwhelmed by the idea of meeting dozens of people.

Real-life example: You're attending a work conference, and the thought of mingling with so many new people feels daunting. Instead of trying to network with everyone, you set a goal to meet just two people. During the networking session, you approach someone near the coffee station and ask, "What's been the highlight of the conference for you so far?" This leads to a relaxed, enjoyable conversation, and by the end of the day, you've met two new contacts—without feeling exhausted.

7. Using Body Language to Project Confidence (Even When You Don't Feel It)

Here's the thing about body language: **people believe what they see**. Even if you're feeling anxious or unsure, the way you carry yourself can significantly impact how others perceive you—and, more importantly, how you feel about yourself. By using confident body language, you can **trick your brain into feeling more confident**, and others will respond to the energy you're projecting.

Here's how to use body language to project confidence, even when you're not feeling it:

Pro Tip #1: Open Your Posture Confident body language starts with an **open posture**. Keep your shoulders relaxed and back, your chest open, and your head held high. Avoid crossing your arms or hunching your shoulders, as this can make you appear closed off or nervous. The more open your posture, the more confident you'll appear (and feel).

Pro Tip #2: Make Eye Contact Making eye contact can feel intimidating, but it's one of the easiest ways to project confidence. When speaking to someone, make steady, but not intense, eye contact. If you're feeling nervous, try looking at the space between their eyebrows rather than directly into their eyes—this gives the illusion of eye contact without the pressure.

Exercise: The "Confident Posture" Practice For the next week, practice using confident body language in everyday interactions. Whether you're in a meeting, talking to a colleague, or even ordering coffee, focus on keeping your posture open, making eye contact, and speaking with clarity. Notice how these small adjustments make you feel more confident, even in casual conversations.

Real-life example: You're at a team meeting, and instead of sitting with your arms crossed and your head down, you decide to project confidence through your body language. You sit up straight, uncross your arms, and make eye contact with the person speaking. When it's your turn to contribute, you speak clearly and hold eye contact with your colleagues. By the end of the meeting, you feel more confident and notice that people are responding positively to your energy.

8. Taking Breaks Without Disappearing

For introverts, social situations can be draining, especially when they stretch on for hours. But here's the thing: **it's okay to take breaks**, even in the middle of a busy event or workday. The key is to step away and recharge without completely disappearing or isolating yourself. By learning how to take quick, strategic breaks, you can stay engaged without burning out.

Pro Tip #1: Find a Quiet Spot When you start to feel overwhelmed or drained, look for a quiet corner, hallway, or even a bathroom stall where you can take a few minutes to breathe and reset. These mini-breaks will help you recharge so you can re-enter the social situation with renewed energy.

Pro Tip #2: Set a Time Limit for Breaks While it's important to take breaks, you don't want to disappear for too long and risk losing momentum. Set a time limit for yourself—whether it's five or ten minutes—and use that time to step away, recharge, and mentally reset before returning to the event or meeting.

Exercise: The "Recharge Break" At your next social event, practice taking short, strategic breaks when you need to recharge. Find a quiet spot, take a few deep breaths, and allow yourself to step away for five minutes. When you're ready, return to the group feeling refreshed and more engaged.

Real-life example: You're at a work retreat, and after hours of socialising and team-building activities, you start to feel drained. Instead of pushing through the exhaustion, you step away for a quick break, find a quiet spot outside, and take a few minutes to recharge. After five minutes of fresh air, you feel more centred and ready to rejoin the group with a clear head.

Now that you've learned the fine art of faking confidence in high-pressure situations, it's time to tackle the most intimidating, and let's be honest, the most universally dreaded extrovert activity: **public speaking**. Whether it's a formal presentation at work, a toast at a wedding, or just being called on in a meeting, the fear of public speaking is something that unites introverts and extroverts alike.

But here's the truth that no one really talks about: **even people who seem natural at public speaking are often faking it too**. The difference is they've learned how to use a few simple tricks to project confidence and keep their nerves in check. The good news? These tricks aren't some extrovert-only club secret—you can use them too. Ready to learn how to fake your way through public speaking and come out looking like a pro?

9. Public Speaking: How to Nail It Without Fainting

Okay, here's the deal: **public speaking is a performance**. And, like any performance, it's all about preparation, mindset, and faking a little confidence when you need to. You don't need to be a natural orator to give a great speech—you just need to know how to **project confidence**, **connect with your audience**, and **stay calm under pressure**. Let's break it down.

Pro Tip #1: Preparation Is Key The more prepared you are, the more confident you'll feel when it's time to speak. Write down key points or bullet points you want to cover, and rehearse them out loud. Don't memorise your entire speech word-for-word; instead, focus on mastering the flow and structure of what you want to say. This way, you can speak more naturally, without the pressure of reciting a script.

Pro Tip #2: Visualise Success Before you get up to speak, take a moment to **visualise yourself delivering a great speech**. Imagine the audience responding positively, imagine yourself speaking with confidence, and imagine the feeling of success once you're done. This mental rehearsal can help reduce anxiety and set you up for success.

Pro Tip #3: Focus on Your Audience, Not Yourself Here's the trick to calming your nerves during public speaking: **focus on your audience, not yourself**. Instead of worrying about how nervous you feel or how you're coming across, shift your focus to how you can serve your audience. What do they need to hear? How can you connect with them? By taking the focus off yourself and putting it on the people in front of you, you'll feel less self-conscious and more engaged with your audience.

Exercise: The "Rehearse and Visualise" Technique Before your next presentation or public speaking opportunity, take some time to rehearse your key points out loud. Then, spend a few minutes visualising yourself delivering a great speech—imagine how you'll feel, how the audience will respond, and how successful the experience will be.

When it's time to speak, use this mental preparation to calm your nerves and project confidence.

Real-life example: You've been asked to give a brief presentation during a team meeting. Normally, the idea of speaking in front of your colleagues would make you want to disappear, but this time, you try something different. You prepare by jotting down a few key points and practising them out loud. Before the meeting, you take a few minutes to visualise yourself giving a confident, engaging presentation. When it's your turn to speak, you focus on connecting with your audience and sharing valuable information, rather than worrying about how you're coming across. The result? You nail the presentation and feel surprisingly good about it.

10. Handling Q&A Like a Pro

Nothing makes public speaking more nerve-wracking than the dreaded **Q&A session**. After all, it's one thing to deliver a prepared speech, but answering unexpected questions on the spot? That's a whole different level of scary.

But don't worry—there's a way to fake your way through a Q&A session too. Here's how to handle audience questions like a pro, even if you're caught off guard:

Pro Tip #1: Take a Pause Before Answering When someone asks you a question, it's natural to feel like you need to respond immediately. But here's the thing: **it's perfectly okay to pause** and take a moment to gather your thoughts before answering. In fact, pausing can make you seem more thoughtful and composed. Don't be afraid to take a breath, think for a second, and then respond.

Pro Tip #2: If You Don't Know the Answer, Be Honest One of the biggest fears during a Q&A session is getting a question you don't know the answer to. But here's the secret: **it's okay not to know everything**. If someone asks you a question you're unsure of, it's perfectly fine to say, "That's a great question—I'll need to look into that and get back to you." Being honest about not knowing something doesn't make you look unprepared—it makes you look authentic.

Pro Tip #3: Reframe the Question if You're Stumped If a question catches you off guard and you're not sure how to answer, one trick is to **reframe the question** in a way that plays to your strengths. For example, if someone asks you a complex technical question you don't know much about, you could respond by saying, "That's a really important point, and it reminds me of something we've been working on..." Then pivot the conversation to something you're more comfortable discussing.

Exercise: The "Pause and Pivot" Technique At your next Q&A session, practice taking a pause before answering questions. If you're unsure of an answer, be honest about needing more time to look into it. If you feel stumped, try reframing the question in a way that allows you to share what you do know, rather than focusing on what you don't.

Real-life example: You've just finished giving a presentation, and now it's time for the Q&A. Someone asks a question that you're not entirely sure how to answer. Instead of panicking, you take a deep breath, pause for a moment, and think it over. You decide to be honest and say, "That's a great question. I'll need to look into that and follow up with you afterward." By staying calm and composed, you handle the question like a pro—even without having all the answers.

11. The Art of Small Wins

Here's the thing about faking it 'til you make it: **it doesn't have to be an all-or-nothing approach**. Sometimes, the best way to build confidence is by racking up a series of small wins over time. These small victories—whether it's successfully navigating a conversation with a stranger or giving a presentation without breaking into a cold sweat—can add up to something bigger.

Instead of putting pressure on yourself to become an extrovert overnight, focus on **small wins** that will help you build confidence in a way that feels authentic to you.

Pro Tip #1: Celebrate Every Victory No matter how small, every step you take toward becoming more confident is worth celebrating. Did you manage to start a conversation with a new colleague? Celebrate that! Did you make it through a meeting without feeling overwhelmed? Celebrate that too! Recognizing and celebrating these small wins will help you stay motivated and build confidence over time.

Pro Tip #2: Focus on Progress, Not Perfection Nobody is perfect—not even the most extroverted people you know. So don't focus on trying to be perfect in every social situation. Instead, focus on making progress. Each time you push yourself a little outside your comfort zone, you're making progress, and that's what matters.

Exercise: The "Small Wins" Journal For the next week, keep a journal of your small wins. Each time you step outside your comfort zone—whether it's initiating a conversation, giving a presentation, or attending a social event—write it down. At the end of the week, review your wins and celebrate how far you've come.

Real-life example: You've been working on faking confidence in social situations for a few weeks now, and while you're not exactly the life of the party, you've noticed some small victories along the way. You've managed to strike up conversations with new people, give a presentation without panicking, and even handle a few Q&A sessions like a pro. As you reflect on these wins, you start to realise that what once felt like faking it now feels more natural—and that's worth celebrating.

Awesome! Now that we've worked through some of the core areas where "faking it 'til you make it" can really help (like public speaking, handling Q&A, and celebrating those small wins), it's time to talk about something equally important: **building momentum**. The more you practise these strategies, the easier they become. What starts as "faking it" begins to transform into something real—a sense of confidence that actually sticks around.

In this final part of the chapter, we'll dive into how to **maintain your progress**, stay consistent, and use momentum to help you keep growing. Plus, we'll look at the importance of **self-care** during this process, because let's face it, "faking it" takes energy, and it's important to make sure you're not running on empty.

12. Building Momentum: Turning Small Wins into Big Gains

As you continue practising confidence-boosting techniques and pushing yourself out of your comfort zone, something interesting starts to happen: you begin to **build momentum**. Those small wins we talked about earlier? They start adding up, and before you know it, the things that once felt intimidating begin to feel like second nature.

This is the power of momentum. Once you've faked your way through a few successful social interactions, presentations, or networking events, it becomes easier to approach the next challenge. Each win fuels the next, and your confidence grows with each experience.

Pro Tip #1: Keep Pushing Your Comfort Zone Momentum only builds when you keep moving. That means continuing to push yourself, even when it feels uncomfortable. If you've gotten comfortable with small talk, challenge yourself to go a little deeper in conversations. If you've mastered public speaking in front of small groups, try speaking in front of a larger audience. The more you push your boundaries, the more your confidence will grow.

Pro Tip #2: Reflect on Your Progress As you build momentum, take time to reflect on how far you've come. Look back at your initial struggles and compare them to where you are now. Chances are, the things that once felt impossible now seem totally manageable. This reflection will help reinforce your progress and keep you motivated to keep going.

Exercise: The "Momentum Builder" For the next month, challenge yourself to take one small step each week that pushes you out of your comfort zone. It could be anything from speaking up more in meetings to attending a social event you'd normally avoid. At the end of each week, reflect on what you learned and how it's helping you build momentum for the future.

Real-life example: You've been working on faking confidence for a few months, and it's starting to pay off. Where you once dreaded networking events, now you can walk in with a plan and actually enjoy meeting new people. You're even handling presentations and Q&A sessions like a pro. By continuing to push your comfort zone and reflect on your progress, you're building momentum that's helping you tackle bigger and more challenging situations with confidence.

13. Staying Consistent: The Key to Long-Term Confidence

Once you've started building momentum, the next challenge is **staying consistent**. It's easy to fall back into old habits, especially when life gets busy or stressful. But the key to long-term confidence is consistency—continuing to practise these strategies, even when you feel like you've "made it."

Here's how to stay consistent without burning out:

Pro Tip #1: Create a Routine One of the best ways to stay consistent is by creating a routine. This doesn't mean you have to schedule daily confidence-boosting activities, but it does mean finding ways to integrate these practices into your everyday life. For example, you could set a goal to initiate at least one conversation each day or to contribute a comment during every meeting. By making these small actions a regular part of your routine, you'll keep your confidence-building muscles strong.

Pro Tip #2: Don't Get Discouraged by Setbacks Confidence-building is a process, and setbacks are a natural part of it. There will be days when things don't go as planned, and that's okay. The important thing is to not let one bad day undo all the progress you've made. Use setbacks as learning experiences, and remind yourself that every step—whether forward or backward—is part of the journey.

Exercise: The "Daily Confidence Habit" For the next 30 days, commit to practising one small confidence-boosting habit each day. It could be anything from initiating a conversation to practising a power pose before a meeting. The goal is to build consistency and make confidence a natural part of your daily life.

Real-life example: After building up momentum, you realise that staying consistent is the key to maintaining your confidence. You decide to make small, daily habits part of your routine—like speaking up during meetings, taking breaks to recharge, and reflecting on your progress each week. By sticking to these habits, you continue to build confidence over time, and what once felt like "faking it" now feels like a genuine part of who you are.

14. Self-Care: Avoiding Burnout While Faking It

Let's get real for a second: **faking it 'til you make it can be exhausting**. As an introvert, social interactions and projecting confidence can drain your energy, and if you're not careful, it's easy to burn out. That's why it's crucial to balance your efforts with **self-care**—making sure you're recharging your batteries and taking time for yourself.

Here's how to avoid burnout while faking it:

Pro Tip #1: Schedule Regular Downtime Just as you schedule meetings and social events, make sure you're also scheduling regular downtime. Whether it's a quiet evening at home, a solo walk in nature, or simply reading a book in your favourite cosy spot, these moments of solitude are essential for recharging your introverted energy.

Pro Tip #2: Listen to Your Body Your body is always sending you signals about how much energy you have left, so it's important to listen to it. If you start to feel drained or overwhelmed, give yourself permission to step away and take a break. Pushing through when you're exhausted will only lead to burnout, so prioritise self-care when you need it.

Exercise: The "Recharge Ritual" creates a personal recharge ritual that you can use after big social events, presentations, or any situation where you've had to fake it for an extended period. This could be a relaxing bath, watching your favourite show, or spending time alone in nature. The goal is to give yourself a chance to unwind and recharge after expending a lot of social energy.

Real-life example: You've been faking it 'til you make it for a while now, and while it's helped you grow in confidence, you've also noticed that you're feeling more drained than usual. To avoid burnout, you start scheduling regular downtime—quiet evenings with no social obligations, time spent reading, and solo walks to clear your head. By balancing your confidence-building efforts with self-care, you're able to keep growing without running out of steam.

15. Embracing Authentic Confidence: The End of "Faking It"

At some point in your journey, something amazing happens: **you stop faking it**. The confidence you've been practising and projecting starts to feel more real. Those situations that once made you anxious—public speaking, networking, meeting new people—no longer feel like obstacles. Instead, they feel like opportunities.

This is the end goal: **authentic confidence**. It's the point where you realise you no longer need to put on an extroverted persona to get through social situations. You've developed the skills, habits, and mindset to navigate the world as a confident introvert.

Pro Tip #1: Own Your Progress When you reach the point where "faking it" turns into genuine confidence, take a moment to recognize how far you've come. Celebrate your progress and take pride in the fact that you've built something real. You're no longer faking confidence—you've earned it.

Pro Tip #2: Keep Growing Even when you've reached a place of authentic confidence, there's always room to grow. Keep challenging yourself to step outside your comfort zone, build new skills, and embrace new opportunities. Confidence is a lifelong journey, and the more you grow, the more you'll discover about yourself.

Exercise: The "Confidence Reflection" Take some time to reflect on your journey from faking it to making it. Write down the key moments that helped you grow, the skills you've developed, and the wins—big and small—that you've achieved along the way. Use this reflection to fuel your continued growth and remind yourself of what you're capable of.

Real-life example: After months of faking it, you realise something has changed. You're no longer nervous about attending social events, giving presentations, or meeting new people. The confidence you once had to fake now feels authentic and natural. As you reflect on your journey, you're proud of the progress you've made and excited about where your newfound confidence will take you next.

11

Public Speaking for People Who Hate Speaking

(or the Public)

So, you've made it this far. Kudos! You've tackled small talk, worked your way into handling social situations, and might even feel a little more confident about pretending to be an extrovert. But now, we're going to hit on the big one: **Public Speaking.** And, yes, I know what you're thinking— "Why would anyone in their right mind willingly want to speak in front of a crowd?" You're an introvert, after all, and the idea of standing in front of a group—eyes on you—probably feels like some kind of social torture.

But here's the thing: **public speaking isn't as terrifying as it seems**—and I swear, I'm not just saying that to mess with you. With the right approach, you can tackle public speaking just like you've been handling everything else—by faking it until you're no longer faking it. And I'm here to guide you through it in the most introvert-friendly way possible.

1. The Myth of Extroverts Being Better Public Speakers

Let's start by debunking a common myth: **extroverts aren't necessarily better public speakers**. Sure, they may have more practice putting themselves out there, but public speaking is a skill—one that can be learned, developed, and mastered by anyone. In fact, many of the world's best public speakers are introverts. Why? Because introverts tend to be better at **preparing, focusing, and reflecting** on their presentations. Extroverts might wing it with charisma, but introverts? We come prepared, and preparation is half the battle.

Take **Barack Obama**, for example. An introvert by nature, his public speaking is world-renowned—not because he loves being in front of a crowd, but because he prepares meticulously and knows how to deliver a message with clarity and calm. This means **you**, the introvert, have just as much (if not more) potential to knock it out of the park when it comes to public speaking.

2. Why Public Speaking Feels So Awful (and How to Change That)

Let's be real: The idea of public speaking often ranks high on lists of common fears, right next to spiders, heights, and *accidentally hitting "Reply All"* on a sensitive email. But why is it so intimidating? Well, it's mostly due to one big factor: **fear of judgement**.

Public speaking makes us feel vulnerable, like everyone is analysing our every word, gesture, and stammer. And as introverts, we're often more introspective, so the anxiety builds up in our heads. What if I mess up? What if I sound stupid? What if they all hate me?

The key here is understanding that **most people aren't paying as much attention as you think they are**. I know, shocking, right? But here's a truth bomb: your audience is often too focused on themselves or their own thoughts to dissect every detail of your speech. And even if you do slip up, most people won't even notice—or care. They're not waiting for you to fail; they're hoping for a good experience, and most of the time, they're rooting for you.

3. Public Speaking Starts With Preparation

As an introvert, one of your greatest strengths is your ability to prepare. Use it to your advantage. Unlike extroverts who might rely on their natural social abilities, you have the edge when it comes to **planning, structure, and focus**. And public speaking is a game of preparation. The more prepared you are, the less anxious you'll feel, and the more you can "fake" that confidence on stage.

Pro Tip #1: Plan the First 30 Seconds One of the hardest parts of public speaking is getting started. Those first 30 seconds are when nerves are at their highest, and that's when people tend to get tripped up. So here's a tip: **plan and memorise the first 30 seconds of your speech**. Whether it's an engaging introduction, a joke, or a compelling story, knowing exactly how you're going to start will give you the confidence to get past the initial jitters.

Pro Tip #2: Practice, Practice, Practice. You've probably heard this a million times, but it's true: **practice makes perfect**. The more you rehearse your speech, the more comfortable you'll feel delivering it. But don't just rehearse in your head—**practice out loud**. Stand in front of a mirror, record yourself on your phone, or present to a trusted friend. Hearing your voice and seeing yourself in action will help you get used to how you'll sound and look when you're up there.

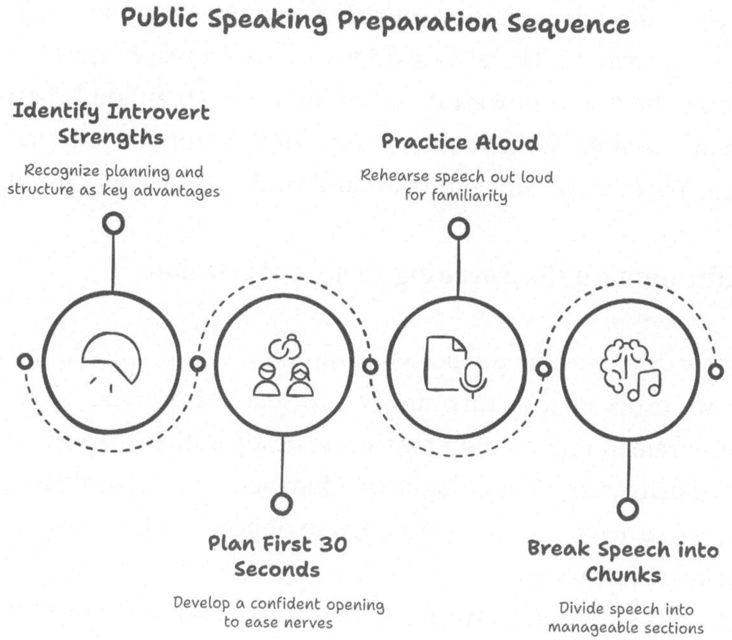

4. Use Your Introvert Superpowers (Yes, You Have Them)

You might think that public speaking is a job best suited for extroverts, but introverts have some serious **superpowers** when it comes to giving presentations. Here are a few ways you can use your natural introverted traits to your advantage:

Superpower #1: Thoughtful Communication Introverts tend to think before they speak, which means you're more likely to be clear, concise, and thoughtful in your delivery. Use this to your advantage by focusing on the **quality of your message** rather than trying to dazzle the audience with flair.

Superpower #2: Empathy Introverts are often more in tune with how others are feeling, which makes you great at reading the room. Use this skill to adjust your tone, pace, and energy based on how the audience is responding. If they seem bored or confused, switch things up—tell a joke, ask a question, or shift to a more engaging story.

Superpower #3: Quiet Confidence Here's a secret: **quiet confidence** can be just as powerful—if not more so—than loud charisma. You don't need to be the loudest person in the room to command attention. Speak with calm authority, and your audience will listen.

5. Reframing Public Speaking as a Conversation

One of the reasons public speaking feels so overwhelming is because we think of it as this massive, formal performance. But what if you reframed it as a **conversation** instead? Rather than imagining yourself delivering a monologue to a bunch of stone-faced strangers, think of it as having a chat with a group of people who are interested in what you have to say.

Pro Tip #1: Ask Questions Even if you're giving a speech or presentation, you can still make it feel like a conversation by **asking questions**. They don't have to be actual questions you expect answers to—they could be rhetorical. Questions like, "How many of you have ever felt nervous speaking in public?" or "Raise your hand if you can relate to this," can help create a more engaging, interactive atmosphere.

Pro Tip #2: Make Eye Contact (But Not Too Much) I know, I know—eye contact is the ultimate nightmare for introverts. But here's the thing: making eye contact with your audience doesn't mean staring into their souls. It's more about glancing at different people in the room to create a sense of connection. If eye contact makes you nervous, try this trick: **focus on someone's forehead** or look just above their heads. It'll give the illusion of eye contact without making you feel as uncomfortable.

6. The Power of Pauses: Silence is Your Friend

One of the biggest mistakes people make in public speaking is rushing through their presentation because they're nervous. But here's a secret: **pauses are powerful**. They give you time to breathe, think, and gather your thoughts. And they give your audience time to absorb what you've said.

When you're feeling nervous, it's tempting to fill every second with words, but don't be afraid of silence. Pausing after an important point can help emphasise your message and give your audience a chance to reflect on it.

Pro Tip: Use the 3-Second Rule If you feel like you're speaking too fast or getting ahead of yourself, use the **3-second rule**: after you make an important point, pause for three seconds before continuing. It'll slow you down, make you seem more confident, and give your audience a moment to absorb what you've just said.

Alright, you're still with me, which means you're ready to keep tackling this whole public speaking thing head-on. We've talked about how to reframe public speaking as a conversation, how to take advantage of your introverted superpowers, and how to slow things down with strategic pauses. But now, let's get into the practical stuff—**how to actually keep your nerves under control when the big moment comes** and you find yourself standing in front of that room full of people.

Don't worry, I'm not going to tell you to "just relax" (because let's be real, that advice has never worked for anyone, ever). Instead, I'm going to give you some **scientific and practical techniques** you can use to calm your nerves and channel that anxious energy into something useful.

7. Controlling Your Nerves: Channelling Your Energy Instead of Fighting It

Here's a secret about nerves: **everyone feels them**. Even professional speakers who seem cool, calm, and collected on stage feel nervous before they get up to speak. The trick isn't to try and eliminate your nervous energy—that's impossible. Instead, it's about **channelling those nerves** into something productive.

Think of nervousness as energy. Rather than trying to suppress it, use it to your advantage. Let it give you a sense of alertness, focus, and even excitement about what you're going to say. **Nervous energy is a sign that you care about what you're doing**—and that's a good thing!

Pro Tip #1: Reframe Nervousness as Excitement This might sound silly, but one of the best ways to deal with nerves is to **reframe them as excitement**. Instead of telling yourself, "I'm so nervous," try saying, "I'm excited about this." The physical sensations of nervousness (racing heart, sweaty palms) are almost identical to the sensations of excitement, so your brain can be tricked into thinking you're just pumped up for the speech instead of terrified.

Pro Tip #2: Embrace the "Butterflies" You know that feeling of butterflies in your stomach before you speak? Rather than fighting it, **embrace it**. It's a sign that you're alive, you're present, and you're about to do something that matters. And remember, most of the time, those butterflies settle down after the first minute or two. Just get through the beginning, and you'll find your groove.

Exercise: The "Excitement Reframe" Before your next presentation, when you start to feel those nerves kicking in, practice reframing them as excitement. Say to yourself, "I'm excited to share this information," or "I can't wait to connect with my audience." Notice how this shift in mindset helps calm your nerves and get you in a more positive headspace.

Real-life example: You're about to present to a large group, and the familiar wave of nerves hits you—racing heart, sweaty hands, the works. But instead of spiralling into anxiety, you take a deep breath and reframe it as excitement: "I'm excited to give this presentation!" Once you start speaking, the nerves melt away, and you find yourself actually enjoying the moment.

8. Breathing Techniques: Your Secret Weapon for Staying Calm

When it comes to controlling nerves, **breathing is everything**. Shallow, fast breathing is a sure sign that your body is in panic mode, and it only fuels your anxiety. But deep, slow breathing tells your brain that everything is okay, which helps calm your nerves and slows down that racing heart.

Pro Tip #1: Use Box Breathing One of the most effective breathing techniques for calming nerves is called **box breathing**. It's simple but powerful. Here's how it works:

- Inhale for 4 counts.
- Hold your breath for 4 counts.
- Exhale for 4 counts.
- Hold again for 4 counts.
- Repeat until you feel more centred.

This controlled breathing slows down your heart rate, calms your nervous system, and gives you something to focus on besides your anxiety.

Pro Tip #2: Breathe from Your Diaphragm When you're nervous, it's easy to fall into shallow, chest-level breathing. But to calm your nerves, you want to breathe **from your diaphragm**—the muscle located just below your lungs. Diaphragmatic breathing allows you to take deeper, fuller breaths, which helps relax your body and mind.

Exercise: The "2-Minute Calm-Down" Before your next public speaking engagement, take two minutes to practise box breathing. Find a quiet spot, close your eyes, and focus on your breath. Inhale for 4 counts, hold for 4, exhale for 4, and hold again. Repeat until you feel your nerves start to settle.

Real-life example: You're standing backstage, about to be introduced for your big presentation. The nerves are building, but instead of letting them take over, you take a few minutes to practise box breathing. Inhale for 4 counts, hold, exhale, hold—by the time your name is called, you feel calm, collected, and ready to speak.

9. Visualisation: Seeing Success Before It Happens

Here's another trick used by athletes, performers, and yes, even public speakers: **visualisation**. The idea is simple—before you step up to the podium, **visualise yourself giving a successful presentation**. Imagine yourself speaking clearly, confidently, and engaging your audience. Picture the audience responding positively, smiling, nodding, maybe even laughing at your jokes (hey, it could happen!).

Visualisation helps reduce anxiety because it tricks your brain into believing you've already done the thing you're afraid of—and that it went well.

Pro Tip #1: Picture the Entire Experience When you're visualising your success, don't just focus on your speech. Imagine the entire experience, from walking up to the stage to making eye contact with the audience to finishing with a round of applause (because, let's be real, you deserve it). The more vivid and detailed your visualisation, the more effective it will be.

Pro Tip #2: Focus on Positive Outcomes Your brain has a habit of focusing on worst-case scenarios—what if I forget my lines? What if I trip on my way to the podium? What if the audience hates me? But when you're visualising, you want to focus on the **positive out-**

comes. Picture everything going right: your speech flows smoothly, the audience is engaged, and you feel proud of your performance.

Exercise: The "Pre-Speech Visualization" Before your next presentation, spend a few minutes in a quiet place and close your eyes. Picture yourself walking up to the stage, delivering your speech with confidence, and receiving positive feedback from the audience. Focus on the feeling of success and let that energy carry you through your presentation.

Real-life example: You've been anxious about a presentation all week, so the night before, you take a few minutes to practise visualisation. You close your eyes and picture yourself standing confidently in front of the room, speaking with ease, and getting positive reactions from the audience. The next day, when it's time to present, you feel a sense of calm—you've already seen yourself succeed, and now it's just a matter of following through.

10. The "Power Pause" Technique: How to Buy Yourself Time Without Looking Awkward

Here's a trick that might just save you during a speech: the **power pause**. When you lose your place, stumble over your words, or feel a moment of panic, **take a pause**. Instead of trying to fill the silence with ums, ahs, or panicked improvisation, use that pause to collect yourself, gather your thoughts, and breathe.

Pauses actually make you look more confident, not less. When you take your time to think before you speak, you give off an air of authority and control. Plus, a well-timed pause can add emphasis to your message, making your audience hang on to your every word.

Pro Tip #1: Use Pauses to Emphasise Key Points If you're delivering a powerful point or key takeaway, let it sink in by pausing after you say it. This gives your audience time to absorb the message and makes you look more intentional in your delivery.

Pro Tip #2: Pausing Isn't Awkward—It's Powerful When you're up on stage, it's easy to feel like every second of silence is painfully awkward. But to the audience, those pauses don't feel nearly as long as they do to you. In fact, they likely appreciate the breathing room between points. So don't be afraid to take a pause when you need it.

Exercise: The "Power Pause" Practice During your next presentation or conversation, practice using pauses deliberately. When you make an important point, pause for a few seconds to let it sink in. If you lose your place or need a moment to think, take a breath and pause. Notice how the pause helps you stay calm and collected, rather than scrambling to fill the silence.

Real-life example: You're midway through a speech and suddenly lose track of where you were. Instead of panicking, you remember the power of pausing. You take a breath, collect your thoughts, and after a few seconds, pick up right where you left off. The audience barely notices the pause, and you come across as calm and composed, even though you had a momentary brain freeze

You've got this. By now, you've learned how to channel your nervous energy, calm your body with breathing techniques, and even master the art of pausing to collect your thoughts. You're well on your way to becoming the kind of speaker who can command a room without feeling like a deer in the headlights. But let's take it one step further and dive into how to **connect with your audience**, handle those tricky **unexpected moments**, and finally, how to **end on a high note**.

These next steps are all about going from just "getting through" your speech to actually **enjoying the process** and leaving a lasting impression. After all, public speaking isn't just about delivering information—it's about **engagement** and **connection**.

11. How to Connect with Your Audience (Even If You Feel Disconnected)

Public speaking is often thought of as a one-way street—you stand up there, say your piece, and the audience listens. But here's the truth: **the best public speakers know how to make it feel like a conversation**, even when they're the only ones talking. The key to engaging your audience is to make them feel involved, even if they're not actively participating.

So, how do you create that sense of connection? Here are some tips:

Pro Tip #1: Speak to Individuals, Not the Crowd Even if you're presenting to a room full of people, it helps to **speak as though you're addressing individuals**. Pick a few people in the audience to make eye contact with as you speak, and direct your words to them as if you're having a one-on-one conversation. This creates a sense of intimacy and helps break down the barrier between "you" and "them."

Pro Tip #2: Use Relatable Stories or Examples People love stories—especially ones they can relate to. Rather than just presenting dry facts or information, weave in personal anecdotes or relatable examples. Not only will this make your presentation more engaging, but it will also make you seem more approachable and human. The more your audience can relate to you, the more connected they'll feel.

Pro Tip #3: Use Humor (When Appropriate) Humour can be a powerful tool for creating connection—when used appropriately. You don't have to be a stand-up comedian, but a well-placed joke or lighthearted comment can help put your audience at ease and make you seem more relatable. Just be sure your humour fits the tone of your presentation and feels natural to you.

Exercise: The "Storytelling Connection" Before your next speech or presentation, think about a personal story or example you can include that relates to your message. Practice telling it in a way that feels conversational and engaging. As you speak, notice how your audience reacts when you shift from information to storytelling, and use that connection to keep them engaged throughout.

Real-life example: You're giving a presentation on a somewhat dry topic—let's say, company policies. Instead of diving straight into the technical details, you start with a lighthearted story about a time you accidentally violated one of the policies yourself. The audience laughs, and suddenly, they're more engaged. Throughout the presentation, you continue to weave in small stories and examples, keeping the audience connected and interested.

12. Handling Unexpected Moments (Like a Pro)

Even the most perfectly planned presentation can have its hiccups. Maybe someone asks an unexpected question, maybe the microphone cuts out, or maybe you lose your place halfway through. These moments can feel like your worst nightmare, but here's the thing: **how you handle unexpected moments says more about your confidence than the actual mistake itself**.

Here's how to handle the unexpected with grace and confidence:

Pro Tip #1: Stay Calm (No One Else Knows What's Supposed to Happen) The audience has no idea what your presentation is supposed to look like, so if something doesn't go as planned, **don't panic**. Take a breath, smile, and carry on. Your calmness will signal to the audience that everything is under control, even if things feel chaotic on your end.

Pro Tip #2: Laugh It Off If something funny happens—like tripping over your words or knocking over your water bottle—**laugh it off**. A little humour can go a long way in making you seem more relatable and relaxed. Plus, it helps ease the tension in the room and shows your audience that you're human too.

Pro Tip #3: Have a Backup Plan While you can't predict every possible mishap, it's helpful to have a few **backup strategies** in place. If you lose your train of thought, have a cue card or key point written down that you can quickly refer to. If technology fails (because it will, at some point), be prepared to deliver your presentation without slides. The more prepared you are, the less stressful these moments will feel.

Exercise: The "Laugh It Off" Practise The next time you practise a presentation, intentionally throw in a small mistake—like pausing awkwardly or pretending to forget your next point—and practice laughing it off or calmly moving on. This will help you feel more comfortable with the idea that mistakes happen, and they don't have to derail your confidence.

Real-life example: You're in the middle of presenting when you accidentally skip over an entire section of your slides. Instead of freezing, you smile and say, "Well, that escalated quickly—let's go back for a second." The audience chuckles, and you smoothly return to the missing section. Your calm, lighthearted response turns what could have been an awkward moment into a moment of connection.

13. Ending on a High Note: How to Leave a Lasting Impression

Just as those first 30 seconds of your presentation are crucial for grabbing attention, **the last 30 seconds are just as important** for leaving a lasting impression. The way you close your presentation sets the tone for how your audience will remember you and your message, so it's worth putting some thought into how you'll wrap things up.

Here's how to end your presentation with confidence and leave a lasting impact:

Pro Tip #1: Summarise Your Key Points A strong conclusion often involves a brief **summary of your key points**. This doesn't mean repeating everything you just said—it's about giving the audience a quick, memorable takeaway that reinforces your message. Think of it as the final bow at the end of a performance—it should be clear, confident, and leave no doubt about your message.

Pro Tip #2: Give a Call to Action If your presentation is meant to inspire change or action, **end with a clear call to action**. What do you want your audience to do after they leave the room? Whether it's signing up for something, making a change in their behaviour, or simply reflecting on a new idea, be specific about what you want your audience to take away from your presentation.

Pro Tip #3: End with a Memorable Quote or Story Another way to leave a lasting impression is by ending your presentation with a **powerful quote** or a **final story** that ties everything together. A well-chosen quote can add weight to your message, while a closing story can leave your audience with something to think about after they leave. The goal is to end on a note that feels complete and impactful.

Exercise: The "Closing Statement" Practice Write out a clear, concise closing statement that summarises your key points and reinforces your message. Practice delivering this closing with confidence and intention, making sure it feels like a natural conclusion to your presentation. If it feels right, add in a call to action or a final story to make your closing even more memorable.

Real-life example: You're wrapping up a presentation, and instead of ending with a simple "Thank you," you close with a powerful quote that ties back to your main message: "As Maya Angelou once said, 'People will forget what you said, but they will never forget how you made them feel.'" The audience nods, and you can see that the quote resonates. You finish with a brief call to action: "So, let's go out there and make sure we leave people feeling inspired." You walk off the stage to applause, confident that your message will stick.

14. Final Thoughts: You've Got This

Public speaking might never be your favourite activity—and that's okay. But with the right tools, preparation, and a little bit of confidence (even if it's faked), you can handle any presentation that comes your way. The more you practise, the more you'll find that public speaking isn't the terrifying monster it once was. In fact, you might even start to enjoy it—just a little.

Remember: **nobody is expecting perfection**. The audience is rooting for you, and most of the time, they're just happy it's you up there and not them. So take a deep breath, stand tall, and give it your best shot. You've got this.

practical tips for handling public speaking situations, especially when you're not fully in control of the environment. From **managing unexpected technical issues** to dealing with **difficult audience members**, we'll cover how to keep your cool and maintain confidence no matter what happens. By the end of this page, you'll be armed with everything you need to **fake it**—or, who knows, maybe even start to feel like a natural up there.

15. Handling Technical Issues: When the Mic Dies and the Slides Won't Load

Let's face it—technology is great, but when it fails during a presentation, it can feel like a nightmare. Whether the projector stops working, the microphone cuts out, or your slides won't load, these are the moments that can throw even the most seasoned speakers off their game. But don't worry! There are ways to **handle technical issues like a pro** without losing your cool.

Here's what to do when things go wrong:

Pro Tip #1: Keep Talking (If You Can) If your slides or tech aren't working, the best thing you can do is **keep talking**. Rather than standing awkwardly while someone fixes the problem, continue delivering your message as best you can. If you've prepared properly, you should be able to speak confidently without relying too much on your slides. This keeps the momentum going and shows the audience that you can handle setbacks with grace.

Pro Tip #2: Acknowledge the Problem, Then Move On Sometimes, the audience will notice the technical issue before you do. It's okay to acknowledge it with a quick comment like, "Looks like the slides are taking a coffee break," but don't dwell on it. The more relaxed you are about the situation, the more comfortable your audience will feel. After acknowledging the issue, keep the focus on your message.

Pro Tip #3: Have a Backup Plan If you're relying heavily on slides or tech, it's always a good idea to **have a backup plan**. This could be a printed version of your presentation, notes on a cue card, or even a simplified version of your talk that you can deliver without visuals. Being prepared for the worst-case scenario will help you stay calm if things go south.

Exercise: The "Tech-Free Practice" Before your next presentation, practice delivering it **without any slides** or technology. Focus on your words, your message, and your connection with the audience. This way, if the technology fails during the real thing, you'll still feel confident and prepared to keep going.

Real-life example: You're giving a presentation at a conference when suddenly the projector stops working, and your slides disappear. Instead of panicking, you acknowledge the problem with a smile: "Looks like technology has decided to take a break," you say, which gets a laugh from the audience. You continue speaking, relying on your preparation and engaging the audience with your words alone. By the time the tech is fixed, you've already delivered most of your message, and the audience is impressed by your composure.

16. Dealing with Difficult Audience Members: When Someone Won't Stop Interrupting

Every speaker's worst nightmare: the **difficult audience member**. Whether it's someone who won't stop asking questions, constantly interrupts, or is just visibly uninterested, difficult audience members can throw you off your game. But guess what? You can handle them without losing your cool.

Here's how to deal with challenging audience members:

Pro Tip #1: Stay Polite, but Firm When someone interrupts or derails your presentation, it's important to stay polite but **take control of the situation**. You can say something like, "That's a great question. I'd love to address it during the Q&A at the end." This acknowledges their comment but sets a boundary to keep the presentation on track.

Pro Tip #2: Don't Let One Person Hijack the Room Sometimes, an audience member will try to turn your presentation into a personal conversation. If this happens, politely bring the focus back to the group. For example, you could say, "That's an interesting point. Let's hear what others think," or "I'll make sure to follow up with you after the presentation so we can dive deeper into that."

Pro Tip #3: Redirect Negative Energy If someone is being negative or difficult, one strategy is to **redirect that energy** back into something positive. Acknowledge their frustration or concern, but then shift the focus back to the value of your message. For example, you could say, "I understand that this topic might be challenging, but let's focus on how we can use this to improve our approach."

Exercise: The "Tough Crowd" Rehearsal Before your next presentation, practice handling a difficult audience member by asking a friend or colleague to interrupt you with tough questions or comments. Practice staying calm, redirecting the conversation, and keeping the presentation on track.

Real-life example: You're midway through a presentation when an audience member keeps interrupting with questions that are slightly off-topic. You smile and say, "I really appreciate your enthusiasm. Let's save the rest of your questions for the Q&A so we can keep moving through the material." The audience member nods, and you regain control of the room, finishing the presentation smoothly.

17. Knowing When to Stop Talking: The Power of a Strong Finish

One of the most common mistakes in public speaking is **talking too long**. When nerves are high, it's easy to ramble, repeat yourself, or go off on tangents. But here's the truth: **less is often more** when it comes to public speaking. Ending your presentation on a strong, concise note leaves a lasting impression.

Here's how to end your presentation with impact:

Pro Tip #1: Know Your Exit The best speakers know exactly when—and how—to end their presentations. Don't wait for someone to give you the "wrap it up" signal. **Plan your ending in advance** and know exactly what your final words will be. Whether it's a memorable quote, a call to action, or a summary of your main points, stick the landing and leave your audience with something to remember.

Pro Tip #2: Don't Over-Explain When you've made your point, resist the urge to over-explain or keep talking. **Trust that your message has landed**. Instead of rambling on, wrap things up confidently and clearly. Your audience will appreciate the brevity, and it'll make your message stick.

Pro Tip #3: End With Confidence Even if you feel a little shaky during your presentation, **end with confidence**. Speak your final words slowly and deliberately, make eye contact with the audience, and smile. This final moment is what people will remember most, so make sure it leaves a positive impression.

Exercise: The "Perfect Ending" Practice Before your next presentation, write out and practise your final closing statement. Make sure it's concise, confident, and leaves a lasting impression. Practice delivering it with intention, and focus on ending on a high note.

Real-life example: You're giving a presentation, and as you near the end, you resist the urge to keep talking or over-explain your points. Instead, you deliver a clear, confident closing statement: "In the end, it's not about how much we say, but the impact we make.

Thank you for your time today." The audience applauds, and you walk off the stage, knowing you left them with something powerful to think about.

18. Bringing It All Together: Confidence Isn't Perfection

Here's the final truth about public speaking: **it's not about perfection**. No matter how much you prepare or how confident you feel, there will always be moments when things don't go as planned. But that's okay. Confidence comes from your ability to handle those moments with grace, humour, and resilience.

Whether you're giving a big speech, a small presentation, or just speaking up in a meeting, remember that confidence doesn't mean being perfect—it means **being willing to try**, even when things feel uncomfortable. And with each attempt, you'll get a little better, a little more confident, and a lot less afraid.

Congratulations! You've made it to the final stretch of Chapter 11, and at this point, you should be feeling a little less terrified and a little more prepared to face the dreaded world of public speaking. But before we close out this chapter, let's talk about how to **practise effectively** so that all the tips and tricks we've covered can really stick. We'll also go over **how to handle post-presentation feedback**—because, let's be honest, hearing people talk about your performance can sometimes be just as nerve-wracking as the actual presentation.

Let's dive into these last few essentials to help you become not only a competent public speaker but a **confident one**.

19. Practising Like a Pro: Turning Rehearsals Into Success

Practice doesn't just make perfect—it makes **progress**. But here's the thing: not all practice is created equal. If you're just running through your speech once or twice in your head, you're probably not getting the full benefit of your rehearsal time. Instead, try to make your practice sessions as close to the real thing as possible.

Here's how to **practise effectively** for public speaking:

Pro Tip #1: Practise Out Loud It sounds obvious, but many people don't actually practise their presentations out loud—they rehearse silently in their heads. But public speaking is, well, **speaking**. Practising out loud helps you get used to the sound of your own voice, the rhythm of your speech, and the natural pauses you'll need to take. It also helps you catch any awkward phrasing or unclear points before you're in front of an audience.

Pro Tip #2: Simulate the Real Environment The closer your practice environment is to the real thing, the better prepared you'll be. If possible, practice in the actual room where you'll be presenting or a similar space. Stand up while you speak, use a remote or clicker if you'll be using slides, and time yourself to make sure your presentation fits the allotted time.

Pro Tip #3: Record Yourself One of the most helpful tools in public speaking practice is recording yourself. Yes, it can be cringeworthy to watch yourself on video, but it's an incredibly useful way to identify areas for improvement. Pay attention to your body language, eye contact, and pacing, and adjust as needed.

Exercise: The "Full Dress Rehearsal" Before your next presentation, do a full dress rehearsal. Stand up, speak out loud, and use any visuals or tech you plan to include. Time yourself and make any necessary adjustments to your pacing or content. If you can, record the rehearsal and watch it back to see how you come across.

Real-life example: You've got a big presentation coming up, and instead of just rehearsing in your head, you decide to do a full dress rehearsal. You stand up in your living room, run through the entire presentation out loud, and even use a timer to check your pacing. When you watch the recording, you notice that you're speaking a little too fast, so you adjust your pace in the next rehearsal. By the time the real presentation rolls around, you feel much more prepared—and it shows.

20. Handling Feedback: Learning Without Cringing

So, you've delivered your presentation, and it's all over. But now comes the part that can be even more uncomfortable than speaking in front of people: **hearing feedback**. For introverts, receiving feedback—especially about something as personal as public speaking—can feel intimidating. But feedback is essential for growth, and learning how to take it in stride will help you continue improving.

Here's how to handle feedback without cringing:

Pro Tip #1: Ask for Specific Feedback Generic feedback like "You did great!" or "That was good!" is nice to hear, but it doesn't really help you grow. If you want to improve, ask for **specific feedback**. For example, ask a trusted colleague or friend, "Was my pacing okay?" or "Did you feel like my key points were clear?" This helps you get actionable insights that you can use to improve.

Pro Tip #2: Focus on the Positive First It's natural to focus on the negatives when receiving feedback, but try to **start by acknowledging the positives**. If someone says, "You seemed a bit nervous at the start, but your delivery was strong by the end," focus on the fact that you finished strong. Positive reinforcement helps build your confidence, so take a moment to recognize what went well.

Pro Tip #3: Don't Take It Personally This one's tough, but it's important: **don't take feedback personally**. Remember, feedback is about your presentation, not about you as a person. Even if you made a mistake or struggled in certain areas, it doesn't define your abilities as a speaker or your value as an individual. Use feedback as a tool for learning, not as a measure of your self-worth.

Exercise: The "Feedback Filter" After your next presentation, ask for feedback from a few trusted colleagues or friends. Listen to their comments, but practice using a "feedback filter." Focus on the points that are most helpful and let go of any overly critical or unhelpful comments. Write down one or two specific actions you can take to improve next time.

Real-life example: You give a presentation at work, and afterward, your manager gives you some feedback: "I liked your main points, but I think you could work on slowing down a bit. You rushed through the middle section." Instead of getting defensive, you thank them for the feedback and note that your pacing is something to work on. For your next presentation, you focus on improving your pacing, and it makes a noticeable difference.

21. Dealing with Post-Presentation Anxiety: What to Do When You Overthink Everything

It's common for introverts to experience **post-presentation anxiety**—that dreaded feeling after a speech where you replay every moment in your head and obsess over what you could have done better. "Did I sound nervous? Did I forget that key point? Did anyone even care about what I said?" Sound familiar? You're not alone.

Here's how to deal with that post-presentation anxiety and move on without overthinking every little detail:

Pro Tip #1: Give Yourself a Break First things first—**give yourself some grace**. Public speaking is hard, and even if it didn't go perfectly, you did it. That alone is an accomplishment. Don't be too hard on yourself if things didn't go exactly as planned. No one is perfect, and your audience is more likely to remember the overall message than the small slip-ups.

Pro Tip #2: Focus on What You Did Well After your presentation, take a moment to **celebrate what went well**. Maybe you handled a difficult question with ease, or maybe you kept your nerves under control. Whatever it is, acknowledge the successes, no matter how small, before diving into what could have been better.

Pro Tip #3: Trust the Process Every presentation, no matter how challenging, is an opportunity to learn and grow. Instead of dwelling on what you think went wrong, **focus on the progress you've made**. Each time you speak, you're getting better, more comfortable, and more confident. Trust that the process is working, even if it feels uncomfortable at times.

Exercise: The "Post-Presentation Review" After your next presentation, take five minutes to write down three things that went well and one thing you'd like to improve next time. This helps you reflect on the experience without getting bogged down by negative overthinking. Focus on the positive takeaways and use the one area of improvement as a goal for your next speaking opportunity.

Real-life example: After giving a presentation at a staff meeting, you find yourself replaying every little detail in your head, worrying about how you came across. But instead of getting stuck in post-presentation anxiety, you decide to focus on what went well: you made eye contact with the audience, your main points were clear, and you handled a tricky question with ease. You write these down and set a small goal to work on your pacing next time, but overall, you feel proud of the progress you've made.

22. Moving Forward: The Journey from Fear to Confidence

Public speaking is one of those skills that will continue to evolve as you grow more comfortable with it. The more you practise, the less terrifying it becomes, and the more confident you'll feel with each presentation. The key is to **keep pushing yourself**, even when it feels uncomfortable. Confidence is built through experience, and with time, you'll go from faking it to truly owning the stage.

As you move forward, remember: **confidence isn't about being perfect**. It's about showing up, doing your best, and learning from each experience. So keep practising, keep pushing yourself, and don't be afraid to make mistakes along the way. You've got this.

12

Small Talk – Making it Big

Alright, introverts, we're diving into the subject you may have been dreading since Page 1—**small talk**. I know, I know. Just the phrase "small talk" might make you want to grab a book, find a cosy corner, and avoid all human interaction for the next week. But here's the thing: **small talk is unavoidable**. It's everywhere—at work, at parties, even in line at the grocery store when the person behind you just has to comment on the weather.

But before you run for the hills, let's look at small talk from a new angle. Instead of seeing it as a social obligation, let's treat it as a **skill**—a tool that, when used well, can open doors, spark connections, and actually (brace yourself) be enjoyable. In this chapter, we'll break down how to make small talk less painful, maybe even fun, and **a whole lot less awkward**.

1. Why Small Talk Matters (Even if You'd Rather Skip It)

Let's address the big question: **Why does small talk even exist?** What's the point of discussing the weather, weekend plans, or the traffic on the way over? Well, here's the deal: small talk isn't really about the topic itself. It's about **building rapport and easing into a**

conversation. Think of it as the warm-up before the main event—it helps people get comfortable, establish trust, and feel connected.

Small talk is a bit like an appetiser. You wouldn't jump straight to the main course without a starter, right? (Okay, maybe you would, but humour me here.) It's a way of setting the stage for a deeper conversation without diving headfirst into personal questions. It gives both people a chance to gauge the other's mood, interest level, and personality.

2. The Secret to Small Talk: Make It Big by Making It Meaningful

Most people think of small talk as "meaningless chatter," but what if I told you that you could actually **make it meaningful**? The key to making small talk less painful is to approach it as more than just filling the silence. Rather than sticking to surface-level topics, look for ways to turn small talk into something that **feels genuine** and leads to a real connection.

Here's how to take the pain out of small talk:

Pro Tip #1: Ask Open-Ended Questions One of the quickest ways to make small talk more interesting is by asking **open-ended questions**. Instead of questions that can be answered with a simple "yes" or "no," try asking questions that encourage the other person to share more about themselves. For example, instead of asking, "Did you have a good weekend?" you could ask, "What was the highlight of your weekend?" This invites the other person to share something meaningful and gives you more to work with in the conversation.

Pro Tip #2: Focus on the Person, Not the Topic People love to talk about themselves, so use that to your advantage. When someone mentions their weekend plans, for instance, dig a little deeper. If they say they went hiking, ask, "Oh, that's cool! Do you hike often, or was this a special occasion?" This shifts the focus from the surface topic (hiking) to the person's interests and experiences, which can lead to a more engaging conversation.

Pro Tip #3: Embrace the Power of Curiosity. Instead of approaching small talk as a chore, try to **get genuinely curious** about the other person. Think of it as a mini-adventure in learning about someone's world. Even if the topic is something as mundane as the weather, you can still show interest. "I've been hearing everyone talk about this heatwave! Do you have any fun ways of keeping cool?" Curiosity makes even the simplest topics feel fresher and more engaging.

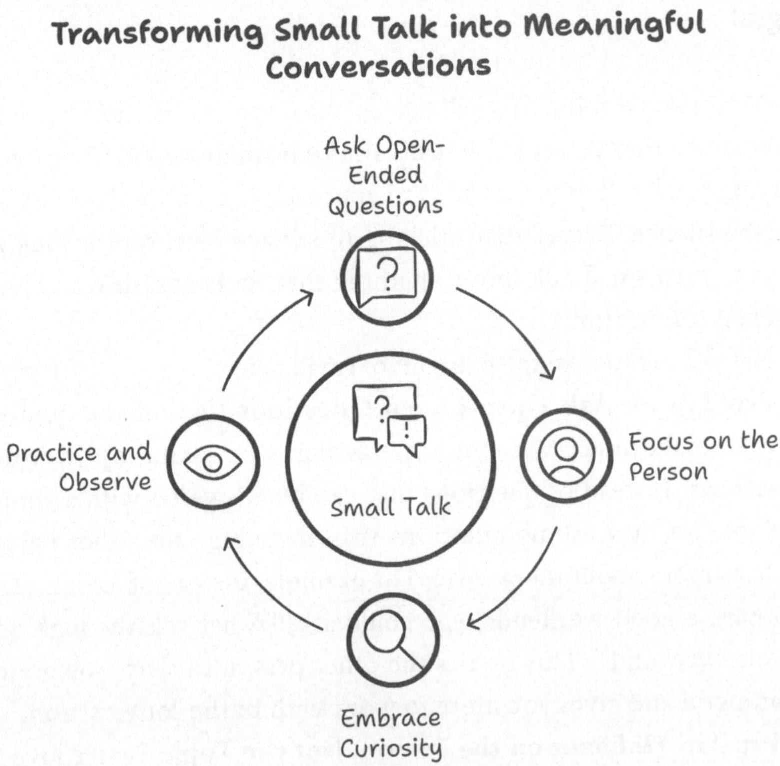

Real-life example: You're at a work event, and someone mentions the local sports team. Instead of nodding politely and letting the topic die, you say, "I don't follow sports much—what got you interested in it?" Suddenly, they're excitedly sharing how they've been a fan since childhood. By showing genuine curiosity, you've transformed small talk about sports into a more personal, engaging conversation.

3. Mastering the Basics: Small Talk Starters That Actually Work

Sometimes, the hardest part of small talk is just **getting it started**. Standing next to someone at a party or in a meeting, it's easy to overthink your opener and worry about sounding awkward. But here's the secret: **most people don't really care what you say**—they're just as happy to have someone break the silence. So instead of stressing over the perfect line, stick to a few tried-and-true small talk starters that will get the ball rolling.

Here are some easy openers that work in almost any setting:

Starter #1: "What's been the highlight of your week so far?" This question works in social and work settings alike, and it's a great way to get people talking about something positive. People enjoy sharing good experiences, and this question often leads to a genuine conversation about their week.

Starter #2: "Are you working on anything exciting right now?" This one is great for work events or professional settings, as it gives people a chance to talk about their current projects, passions, or even challenges. Plus, it's a good way to steer the conversation into areas that could spark common interests.

Starter #3: "I'm always looking for new recommendations—have you seen any good movies or read any good books lately?" This question is perfect for any casual setting, and it often leads to interesting discussions about shared hobbies, movies, or books. Even if you don't share their interests, you'll learn something new and can keep the conversation going by asking follow-up questions.

Exercise: The "Three Starter" Practice Pick one of the three small talk starters above and try using it in a real conversation this week. Notice how the other person responds and how it impacts the flow of the conversation. If it goes well, try another one next time you're in a social situation.

Real-life example: You're at a networking event and feel that familiar anxiety creeping in. Instead of trying to come up with a perfect topic, you ask the person next to you, "What's been the highlight of your week so far?" They smile and start telling you about a recent trip they took, and just like that, you're in a conversation. By using a reliable small talk starter, you've broken the ice and found a comfortable entry point into a larger discussion.

4. Going Beyond the Weather: How to Transition to Deeper Topics

Small talk is meant to be a starting point, not the main event. But how do you move from the surface-level chit-chat to a more meaningful conversation without feeling like you're jumping in too fast? The trick is to use **transitional questions** that bridge the gap between small talk and more engaging topics.

Here's how to turn small talk into something deeper:

Pro Tip #1: Look for Common Ground As you're chatting, pay attention to anything you and the other person have in common. If they mention something that interests you, like a favourite TV show or a shared hobby, use that as a jumping-off point. Say something like, "Oh, I love that show too! Who's your favourite character?" This creates an instant connection and can lead to a deeper conversation.

Pro Tip #2: Ask "Why?" or "How?" Questions One of the easiest ways to shift from small talk to something more engaging is by asking **why** or **how** questions. For example, if someone mentions a hobby, instead of just saying, "That's cool," ask, "How did you get into that?"

or "Why do you enjoy it so much?" These questions invite the other person to share more personal insights.

Pro Tip #3: Listen for Stories People love sharing stories, so give them a chance to tell theirs. If someone mentions a recent experience, say something like, "Oh, that sounds interesting! What happened next?" This shows you're interested and often leads to a more in-depth conversation.

Exercise: The "Transition Question" Challenge The next time you're in a small talk conversation, try asking a "why" or "how" question to see if it opens up a deeper discussion. Notice how this small shift can make the conversation feel more natural and engaging.

Real-life example: You're talking to someone at a party, and they mention they've recently started learning to cook. Instead of leaving it at, "That's nice," you ask, "How did you get into cooking?" They start telling you about a cooking class they took, which leads to a whole conversation about favourite dishes and cooking disasters. By showing interest in their story, you've taken small talk to the next level and created a more enjoyable conversation.

Now that you know the basics of making small talk more meaningful and kicking off with a few good starters, let's talk about how to **keep the conversation flowing smoothly**. Once you've broken the ice, it can sometimes feel challenging to keep things rolling without slipping into those awkward silences we all dread. But don't worry—we're going to cover simple tactics that will help you transition from small talk into something that feels natural and engaging.

Remember, the goal here isn't to turn into a chatterbox overnight. It's to **create a comfortable rhythm** that makes both you and the other person feel more at ease.

5. The Art of Keeping It Flowing

Small talk often fizzles out because people run out of things to say. But keeping a conversation going doesn't have to be a constant scramble for topics. Instead, focus on **following the flow of the conversation** and using simple techniques to keep it alive. Let's dive into a few strategies that make continuing a conversation feel easy and natural.

Pro Tip #1: Follow the "Thread" of the Conversation. Think of conversation like following a thread—each comment or question leads naturally to the next. If someone mentions they recently saw a movie, you could ask what they thought of it or if they'd recommend it. By picking up on what they've said, you're keeping the conversation relevant to their interests and avoiding forced or unrelated questions.

Pro Tip #2: Share Your Own Experience (But Keep It Brief) One way to keep the conversation balanced is to share a **brief story or experience** that relates to the topic. If they're talking about a recent vacation, you might mention a favourite travel memory of your own. Just keep it short—this isn't about stealing the spotlight; it's about showing interest and building a shared connection.

Pro Tip #3: Don't Fear the Pauses Sometimes, silences are inevitable, and that's okay. Rather than panicking when there's a pause, take it as a moment to reset. You don't need to fill every silence immediately. Often, the other person will pick up the next part of the conversation. Embracing pauses makes you seem more confident and gives the interaction a relaxed pace.

6. The Fine Line Between Curious and Nosy

Curiosity can be your best friend in small talk, but it's important to keep it **friendly and casual**. When you're just getting to know someone, aim for questions that feel natural and aren't too probing. This way, the conversation feels light rather than crossing into territory that might feel uncomfortable for the other person.

7. Knowing When (and How) to Wrap It Up

Finally, let's talk about **how to end a conversation gracefully**. Just like a good exit in public speaking, a well-timed wrap-up in small talk leaves a positive impression. You don't need to wait for a lull or run out of things to say. Ending on a high note is not only easier, but it also lets the other person feel that you valued the conversation.

You're making progress, and you're probably noticing that **small talk doesn't have to be excruciating**. Now that you know how to kick things off and keep the conversation flowing, let's talk about building some finesse. In this part, we'll focus on **deepening the conversation in a natural way** without feeling forced. This is the key to making small talk feel more like a real connection rather than a task you have to get through.

8. Transitioning to Topics that Matter (Without Making It Awkward)

Once you're comfortable with the basics of small talk, the next step is knowing how to guide the conversation into territory that feels more genuine. This doesn't mean you have to dive into deep topics immediately, but rather **finding ways to make the conversation feel more authentic** and relevant to both of you.

Here are some tips to help ease into more meaningful territory:

Pro Tip #1: Look for "Anchor" Topics As you're chatting, keep an ear out for topics that seem to resonate with the other person. This might be a shared interest, a relatable experience, or even a common frustration. These "anchor" topics give you a point of connection that you can return to, making the conversation feel more substantial and less like a series of random questions.

Pro Tip #2: Use Empathy to Connect One of the best ways to make small talk feel deeper is by showing **empathy and understanding**. If someone mentions a challenge or a tough day, take a moment to acknowledge it with a simple, "That sounds really frustrating" or "I totally get that." Empathy allows you to connect on an emotional level, which can make even light conversation feel meaningful.

Pro Tip #3: Reflect on Their Responses Instead of jumping to the next question or topic, try reflecting back on what they've just shared. If someone tells you about a hobby they're passionate about, for instance, you might say, "That's amazing—I can see why you're so into it!" Reflecting their responses not only shows that you're listening but also helps deepen the exchange.

9. Building Your Confidence with Each Interaction

The more you practise these small talk strategies, the more confident you'll become in social situations. With each conversation, you're building a toolkit of skills that you can use to navigate future interactions with ease. Remember, confidence in small talk doesn't come from knowing all the right things to say—it comes from feeling comfortable in the flow of the conversation.

Pro Tip #1: Start Small, and Build Up If you're new to small talk, start with shorter conversations or situations that feel low-pressure, like chatting with a barista or making a quick comment to a colleague. As you become more comfortable, you'll feel ready to try these techniques in longer or more social settings.

10. Practice Makes Perfect (or at Least, More Comfortable)

Like any skill, getting better at small talk takes practice. The more you engage in these brief conversations, the more natural they'll feel. You don't have to aim for perfection—just aim for progress, and give yourself credit for each positive interaction, no matter how small.

You're getting the hang of small talk, and by now, it should feel less like a chore and more like an opportunity. Now, let's focus on a few **advanced techniques** to help you navigate small talk with different types of people. After all, the same approach doesn't always work for everyone, and part of mastering small talk is learning how to **adapt your style** based on the other person's cues.

11. Reading Social Cues: When to Keep Going (and When to Wrap It Up)

One of the biggest keys to successful small talk is knowing when to continue the conversation—and when to gracefully step away. Social cues are subtle but powerful indicators that can tell you if someone is engaged or if they're ready to move on. By paying attention, you can make sure your small talk hits the right note every time.

Pro Tip #1: Watch Their Body Language If someone is facing you directly, maintaining eye contact, and responding actively, they're likely interested in the conversation. On the other hand, if they're glancing around the room, crossing their arms, or giving short answers, it might be a sign that they're ready to wrap it up. Adjust accordingly based on their level of engagement.

Pro Tip #2: Use Your Exit Lines Smoothly When you sense it's time to end the conversation, having a smooth exit line makes it easier. Try something friendly like, "It was great talking with you! I'll let you get back to things," or "I've got to run, but I really enjoyed chatting!" This helps you exit without any awkwardness and leaves a positive impression.

Pro Tip #3: Don't Overthink It Not every conversation has to end perfectly or lead to a deeper connection. Small talk is often just that—small. Sometimes it's okay to have a quick, light exchange and move on. Don't put pressure on yourself to make every interaction meaningful; the goal is simply to make each one comfortable.

12. Adapting to Different Personality Types

Not everyone approaches small talk the same way, and understanding different personality types can make it easier to **adjust your style**. Whether you're talking to an extrovert who loves to chat or a fellow introvert who might be feeling just as reserved, knowing how to tailor your approach helps make the interaction smoother.

13. Making Small Talk Feel Natural (Even When It's Not)

Finally, remember that small talk can sometimes feel awkward, and that's perfectly normal. What matters is that you're putting in the effort to connect. The more you practise, the more natural it will feel over time.

Here we are at the final stretch of Chapter 12! By now, you've learned how to start, navigate, and wrap up a small talk conversation like a pro. For this last part, let's focus on **building confidence in your small talk skills**. Believe it or not, the biggest barrier to successful small talk isn't lack of knowledge or skill—it's the **fear of awkwardness**. But the more you engage in these brief, everyday conversations, the less intimidating they become.

Let's wrap up by discussing how to keep improving and embracing the fact that small talk is simply a skill to practise and enjoy, not something to fear.

14. Embracing the Awkward Moments

No matter how polished your small talk skills become, there will always be moments that feel awkward. Maybe someone gives a short answer, or maybe there's a pause you didn't expect. Instead of fearing these moments, learn to **embrace them**. A quick smile or lighthearted comment like, "Well, I guess I've run out of my best material!" can turn an awkward silence into a moment of humour.

Awkwardness is part of being human, and sometimes it can even make you seem more relatable. So, when these moments happen (and they will), take them in stride and move on without letting them derail your confidence.

15. Practising Small Talk in Everyday Situations

The best way to improve at small talk is to **practise in low-stakes situations**. Chat with the barista at the coffee shop, say a quick hello to a neighbour, or make small talk with a colleague in the break room. These brief interactions may not lead to deep conversations, but they'll help you become more comfortable with the rhythm of small talk. Over time, you'll feel more at ease starting conversations with anyone, anywhere.

16. Remembering the Power of Genuine Interest

The best small talk doesn't come from knowing the "right" questions to ask; it comes from showing a **genuine interest in the other person**. People can tell when you're really listening, and they're much more likely to open up if they feel you're truly engaged. So instead of focusing too much on what to say, focus on being present in the conversation. This approach will not only make the exchange more enjoyable for both of you, but it will also help you form authentic connections.

Pro Tips for Mastering Small Talk:

1. **Practice Curiosity** – Approach each conversation with a curious mindset, and let your interest guide the questions you ask.
2. **Keep It Light** – Remember, small talk doesn't have to be deep. Light topics are perfect for making a positive first impression.

3. **Let Go of Perfection** – Don't worry about getting everything "right." Small talk is meant to be easy-going, so relax and enjoy it.

13

How to Be the Life of the Party

Without Losing Your Mind

Alright, introverts, we're about to dive into one of the most intimidating social events out there—the **party**. I know, for many of you, the idea of being at a party, let alone standing out at one, might sound more like a nightmare than a good time. But here's the truth: **you don't have to be the loudest or the most outgoing person in the room** to be the life of the party. In fact, some of the most magnetic people are those who know how to be genuinely present, listen well, and bring their own calm energy to the chaos around them.

In this chapter, we'll cover how to **navigate parties without losing your mind, find your own way to shine**, and maybe even enjoy yourself a little along the way. The goal isn't to turn you into a party animal; it's to help you feel comfortable and confident, regardless of the crowd around you.

1. Reframing the Party Mindset

The first step to surviving (and thriving) at a party is **reframing your mindset**. Instead of seeing the event as an overwhelming social obligation, try to approach it as an opportunity to connect. You don't have to be the centre of attention, and you don't need to talk to everyone in the room. The goal is simply to find a few moments that feel enjoyable or meaningful to you. By changing your expectations, you'll feel less pressure to perform and more freedom to just be yourself.

2. Finding Your Comfort Zone Within the Crowd

At any party, there are usually pockets of people with different levels of energy. Some groups are laughing loudly by the bar, others are chatting in smaller clusters on the couch, and a few might even be outside, enjoying a quieter space. Look for an area that feels comfortable to you—a quieter corner, a casual group, or even the food table where you can strike up easy conversations with people passing by.

Remember, you don't have to be everywhere at once. Find a spot where you feel at ease, and let the conversation come to you. This way, you can avoid feeling overwhelmed by the crowd and still participate at your own pace.

3. The Power of Being Genuinely Present

Parties are often filled with people talking past each other, everyone trying to be heard. But one of the best ways to make an impression at a party is by **being genuinely present**. When you're engaged in a conversation, really listen, ask questions, and show interest. People will remember you for being someone who paid attention, which is surprisingly rare in a party setting. This approach also takes the pressure off you to "perform" and allows you to connect on a more authentic level.

Now that you're approaching the party with a healthier mindset and have found a comfortable spot in the crowd, let's talk about how to **create moments that make you stand out—without exhausting yourself**. Being the life of the party doesn't mean being the loudest; it can mean creating memorable, genuine interactions that leave people glad they met you.

Here's how to keep things lively while still staying true to your introverted nature.

4. Starting Conversations Without the Pressure

Starting conversations at a party can feel intimidating, especially when the energy is high. But remember, you don't have to dive into deep topics or impress everyone with clever jokes. A simple, friendly comment on something going on around you—like the music, the food, or the atmosphere—can be a perfect icebreaker.

Example: If you're at the snack table, you might say to the person next to you, "I think I came here just for the food!" This kind of light comment makes it easy for others to respond without feeling pressured. Plus, it gives you a natural way to ease into a conversation without feeling like you have to entertain.

5. Embracing Small Wins: Quality Over Quantity

At a party, it's easy to feel like you should be mingling with everyone, but that's just going to leave you drained. Instead, focus on having a few quality conversations rather than trying to meet the entire guest list. **Small wins, like one good conversation or a few shared laughs**, can make the entire night feel worthwhile.

By focusing on quality over quantity, you'll also come across as more sincere and approachable—traits people will remember long after the party is over.

6. Taking Breaks to Recharge

Even with the best mindset, parties can be overwhelming. When you start to feel drained, find a quiet spot where you can take a few minutes to breathe, grab some water, or just enjoy a moment of solitude. Think of it as a way to **refresh and reset** so that you can jump back into the crowd without feeling exhausted. This little act of self-care can make a big difference in how much energy you have to keep enjoying the night.

Great! Now that you know how to enter the party scene with confidence, create genuine connections, and take breaks when needed, let's talk about **adding your own unique flavour to the event**. You don't have to be the loudest person in the room to stand out. Instead, finding small ways to share your personality can make you memorable and help you enjoy the experience even more.

7. Adding Humor Without Forcing It

Humour can be a fantastic way to connect with people, but you don't need to tell great stories or crack a ton of jokes to be funny. **Subtle humour—like a well-timed comment or playful observation**—can leave a lasting impression. If something funny happens in the moment, share a quick laugh with someone nearby. This kind of humour doesn't require you to be "on" all the time; it just allows you to enjoy the moment.

Example: If the playlist switches to an unexpected song, you could say with a grin, "Looks like the DJ's got some hidden talent!" Small moments of shared humour can make you approachable and help build a comfortable vibe.

8. Finding a Few Allies

Every party has at least one or two people who are also looking for a quieter, more relaxed experience. **Finding a few "party allies"** who share your energy level can make the entire experience feel easier and more enjoyable. These might be the folks sitting in a cosy corner, chatting by the snacks, or people-watching from the sidelines.

Having a few allies means you'll have a go-to group if things get overwhelming, and you can easily enjoy smaller conversations without feeling like you need to work the entire room.

9. Knowing When It's Time to Make Your Exit

Finally, knowing when to leave is just as important as knowing how to enter the party. There's no need to feel guilty if you're ready to head out before everyone else—**leaving on your own terms can actually make the experience more enjoyable**. If you've had a good time and made some connections, trust that you've accomplished what you came for. And who knows? You might even leave with an invitation to the next gathering.

Now that you're mastering the art of making a low-key but memorable impression at parties, let's talk about **maintaining your energy throughout the event**. Parties can be a marathon, not a sprint, and knowing how to manage your social energy can help you enjoy the entire experience without burning out. Remember, being "the life of the party" for an introvert isn't about being everywhere at once—it's about making the most of each moment while still feeling true to yourself.

10. Balancing High-Energy and Low-Energy Interactions

One of the best ways to preserve your energy at a party is by **balancing high-energy interactions with quieter moments**. If you've just spent time in a lively conversation with a large group, take a few minutes afterward to chat with one person or step outside for a breather. This alternating rhythm of social activity and solitude can help keep your energy steady and prevent you from feeling drained.

Example: After talking with a group around the food table, you could excuse yourself to get a drink, then join a smaller group or have a quiet one-on-one chat. By pacing yourself, you'll avoid burnout and enjoy each interaction more.

11. Giving Yourself Permission to Observe

If you're at a high-energy event, it's okay to step back and simply observe from time to time. **Being an observer is a strength**—you're likely to pick up on details, notice dynamics, and appreciate the atmosphere without feeling pressured to be involved every moment. Plus, people often feel more comfortable approaching you when you're relaxed and observing, making it easier to form connections naturally.

12. Creating Your Own Fun

Finally, don't be afraid to bring your own twist to the party. Whether it's starting a game, suggesting a group activity, or just sharing an interesting fact, adding a bit of your own flair helps create memories for everyone. Parties are about enjoying the experience together, and by finding little ways to add fun, you make the event enjoyable for both yourself and those around you.

Here we are at the final page of Chapter 13! Now that you've learned how to balance your energy, connect with others in ways that feel genuine, and create your own fun, let's talk about **leaving a lasting impression**. When you're at a party, you don't need to "wow" everyone you meet; you just want to leave a positive, memorable impression on a few people. This final page focuses on how to end the night on a high note, ensuring you feel good about the connections you made and the time you spent.

13. Leaving on a High Note

Ending your night with a positive interaction can make the entire experience feel more rewarding. Before you leave, take a moment to say a sincere goodbye to the people you enjoyed talking to, thank the host, and maybe even share a quick laugh or memory from the night. This kind of small gesture shows that you valued the time you spent with them and leaves a great impression.

Example: "Hey, it was great chatting with you—hope to see you at the next one!" or "Thanks for hosting! Had a blast and loved the music." Little touches like this make you memorable without requiring a lot of extra energy.

14. Reflecting on What Went Well

Once you've left the party, take a few minutes to **reflect on the positive interactions and moments** you experienced. Did you connect with someone new? Did you step out of your comfort zone? Did you actually enjoy yourself (surprise!)? Reflecting on what went well helps reinforce the progress you're making and reminds you that social events can be enjoyable, even for an introvert.

15. Building Confidence for Future Events

Each party you attend is another opportunity to build confidence. The more you put these strategies into practice, the more comfortable you'll feel in social settings. By gradually becoming more familiar with parties and social events, you'll find yourself looking forward to these gatherings, knowing you can navigate them in a way that feels good for you.

Pro Tips for Party Survival:

1. **Create Small Goals** – Set small, achievable goals for each party, like talking to three new people or staying for an hour.
2. **Balance Social Energy** – Alternate between group interactions and quieter moments to avoid feeling overwhelmed.
3. **Make Your Exit Memorable** – Thank the host, say goodbye to friends, and leave with a smile to create a positive impression.

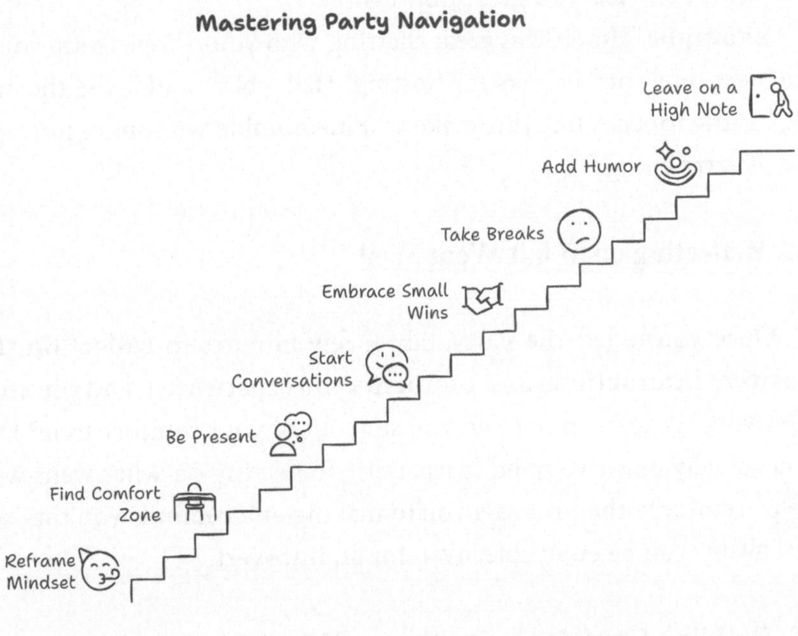

14

Becoming Comfortable with Uncomfortable Situations

Let's be honest: life is full of awkward, uncomfortable situations, and it's practically impossible to avoid them all. For introverts, these moments can feel magnified—a room full of strangers, an unexpected question in a meeting, or even a surprise invitation to dinner can create a wave of discomfort. But here's the thing: **getting comfortable with the uncomfortable** can be one of the most liberating skills you develop.

In this chapter, we'll cover how to **navigate awkward situations without shrinking away**. You don't have to love these moments, but learning to face them with a bit more confidence can make life a lot easier and even a little more enjoyable.

1. Understanding the Power of Adaptability

One of the best things you can do to become more comfortable in uncomfortable situations is to **embrace adaptability**. Life is unpredictable, and while it's natural to want to feel prepared, adaptability is often more valuable than preparation. Embracing the idea that not everything will go as planned gives you a bit of freedom to go with the flow, even when you'd rather have a clear plan.

The goal here is to **practise flexibility** and remind yourself that it's okay to not have all the answers right away. When you approach an uncomfortable situation with a mindset of "let's see what happens," it can take some of the pressure off.

2. Embracing the Art of the Pause

Awkward situations often feel urgent, like you need to respond immediately to avoid silence. But here's a secret: **pausing is powerful**. When faced with a question or a comment that makes you uncomfortable, give yourself a moment to think. You can take a sip of water, smile, or nod as you gather your thoughts. A short pause not only gives you time to come up with a response but also helps you appear calm and collected, even if you're feeling flustered inside.

Example: If someone catches you off guard with a question in a meeting, pause, smile, and say, "That's a great question—I need a second to think about it." You'll look thoughtful and confident, even if you're secretly glad for the extra moment.

3. Finding the Humour in Awkwardness

Sometimes, the best way to handle an uncomfortable situation is with a bit of humour. Laughing at yourself or the situation can lighten the mood and help you feel more at ease. If you stumble over your words or find yourself in a strange conversation, a quick, lighthearted comment can break the tension and remind everyone that it's okay to be human.

Now that you're embracing adaptability, using pauses to gather your thoughts, and finding humour in the awkwardness, let's focus on a few more strategies for navigating these uncomfortable moments with confidence. The goal here isn't to magically eliminate discomfort but to handle it gracefully, so it doesn't throw you off balance.

4. Staying Present Instead of Overthinking

When we find ourselves in uncomfortable situations, the tendency to **overthink** can kick in almost immediately. You might start analysing every word you say, wondering if you're making the right impression or imagining every possible way the situation could go wrong. The problem with overthinking is that it pulls you out of the moment, making you more self-conscious.

Instead, try to stay present by focusing on what's happening right now, not what you think might happen. A simple trick is to **focus on your senses**—what you see, hear, or feel around you. Grounding yourself in the present helps quiet the overthinking and keeps you engaged with what's actually happening rather than the "what ifs."

5. Shifting the Spotlight to Others

One effective way to reduce your own discomfort in awkward situations is to **shift the focus to the other person**. If you're at a loss for words or feeling self-conscious, try asking a question to redirect the conversation. People usually appreciate the chance to talk about themselves, and this approach gives you a moment to relax while showing interest in them.

Example: If someone's question catches you off guard, you can say, "That's an interesting point—how did you get interested in that topic?" This shifts the spotlight and allows you to regroup without the pressure of being in the hot seat.

6. Building Resilience Through Small Challenges

Facing uncomfortable situations becomes easier with practice. Start by tackling **small social challenges** that push you out of your comfort zone in manageable ways. This could mean striking up a quick conversation with a cashier, offering a suggestion in a group setting, or accepting an invitation you might normally turn down. Each small win builds resilience and makes bigger challenges feel less intimidating over time.

You're making excellent progress, and by now, you should be starting to feel a bit more comfortable with the idea of facing discomfort. The truth is, navigating awkward situations can be a skill all on its own—one that can actually help you build confidence in other areas. On this page, we'll focus on **keeping calm and managing your reactions** when things don't go as planned.

7. Practising a Calm Response

One of the most effective ways to handle an uncomfortable situation is by **keeping your response calm and measured**. This doesn't mean pretending to be okay with everything; it's more about how you respond outwardly, even if you're feeling unsure. A calm tone, a steady pace in your speech, and relaxed body language all signal to the other person—and to yourself—that you're in control.

Example: If someone makes an unexpected comment that throws you off, take a deep breath, and respond with a simple, neutral comment like, "That's interesting. I hadn't thought of it that way." This buys you time, acknowledges the comment, and keeps things moving smoothly.

8. Recognizing and Accepting Your Limits

One of the challenges in uncomfortable situations is knowing when to **accept your limits**. It's okay if you're not always comfortable or if there are certain situations that push you too far. Recognizing when you're reaching your limit and being okay with stepping back is just as important as pushing yourself. The goal is to grow, but also to be kind to yourself and respect when you've had enough.

9. Using Reflection as a Tool for Growth

After facing an uncomfortable situation, take some time to reflect. Ask yourself what went well, what you found challenging, and what you might try differently next time. Reflection helps you turn each experience into a learning opportunity, making it easier to handle similar situations in the future. Remember, progress isn't always about perfection—it's about taking small steps toward feeling more at ease in a variety of settings.

Great work! You're building a solid toolkit for handling awkward or uncomfortable situations, but sometimes, even with the best preparation, these moments can feel overwhelming. On this page, we'll explore a few additional techniques for managing those intense or surprising situations, helping you stay in control even when things take an unexpected turn.

10. Using Body Language to Signal Confidence

Body language is one of the most powerful ways to communicate confidence, even if you're feeling uncertain. Standing tall, keeping your shoulders relaxed, and making gentle eye contact can help you appear self-assured, which in turn makes you feel more comfortable. Plus, confident body language often encourages others to respond positively, creating a friendlier environment.

Example: If you're at a networking event and start to feel nervous, try a small body language adjustment: plant your feet firmly on the ground, straighten your posture, and make eye contact with the person speaking. This simple shift helps ground you and shows others that you're present and attentive.

11. Focusing on the Big Picture

When you're in a tense or awkward situation, it's easy to feel like everything rides on that one moment. But if you zoom out a little and **focus on the bigger picture**, it helps put things in perspective. Remind yourself that one uncomfortable moment is just a blip in the grand scheme of things. This mindset can relieve some of the pressure and help you handle the situation with a more relaxed attitude.

12. Ending the Interaction Gracefully

If a situation feels too uncomfortable, there's no harm in ending it politely. Learning to step away gracefully is a skill in itself. A simple line like, "It was great chatting—I'm going to grab a refill!" or "I need to catch up with someone, but enjoy the rest of your evening!" allows you to exit without feeling awkward or rude. Knowing you can leave a situation when needed gives you a sense of control and can make these moments much easier to handle.

Here we are at the final page of Chapter 14! By now, you should feel a bit more equipped to handle life's awkward or uncomfortable moments without letting them throw you off. Let's finish this chapter with a few final strategies for maintaining confidence, even when things don't go exactly as planned. Remember, building comfort with discomfort is a skill that will serve you well in many areas of life, both socially and professionally.

13. Practising Self-Compassion

One of the most valuable things you can do after any uncomfortable experience is to **be kind to yourself**. It's easy to replay awkward moments in your mind and be critical, but remember that everyone experiences these situations from time to time. Instead of focusing on what you could have done differently, acknowledge the effort you put in and give yourself credit for facing the situation. Self-compassion will help you approach future interactions with a positive mindset.

14. Recognizing Growth Over Time

As you continue facing uncomfortable situations, take a moment now and then to reflect on how much progress you've made. Even if these moments still feel awkward, notice how your responses have improved or how much less stress they bring. Recognizing your growth over time is a great confidence booster and reminds you that you're continually improving, even if the changes feel small.

15. Building Resilience Through Repetition

Pro Tips for Embracing Uncomfortable Situations:

1. **Pause Before Responding** – Take a deep breath before you react. It gives you time to gather your thoughts and respond calmly.
2. **Reframe Awkward Moments as Learning Experiences** – Instead of seeing them as mistakes, view them as practice for growth.
3. **Trust in Your Progress** – Remind yourself of how far you've come, and focus on growth rather than perfection.

15

The Psychology of Charm – And How to Fake It

Charm—it's one of those qualities that seems either natural or impossible to fake. But here's the truth: **charm is less about charisma and more about understanding people**. Contrary to popular belief, you don't have to be extroverted, outgoing, or even naturally charismatic to be charming. Often, charm is rooted in subtle behaviours that show you're genuinely interested in the person in front of you.

In this chapter, we're diving into **the psychology of charm** and how introverts can develop this skill without having to reinvent their personalities. Think of charm as a tool you can use when needed, not a personality trait you have to adopt 24/7. Ready to become the person people love talking to? Let's go!

1. Understanding What Makes Someone "Charming"

When we think of charming people, we often imagine those who are witty, magnetic, or the centre of attention. But charm is actually more about **how you make others feel**. People are drawn to those who show genuine interest, listen well, and make them feel comfortable. So, becoming charming is less about impressing others and more about making them feel valued.

Charm often involves three key components: **active listening**, **positive body language**, and **an approachable energy**. You don't have to be loud or bold to be charming—you just need to show that you're fully present and interested in the person you're with.

2. Building Confidence Through Small Interactions

Charm doesn't require grand gestures; it can be as simple as a warm smile, a well-timed compliment, or a thoughtful question. Building confidence in your charm starts with **small interactions**. Practice with short conversations—like with a cashier, a colleague, or even a neighbour. Each time you make an effort to be present and personable, you're practising the art of charm in a manageable, low-pressure way.

Over time, you'll feel more comfortable bringing that same energy into longer conversations or larger social settings.

3. Bringing Positive Energy (Without Faking It)

One of the most effective ways to charm others is by bringing a sense of positive energy. This doesn't mean you have to be upbeat all the time—**positive energy is more about openness than enthusiasm**. When you're willing to engage, smile, and look for the good in conversations, people naturally respond to that energy. The key is to let your positive energy feel authentic, rather than forced. Small gestures like nodding, smiling, or giving thoughtful responses create a warm, welcoming vibe.

Now that you know charm is about making others feel comfortable and valued, let's get into **practical techniques** you can use to bring that charm to life. You don't need to memorise witty lines or act like someone you're not. Instead, these techniques are about being genuinely present, expressing interest, and responding in ways that make the other person feel appreciated.

4. The Power of Eye Contact and a Genuine Smile

Few things communicate interest and warmth like **eye contact and a genuine smile**. When you look someone in the eye and smile, you're sending a signal that you're open, attentive, and interested in what they're saying. Eye contact doesn't mean staring—just a few moments here and there to show you're listening.

When combined with a genuine smile, eye contact helps people feel that they're truly seen and valued. And the best part? You don't need to say a word. This simple, silent interaction can go a long way in creating a positive impression.

Example: During a conversation, try looking the person in the eye when they're speaking, then offering a warm smile. Even if you're nervous, this small gesture shows engagement and approachability.

5. Asking Thoughtful, Open-Ended Questions

One of the most charming qualities is curiosity—genuine interest in the other person's thoughts and experiences. **Asking thoughtful, open-ended questions** shows that you care about what the other person has to say. Questions that start with "what," "how," or "why" often open the door to interesting, engaging conversations.

For instance, instead of asking, "Did you have a good weekend?" try asking, "What was the best part of your weekend?" Open-ended questions encourage people to share more and make them feel valued, which is the foundation of charm.

6. Showing Empathy Through Small Reactions

Sometimes, it's the small reactions that make the biggest impact. Nodding when someone shares something meaningful, offering a supportive "I totally get that," or showing a little excitement when they tell a good story all contribute to a sense of **empathy** and understanding. These subtle reactions make people feel heard and appreciated, and that's incredibly charming.

Fantastic! You're starting to see how small gestures—like eye contact, thoughtful questions, and empathy—can make you naturally charming without needing to be over-the-top. Let's keep building on this by diving into **how to make others feel special** through even more subtle behaviours. Remember, charm isn't about dominating the conversation but rather about making the other person feel valued and seen.

7. Listening More Than You Speak

One of the most charming qualities you can develop is the ability to **listen actively**. When people feel like they're truly being listened to, they often open up more, which makes the conversation deeper and more enjoyable. Charm is about balance, and giving others the chance to share their thoughts shows you're genuinely invested in them.

Active listening is more than just being quiet while the other person speaks. It's about responding with interest, nodding, and maybe even repeating back part of what they said to show you're engaged.

Example: If someone tells you a story about a recent experience, respond with something like, "Wow, that sounds amazing! How did that make you feel?" This shows that you're not just hearing them—you're engaging with what they're saying on a deeper level.

8. Remembering and Recalling Details

One way to make someone feel valued is by remembering small details they've shared with you. Whether it's a mention of their favourite coffee shop, an upcoming trip, or a recent accomplishment, **recalling these details in future conversations** shows that you care enough to pay attention.

When people feel that they're remembered, they're more likely to view you as thoughtful and considerate, both of which are key components of charm. Plus, it's a great way to build rapport over time.

9. Adding a Personal Touch to Compliments

Compliments are a wonderful way to show appreciation, but the most charming compliments are those that feel genuine and specific. Instead of generic comments, **give a compliment that's unique to the person**. Maybe you admire their work ethic, their sense of humour, or their ability to tell a story. By making your compliment personal, it feels more sincere and shows that you're genuinely paying attention.

Example: Instead of saying, "You're good at your job," try, "I really admire how you handle challenges at work—it's inspiring." This small shift makes the compliment feel authentic and meaningful.

You're well on your way to mastering the art of charm in a way that feels genuine and easy to maintain. On this page, we're going to focus on **keeping the conversation balanced and engaging**. One of the simplest ways to charm others is by finding ways to bring positive energy into the interaction, allowing them to feel appreciated and at ease.

10. Finding Common Ground

One of the easiest ways to make a conversation feel natural and engaging is by finding **shared interests or experiences**. When you find common ground, even small details—like a favourite TV show, a recent experience, or a shared hobby—can create a deeper connection. It's like hitting the "fast forward" button on getting to know someone, and it helps you both feel more comfortable.

When you connect over something mutual, the conversation naturally flows because you're both interested. It also takes the pressure off, making it feel more like a shared experience rather than an interview.

Example: If someone mentions they enjoy hiking, you could say, "Me too! Do you have any favourite trails?" This immediately brings the conversation to a shared interest and makes it feel less formal.

11. Letting the Other Person Shine

Charm isn't about showcasing your own qualities—it's about giving others a chance to shine. **Let the other person take the spotlight** by encouraging them to talk about their accomplishments, interests, or unique skills. This doesn't mean downplaying yourself; it simply means creating space for the other person to feel valued.

When people feel encouraged to talk about themselves without judgement, they're more likely to see you as a warm, welcoming presence. This approach helps you form connections that feel genuine and effortless.

12. Ending on a Positive Note

Finally, one of the most charming things you can do is **end the conversation on a positive note**. Whether you're leaving a party or wrapping up a quick chat, finish with a friendly remark or a thank-you. This leaves a lasting impression, making people look forward to seeing you again.

Example: "I really enjoyed talking with you—hope we get a chance to catch up soon!" This simple closing statement shows appreciation and reinforces the positive energy of the conversation.

Great! You've now gathered the skills to become charming in a way that feels natural, focused on listening, encouraging others, and ending on a positive note. For this final page, let's talk about **how to keep building on these skills** so that they become second nature. The goal is for charm to feel less like a practised act and more like a natural part of how you interact with others.

13. Practising Consistency

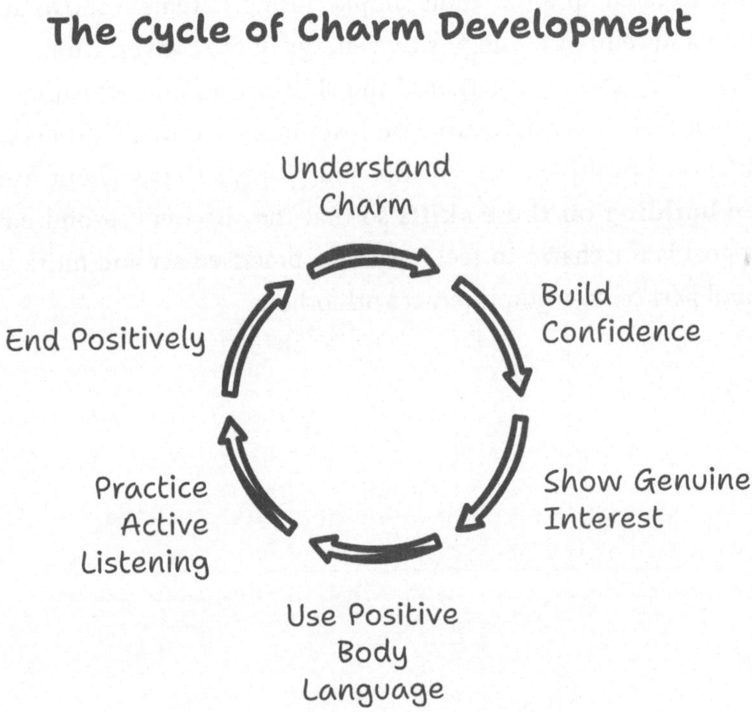

14. Embracing Your Unique Style

Not all charm looks the same. Some people are charming in an enthusiastic, high-energy way, while others bring a calm, thoughtful presence. **Lean into your unique personality** and bring charm in a way that feels comfortable to you. Maybe your strength is in asking great questions, offering sincere compliments, or keeping a conversation balanced. By embracing what feels natural, your charm will be genuine and memorable.

15. Reflecting on Progress

After practising these skills for a while, take some time to reflect. Think about interactions that went well and the moments that felt natural. Reflection helps reinforce what's working and encourages you to keep building on your strengths. Charm is a skill you'll keep refining, and each positive interaction will help you feel more confident in it.

Pro Tips for Faking (and Mastering) Charm:

1. **Ask Genuine Questions** – People love talking about themselves, so ask questions that let them share.
2. **Be Present** – Small moments of focus, like eye contact and nodding, make others feel valued.
3. **End with a Positive Remark** – Wrap up every conversation with a friendly note, leaving a lasting good impression.

16

Travelling as an Introvert while Making Friends

Travelling is an incredible experience—the chance to see new places, explore different cultures, and, yes, meet new people. But for introverts, the "meeting new people" part can feel a bit intimidating. Between hostels, group tours, and shared spaces, travel often involves a lot of social interaction, which can quickly drain your energy. However, there's good news: **travelling as an introvert doesn't mean you have to transform into an extrovert**. Instead, it's about finding ways to connect on your own terms.

In this chapter, we'll dive into **introvert-friendly strategies for meeting people while travelling**—ways to make genuine connections without feeling overwhelmed. Whether you're travelling solo or with friends, these tips will help you enjoy the social side of travel without sacrificing your need for downtime.

1. Setting Boundaries for Social Time

One of the best ways to make travel socialising enjoyable is by setting boundaries around your interactions. Socialising on the road doesn't have to be an all-or-nothing experience; it's perfectly fine to pick and choose when and how you engage with others. Maybe you're up for a group dinner, but you'd rather skip the pub crawl afterward, or perhaps you want to join a guided tour but plan a solo walk later.

Example: When staying in a hostel, consider joining group events you're genuinely interested in and balancing them with solo activities, like a morning walk or reading time. This approach keeps socialising manageable and ensures you're getting the downtime you need.

2. Choosing Introvert-Friendly Accommodations

The place you stay can make a big difference in how comfortable you feel meeting people. **Some accommodations are more introvert-friendly than others**. Hostels with smaller dorms or common areas that encourage quieter interactions can be ideal. Boutique hotels, private rooms in hostels, or Airbnb stays with friendly hosts also provide a mix of privacy and social opportunities. By choosing the right setting, you can socialise when you're up for it and retreat when you need a break.

3. Finding Common Interests with Fellow Travelers

One of the easiest ways to connect with others while travelling is through **shared interests**. Many travellers love exchanging tips, sharing stories, or discussing favourite activities. Look for natural ways to engage, like asking about someone's favourite spot in the city, a hike they recommend, or any must-try local food. Finding common ground makes conversations feel organic and gives you an instant connection.

Now that you know how to set boundaries, choose introvert-friendly accommodations, and connect through shared interests, let's explore **strategies for making travel interactions more relaxed and enjoyable**. Socialising while travelling doesn't have to mean forced small talk or exhausting group activities; it can be about connecting with people in ways that feel comfortable and meaningful.

4. Using Activities to Create Low-Key Social Opportunities

Group activities can be a great way to meet people without the pressure of constant conversation. **Activities like cooking classes, hiking tours, or local workshops** allow you to engage with others naturally, focusing on the experience rather than filling the silence. This approach helps you connect with fellow travellers without the pressure of a purely social setting.

Example: Joining a cooking class offers a way to bond with others over shared tasks, like chopping vegetables or tasting dishes. The conversation flows naturally around the activity, making it easier to connect without feeling drained.

5. Connecting with Locals for Unique Insights

Sometimes, connecting with locals rather than other travellers can provide a refreshing break from constant socialising. Locals often have a different perspective and can introduce you to hidden gems, local customs, or must-try foods. This approach lets you experience the culture more deeply without the expectation of forming long-term friendships.

Consider joining a local tour, attending a cultural event, or even visiting a café where locals hang out. These small interactions offer the chance to connect meaningfully without feeling like you're on a networking spree.

6. Taking Breaks to Recharge

When travelling, it's easy to get caught up in the excitement and feel like you have to be "on" all the time. But taking regular breaks to **recharge your social energy** is essential. Whether it's finding a quiet park, spending time with a book, or exploring a new area solo, breaks help balance socialising with the solitude that keeps you refreshed.

Excellent! You're building a great balance of socialising and recharging, which can make travel experiences richer and more comfortable for an introvert. Now, let's dive into **ways to make social interactions feel more personal and genuine**. When you're travelling, it's often the meaningful conversations and genuine connections that leave the biggest impact, so let's explore how to make those moments happen naturally.

7. Focusing on One-on-One Conversations

While group interactions can be fun, **one-on-one conversations** often feel more relaxed and meaningful for introverts. When you connect with one person, you're less likely to feel overstimulated, and the conversation usually has more depth. If you find someone interesting at a group activity or hostel, try suggesting a coffee or a walk—it's a low-pressure way to enjoy more personal interaction.

Example: After chatting with someone during a group tour, you might say, "I'd love to hear more about your travels—are you free for a coffee later?" This shifts the focus to a calmer setting and allows you to connect on a deeper level.

8. Embracing the Art of Listening

One of the most charming qualities you can bring to travel conversations is your ability to **listen actively**. People appreciate being heard, and listening carefully to someone's stories or experiences makes the interaction more enjoyable for both of you. When you're not rushing to fill silences, conversations often feel more authentic, and you leave a positive impression without having to say much.

9. Staying Open to Short but Memorable Connections

Not every connection you make while travelling has to be long-term. Sometimes, the best travel moments come from brief but memorable interactions—a shared laugh with a stranger, a quick exchange of travel tips, or a random conversation that brightens your day. Embrace these short encounters for what they are, without the pressure to turn them into lasting friendships.

Great! Now that you're getting comfortable with one-on-one interactions, embracing the power of listening, and appreciating short but meaningful connections, let's talk about **keeping travel interactions light and fun**. You don't have to force deep conversations every time you meet someone new. In fact, lighthearted exchanges can be some of the most enjoyable and memorable parts of travel.

10. Embracing Playfulness in Conversations

Travel offers a unique opportunity to let go of everyday routines and embrace a bit of playfulness. Use this freedom to bring a **lighthearted energy to your conversations**. Whether it's a shared joke about the unpredictable weather, a laugh over local customs, or a funny observation about travel mishaps, keeping things light can help both you and the other person feel more at ease.

Example: If you're exploring a quirky local market and notice something unexpected, make a humorous comment like, "I think I just found the world's strangest souvenir!" Playfulness creates a friendly vibe and makes conversations more fun and memorable.

11. Taking Advantage of Shared Experiences

One of the easiest ways to bond with other travellers is by **sharing in the experience**—whether it's admiring a sunset, tasting new foods, or exploring a local landmark. Talking about something you're both experiencing in real time takes the pressure off small talk and keeps the conversation naturally engaging. Plus, shared experiences often become the highlight of your trip, especially when you're enjoying them with others.

12. Letting Go of Perfection

When you're meeting new people on the road, remember that you don't need to be "perfectly social" or impress everyone you meet. Travel conversations are often relaxed and low-pressure, so **embrace imperfection** and just be yourself. Not every interaction will be amazing, and that's perfectly fine. By letting go of the need to be "on" all the time, you can enjoy the social side of travel more naturally.

You've reached the last page of Chapter 16, and by now, you should have a solid grasp of how to balance connection and solitude while on the road. Let's wrap up with some **final tips for maintaining social energy** and making your travel experiences both enriching and comfortable. Remember, travelling as an introvert doesn't mean missing out on connections—it means creating them in a way that works best for you.

13. Creating a Routine to Recharge

When you're travelling, it's easy to get caught up in the excitement and feel the need to constantly be "on." But keeping a small routine, like setting aside quiet time each day, can make a big difference. **A regular time to recharge**—whether it's morning coffee alone, an evening walk, or a quick journal session—helps you feel balanced and ready to engage when you're in social settings.

14. Finding a Balance Between Solo and Social Activities

You don't have to choose between solitude and socialising. Instead, try to **alternate between solo adventures and group activities**. For example, spend a morning exploring a city on your own, then join a group dinner in the evening. This balance allows you to experience the best of both worlds without feeling overwhelmed or isolated.

15. Ending Conversations Gracefully

Knowing when to wrap up a conversation is key to keeping your energy levels up. If you're ready to end a chat, do it with a friendly closing remark. **Ending on a positive note** leaves the other person feeling appreciated and lets you move on without lingering awkwardness.

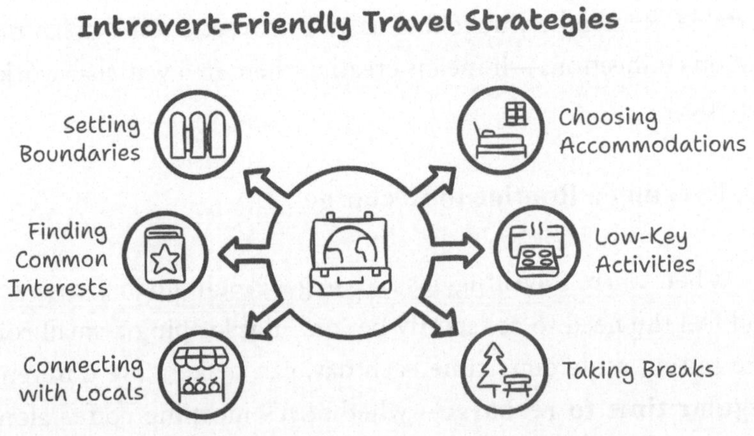

Pro Tips for Introvert-Friendly Travel:

1. **Plan Recharge Time** – Carve out daily moments to unwind, giving you energy for social interactions.

2. **Embrace Casual Connections** – Enjoy brief interactions for what they are, without pressure for lasting friendships.
3. **Mix Solo and Social Activities** – Balance independent adventures with group events to keep things enjoyable.

17

How to Make a Killer First Impression

(Without Killing Yourself Over It)

First impressions: love them or hate them, they matter. Whether it's a job interview, meeting a friend's friend, or introducing yourself at a networking event, **the way we present ourselves in the first few minutes sets the tone**. But let's be honest—making a great first impression can feel like a lot of pressure, especially if you're someone who prefers to ease into conversations.

The good news? First impressions don't require you to reinvent yourself or become someone you're not. It's about small adjustments that help you show up confidently and genuinely. In this chapter, we'll explore simple, approachable ways to **make a strong first impression** without feeling like you're putting on an act.

1. Understanding the Basics of First Impressions

The first impression isn't about saying the perfect thing or being outrageously charming—it's about **being memorable in a positive way**. People often decide how they feel about someone in the first few minutes, and this decision is based on more than just words. Body language, tone, and energy all play a role.

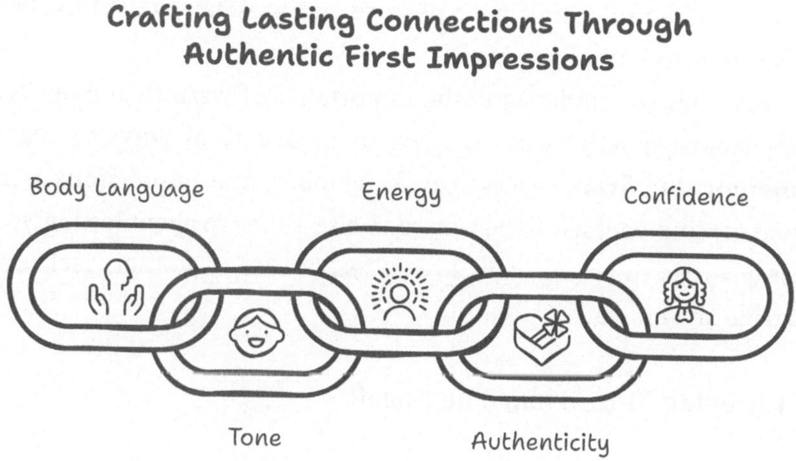

2. The Power of Warmth Over Perfection

One of the biggest mistakes people make is trying to be "perfect" when making a first impression. But in reality, people respond more to warmth and friendliness than to perfection. A friendly smile, relaxed posture, and easy-going attitude go a lot further than rehearsed lines or a polished exterior.

Example: When meeting someone for the first time, start with a smile and a relaxed greeting. Something as simple as, "Hi, I'm [Your Name]—it's great to meet you!" makes the other person feel welcome and takes the pressure off both of you.

3. Using Positive Body Language

Body language speaks volumes, often before you even say a word. Standing tall, making eye contact, and keeping your arms open (not crossed) show that you're approachable. These subtle cues help others feel comfortable around you, creating a friendly atmosphere from the start.

Positive body language can help you feel more confident too. When you're mindful of your posture and presence, you're likely to feel calmer and more grounded

Now that you understand the importance of warmth and positive body language, let's focus on a few more **practical ways to create a memorable first impression**. Remember, first impressions aren't about forcing yourself to be someone else—they're about letting your best qualities shine through, so you feel at ease and others feel comfortable around you.

4. Listening More Than You Speak

One of the simplest and most effective ways to make a great first impression is by **listening attentively**. When you focus on the other person rather than trying to think of the "perfect" response, it shows that you're genuinely interested in what they have to say. People love to feel heard, and attentive listening is a skill that makes you instantly likeable.

Example: If you're meeting someone for the first time and they mention a hobby or experience, ask a follow-up question like, "That sounds interesting—how did you get into it?" This approach shows curiosity and keeps the conversation flowing without pressure.

5. Finding Small Points of Connection

People tend to remember interactions where they felt a sense of connection, even if it's over something small. Look for shared interests, experiences, or even mutual acquaintances to build a connection that feels natural. Finding common ground, even on a minor detail, can help make the conversation memorable and create an instant bond.

For instance, if someone mentions they love coffee and you're a coffee fan too, a simple, "Oh, me too! Do you have a favourite place?" can spark a deeper conversation. Small connections often lead to memorable exchanges without feeling forced.

6. Staying Present in the Conversation

In any first meeting, it's easy to get caught up in your own thoughts, wondering if you're making a good impression or worrying about what to say next. But **staying present**—focusing on the person in front of you and the current conversation—makes a huge difference. When you're fully engaged in the moment, you come across as relaxed and authentic, which others naturally respond to.

Awesome! You're doing great with creating genuine, comfortable first impressions. Now, let's dive into **ways to leave a lasting impact**. Making an impression isn't just about what happens in the first few seconds; it's about keeping the interaction memorable so that the other person leaves feeling positive. Let's focus on how to make each connection feel meaningful without the need for grand gestures.

7. Making Your Words Count

You don't need to be a master conversationalist to leave an impact. Sometimes, saying something simple but sincere can make you memorable. **Genuine compliments, expressions of gratitude, or positive observations** go a long way. When you make a comment that's thoughtful, it shows you're not just trying to impress; you're making a real connection.

Example: If someone helped you with a small favour or even just shared an interesting story, say something like, "Thanks for sharing that—it really made my day!" or "I appreciate you taking the time to chat with me." Simple words of appreciation can create a warm and lasting impression.

8. Embracing Pauses Without Feeling Awkward

Pauses in conversation aren't always a bad thing. In fact, **embracing brief silences** can make the conversation feel more relaxed. You don't need to fill every pause—sometimes, letting a moment breathe adds a sense of calm to the interaction. It also shows that you're comfortable enough not to rush or force the conversation.

By allowing for natural pauses, you give the other person space to reflect or continue sharing, making the exchange feel more balanced and less pressured.

9. Being Yourself (Cliché but True)

Finally, remember that there's no need to put on a show or act like someone else to make a great first impression. People are naturally drawn to authenticity, so **be yourself**—quirks and all. Instead of trying to fit a specific mould, focus on letting your natural personality come through. When you're true to yourself, others sense it, and it often leaves the most genuine, lasting impression.

Great! You're mastering the essentials of a genuine, memorable first impression. Now, let's talk about **managing nerves and bringing positive energy** to interactions. Nerves can sometimes get in the way, especially in high-stakes settings like job interviews, important introductions, or networking events. The goal here is to **channel any nervous energy** into a positive presence that others feel comfortable around.

10. Turning Nervous Energy into Enthusiasm

When we're nervous, it's common to feel tense or withdrawn, which can make others feel uncomfortable too. Instead of trying to suppress your nervous energy, try **redirecting it into enthusiasm** for the conversation. This doesn't mean you need to be overly animated, but a little extra energy—like a warm smile, active listening, or an upbeat tone—can help turn your nerves into a positive vibe.

Example: If you're meeting someone new and feel a bit anxious, greet them with a big smile and show genuine interest in what they're saying. Even a simple, "I'm really excited to meet you!" adds positive energy and takes the edge off your nerves.

11. Using Deep Breaths to Stay Grounded

Breathing might seem like a small thing, but **deep breaths can work wonders** for calming nerves. If you feel anxious, try taking a few slow, deep breaths before or even during the conversation. This helps ground you, keeping you centred and present. A calm breathing rhythm sends a subtle signal of confidence to both your mind and the people around you.

12. Staying Open to Imperfection

First impressions don't have to be flawless to be memorable. Often, small, genuine moments—like a laugh over a minor mistake or a shared smile during a pause—make you more relatable. **Embrace imperfection** by letting yourself relax, laugh at little flubs, and stay comfortable with minor mistakes. This makes the interaction feel more real and takes the pressure off both you and the other person.

You're almost a pro at this! By now, you've learned how to turn nervous energy into enthusiasm, stay grounded, and keep things genuine. Let's wrap up this chapter with **final tips on leaving a positive, lasting impact**. The ultimate goal is to make a memorable impression that doesn't feel forced, so both you and the other person walk away with a good feeling.

13. Wrapping Up with a Positive Remark

Ending the interaction on a positive note can reinforce a great first impression. Whether it's a compliment, a thank-you, or a simple "It was great meeting you," a warm closing leaves a lasting impression. People remember how a conversation made them feel, and ending with a kind remark helps you stand out in a subtle but impactful way.

Example: If you've had an enjoyable chat, try saying, "I really enjoyed our conversation—hope we get to chat again soon!" This lets the other person know you appreciated their time and keeps the energy positive.

14. Reflecting on What Went Well

After any first interaction, take a moment to **reflect on what went well**. Focusing on the positive parts—whether it was a genuine laugh, a shared interest, or just showing up as yourself—reinforces your confidence. Remember, first impressions get easier with practice, and each successful interaction builds your self-assurance for the next one.

15. Practicing in Low-Stakes Situations

If you're still working on making a great first impression, try practicing in low-stakes situations like chatting with a barista, saying hello to a neighbour, or introducing yourself to a friend's friend. These casual settings are great for building confidence without any pressure. Over time, these small interactions make it easier to bring the same confidence to more important introductions.

Pro Tips for Making a Great First Impression:

1. **Smile and Be Present** – Small gestures like a warm smile and eye contact make others feel valued.
2. **Use Positive Closing Statements** – End with a kind remark to leave a memorable impact.
3. **Focus on Progress, Not Perfection** – Each interaction is practice, so celebrate your progress.

18

The Science of Making Friends

(It's Not Rocket Science)

Making friends—it sounds easy enough, but for introverts, it can feel like navigating uncharted waters. Sure, we're all wired to connect in some way, but **building friendships takes a little science and a bit of practice**. The good news? Making friends isn't about becoming a social butterfly or changing who you are. It's about finding people who genuinely resonate with you and building connections in a way that feels natural.

In this chapter, we're diving into **the science of friendship**—why we connect, what makes friendships last, and how to make meaningful connections without trying to be someone you're not. Think of it as a friendly roadmap for making new friends without the pressure.

1. Understanding Why Friendships Matter

Friendships aren't just a "nice to have"; they're essential for our well-being. Research shows that having close friends **improves men-**

tal health, reduces stress, and even boosts physical health. But beyond science, friendships bring joy, laughter, and support into our lives. Knowing the value of friendship can take the pressure off, reminding you that it's worth putting in a little effort to build these connections.

2. The Power of Familiarity

One of the main drivers of friendship is simply spending time together. Psychologists call this the **mere exposure effect**—the idea that we tend to like people we see regularly. So, instead of focusing on instant connections, prioritise being present and showing up. Whether it's a weekly class, a shared hobby, or a recurring meetup, these settings help friendships grow naturally over time.

Example: If you attend a yoga class every Saturday, over time, you'll likely recognize familiar faces and start to feel more comfortable initiating small conversations. Familiarity paves the way for connection without the need for big gestures.

3. Embracing Small Acts of Friendship

Friendship doesn't usually start with grand declarations or deep talks—it begins with **small acts of kindness**. Simple gestures like offering a compliment, remembering someone's name, or lending a hand when needed all signal friendliness. These small acts often lead to more significant connections, creating a foundation for genuine friendship.

You're off to a great start, understanding the value of friendships, the power of familiarity, and how small acts can make a big difference. Now, let's explore **ways to turn acquaintances into friends**. It's one thing to chat with people casually, but how do you go from polite conversation to genuine connection? Building friendships is like planting seeds; it takes consistency and care to help them grow.

4. Following Up in Simple, Genuine Ways

One of the most effective ways to build a friendship is by following up after a shared experience. **Simple follow-ups show you care** and keep the connection going without any pressure. Whether it's a quick message to check in, a suggestion to meet up, or even sharing something that reminded you of them, following up helps keep the conversation flowing.

Example: If you meet someone at a class or event and enjoy talking, try sending a quick message afterward: "I had a great time chatting—are you up for coffee next week?" It's a low-pressure way to build on the initial connection and bring it closer to a budding friendship.

5. Creating Shared Experiences

Friendships are often built on shared experiences, so look for activities you can enjoy together. Whether it's a hobby, exploring a new place, or trying something fun, **shared experiences help deepen the bond**. The more experiences you have together, the stronger the connection becomes, making the friendship feel natural and enjoyable.

Consider inviting someone to something simple—a movie, a concert, or a new cafe. Shared experiences bring variety to your interactions and create memories that form the foundation of your friendship.

6. Practising Patience in the Process

Friendships don't form overnight, and that's perfectly okay. Building genuine connections takes time, and every interaction adds another layer to the relationship. **Practise patience** by focusing on enjoying each step, rather than rushing toward a specific goal. The best friendships often grow slowly, allowing both people to feel comfortable and authentic.

You're on a roll! Now that you're getting comfortable following up, creating shared experiences, and being patient with the process, let's talk about how to **add depth to these budding friendships**. Building a close friendship isn't about having endless conversations or forcing anything—it's about creating an environment where both people feel understood and valued.

Let's dive into ways to make these friendships feel more meaningful over time.

7. Sharing Your Interests and Passions

One of the easiest ways to deepen a friendship is by **sharing your interests and passions**. When you talk about the things you care about, you're not only giving the other person a chance to know you better but also showing them a unique side of yourself. Whether it's a hobby, a favourite topic, or a personal goal, sharing these interests makes the relationship feel more genuine.

Example: If you love photography, invite your friend to join you on a photo walk. Sharing an activity you're passionate about lets the other person see a more authentic side of you, strengthening the connection.

8. Being Open About Vulnerabilities (When the Time is Right)

True friendship often grows when people feel comfortable sharing both the good and the challenging parts of their lives. This doesn't mean you need to dive into heavy topics right away, but over time, being open about your experiences and feelings can create a stronger bond. **Mutual vulnerability fosters trust**, making friendships feel deeper and more supportive.

When the time feels right, sharing a personal story or challenge shows that you trust your friend enough to let them in. This openness encourages them to do the same, creating a deeper sense of connection.

9. Supporting Each Other's Wins (Big and Small)

Part of being a good friend is celebrating each other's successes, no matter how big or small. Showing genuine enthusiasm for your friend's achievements—whether it's a promotion, a new skill, or a personal milestone—makes them feel appreciated. This support not only strengthens the friendship but also creates an environment where both people can thrive.

Fantastic! You're mastering the basics of building meaningful friendships, sharing your interests, opening up when the time feels right, and celebrating your friend's successes. Now, let's focus on **how to maintain friendships over time**. Friendships are like plants—they need regular care and attention to grow. And for introverts, maintaining friendships doesn't mean constant contact but rather small, thoughtful gestures that show you care.

10. Checking In Regularly (Without Overcommitting)

You don't need to be in touch daily to keep a friendship strong, but **regular check-ins** go a long way in maintaining connections. A simple "How's it going?" or "Thought of you today—how's everything?" keeps the friendship alive and shows your friend you're there for them. This approach also feels low-pressure, making it easy to stay connected without feeling overwhelmed.

Example: If your friend recently mentioned a job interview, send a quick message a few days later to ask how it went. These little gestures make a big difference, helping the friendship feel consistent even when you're both busy.

11. Being Flexible with Plans

Life can get hectic, and sometimes plans fall through. Being flexible and understanding when this happens strengthens the friendship by showing you're not rigid about schedules. Instead, **focus on finding another time** that works. This understanding approach makes friendships feel less demanding and more relaxed, which is especially helpful for introverts.

12. Creating Traditions or Rituals

Creating small traditions or routines within a friendship adds a unique layer to the bond. It could be as simple as a monthly coffee catch-up, a shared hobby, or an annual hike. **Traditions give you something to look forward to**, adding stability to the friendship and helping it feel special over time.

You've got the essentials down, from staying connected with regular check-ins to being flexible and creating special rituals. To wrap up this chapter, let's discuss **final tips on deepening and maintaining friendships** in a way that feels natural. These last few touches will help you build friendships that stand the test of time and make you feel fulfilled.

13. Practising Gratitude in Friendships

Expressing gratitude can strengthen any friendship, reminding both of you why you value each other. **Thanking your friend for being there**, remembering small favours, or simply appreciating their company creates a positive dynamic. It shows that you don't take them for granted, which goes a long way in building a lasting connection.

Example: After spending time together, send a quick message like, "Thanks for hanging out—it's always great catching up with you!" These small gestures reinforce the bond and leave your friend feeling valued.

14. Giving Space When Needed

Sometimes, people need space, and respecting this can actually strengthen the friendship. **Giving your friend room to recharge or handle personal matters** without pressure shows understanding. By respecting each other's boundaries, you create a balanced, low-maintenance friendship that both of you can rely on without feeling drained.

15. Accepting That Friendships Evolve

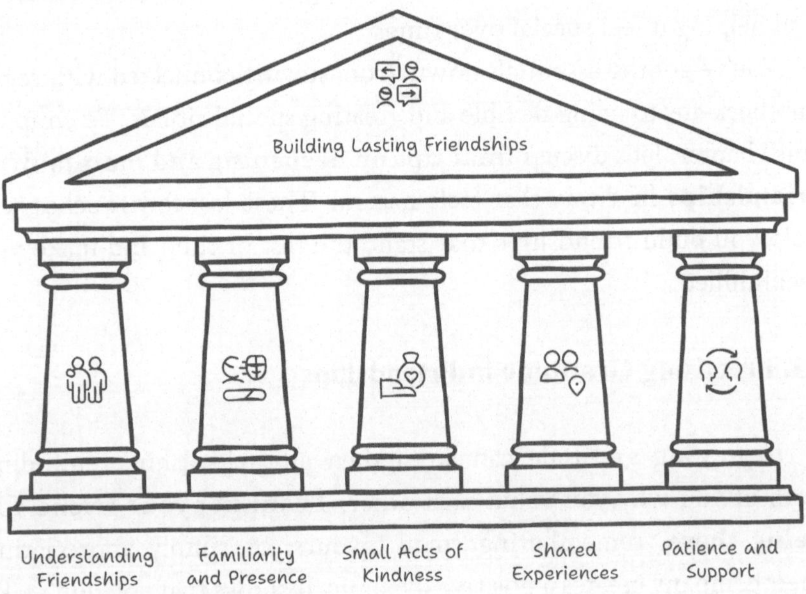

Pro Tips for Building Lasting Friendships:

1. **Express Gratitude** – Regularly let your friend know you appreciate them.
2. **Give and Take Space** – Respect each other's need for downtime without feeling pressured.
3. **Embrace Change** – Friendships evolve, so focus on nurturing those that matter most.

19

Becoming a Conversational Wizard

Ah, conversations—the lifeblood of social interactions, yet often the bane of an introvert's existence. Whether it's the pressure to keep the conversation going, finding the right words, or just not knowing what to say, it can sometimes feel like you're fumbling through the dark. But here's the good news: **being great at conversations doesn't require magic or charisma**. It's simply a skill you can learn, refine, and enjoy.

In this chapter, we'll explore how to become a **conversational wizard**—the kind of person who can effortlessly engage, keep the dialogue flowing, and leave others feeling like they've just had the best conversation of their lives. And the best part? You don't have to change who you are to get there.

1. The Art of Starting a Conversation

For many introverts, the hardest part of a conversation is simply **starting it**. The pressure to find the perfect opener can leave you standing there, hesitating, while your mind races through possible topics. But the secret to starting a conversation isn't about perfection—it's about **keeping it simple**.

A good conversation starter is often right in front of you. It could be a comment on your surroundings, an observation about what's happening, or even a question related to something you both have in common. The goal is to open the door just a crack and see where it leads.

Example: If you're at a party, a simple, "Have you tried the snacks? That dip is incredible!" is often enough to get things rolling. The key is to find something that feels natural rather than rehearsed.

2. The Power of Open-Ended Questions

One of the easiest ways to keep a conversation flowing is by asking **open-ended questions**—questions that can't be answered with a simple "yes" or "no." These types of questions encourage the other person to share more about themselves, which in turn gives you more to work with. They show genuine interest and often lead to deeper, more engaging conversations.

Some great examples of open-ended questions include:

- "What's something exciting you've been working on lately?"
- "What do you enjoy most about what you do?"
- "How did you get interested in [topic]?"

These questions invite the other person to share, making the conversation feel more like a two-way exchange.

3. Listening More Than You Speak

The best conversationalists aren't the ones who talk the most; they're the ones who **listen the best**. When you listen actively—nodding, making eye contact, and responding thoughtfully—you show that you're truly engaged in the conversation. This makes the other person feel valued, which often leads to a more meaningful exchange.

You're off to a great start! Now that you know how to kick off conversations, ask open-ended questions, and practise active listening, let's focus on **how to keep the dialogue engaging and avoid those dreaded awkward silences**. Conversations don't have to feel like a game of verbal ping-pong; they can flow naturally when you're relaxed and focused on the other person.

4. Embracing the "Yes, and..." Technique

A trick borrowed from improv comedy, the **"Yes, and..." technique** is a great way to keep conversations flowing. The idea is simple: when someone shares something, you affirm it ("yes") and then build on it with your own addition ("and"). This approach not only shows that you're listening but also keeps the dialogue dynamic.

Example: If someone mentions, "I just got back from a trip to Spain," you could respond with, "Yes, and I've always wanted to visit! What was your favourite part of the trip?" By adding to their statement, you invite them to keep sharing, making the conversation more interactive.

5. Knowing How to Use Pauses to Your Advantage

Awkward silences can feel uncomfortable, but sometimes a **well-timed pause** can actually enhance a conversation. Instead of rushing to fill every gap with words, give yourself permission to pause, reflect, and then respond thoughtfully. This shows the other person that you're really considering what they've said, which can deepen the conversation.

If you're worried about a silence lasting too long, use it as an opportunity to ask a follow-up question or share a related story. Often, a brief pause gives both people a chance to catch their breath and think, making the conversation feel more relaxed.

6. Bringing in Stories and Personal Examples

One of the best ways to keep conversations interesting is by **sharing personal stories or examples**. Stories are memorable, relatable, and can turn a mundane conversation into something enjoyable. When you share a story, you're inviting the other person into your world, which can make the exchange feel more engaging and authentic.

Example: If someone is talking about their love of cooking, you might share a funny anecdote about the time you tried to make a complicated dish and it turned into a kitchen disaster. Stories like these are not only entertaining but also help the other person feel more connected to you.

You're becoming a pro at keeping conversations lively! Now, let's dive into some strategies for **keeping the other person engaged and making your conversations memorable**. Great conversations aren't just about exchanging words—they're about creating a connection, leaving both parties feeling understood and appreciated.

7. Using Humor to Lighten the Mood

Humour is a fantastic way to break the ice and **lighten the mood** of any conversation. It doesn't mean you have to be a stand-up comedian or constantly crack jokes. Sometimes, just a light-hearted comment, a witty observation, or even poking fun at yourself can make the conversation more enjoyable.

Example: If the conversation is getting a bit serious, you can say something like, "I think we're solving all the world's problems here—one coffee at a time!" Light humour makes you more relatable and helps the other person feel at ease.

8. Mirroring and Paraphrasing

Mirroring is a subtle technique where you **repeat or paraphrase** what the other person has just said to show that you're truly listening. This not only validates their thoughts but also helps deepen the conversation. When someone feels heard, they're more likely to open up and share more.

Example: If someone says, "I've been feeling overwhelmed at work lately," you can respond with, "It sounds like you've been juggling a lot. What's been the most challenging part?" This approach shows empathy and invites the other person to share more details.

9. Knowing When to Shift Gears

Sometimes, conversations can start to feel stagnant or one-sided. Knowing when and how to **change the topic** can breathe new life into the exchange. A simple way to shift gears is to introduce a new, but related, topic. For instance, if you've been talking about work, you might say, "Speaking of busy schedules, have you had time for any hobbies lately?"

This gentle pivot keeps the conversation interesting without feeling abrupt, allowing both of you to explore new territory.

Excellent progress! Now that you've got humour, active listening, and topic-shifting down, let's focus on **how to create a comfortable space for deeper conversations**. Sometimes, the most memorable interactions happen when you move beyond surface-level topics. But how do you do that without making the other person feel pressured or uncomfortable? Let's explore some techniques to navigate this with ease.

10. Reading the Room and Sensing Comfort Levels

Before diving into deeper topics, it's essential to **read the room** and gauge the other person's comfort level. Not everyone is ready to talk about personal topics right away, so it's crucial to take cues from their body language, tone, and responses. If they seem engaged and relaxed, you can slowly steer the conversation toward deeper subjects. But if they're giving short answers or seem distracted, it might be best to keep things light.

Example: If someone opens up about a personal experience, like moving to a new city, you could ask, "What's been the most surprising thing about the change?" This allows them to share more if they're comfortable, without feeling pushed.

11. Finding Balance Between Talking and Listening

Great conversations are like a dance—**it's all about finding the right balance**. You don't want to dominate the conversation, but you also don't want to disappear into the background. Share your thoughts, stories, and opinions, but also give the other person space to do the same. If you notice you've been talking for a while, pause and invite the other person to share their thoughts.

Example: After sharing your own story, ask, "How about you? Have you ever had a similar experience?" This encourages them to participate without feeling like they're interrupting.

12. Wrapping Up a Conversation Gracefully

Sometimes, knowing how to **end a conversation gracefully** is just as important as starting one. If you feel the conversation winding down, it's better to wrap things up on a high note rather than letting it fizzle out awkwardly. Thank the person for their time or for sharing their thoughts, and express genuine interest in speaking again in the future.

Example: "It was great chatting with you—thanks for such an interesting conversation! Let's catch up again sometime." This leaves the conversation on a positive note, making the other person more likely to remember it fondly.

You've made it to the final page of Chapter 19! By now, you should feel confident about starting, maintaining, and deepening conversations. For this last part, we'll focus on how to **leave a lasting impression** in any conversation, ensuring that people remember you for all the right reasons. This isn't about trying to be unforgettable but rather about making others feel valued.

13. Ending on a High Note with a Genuine Compliment

One of the easiest ways to leave a positive impression is to **end the conversation with a sincere compliment**. It doesn't have to be elaborate—just something that shows you appreciated the interaction. Compliments make people feel good and help them remember the conversation fondly.

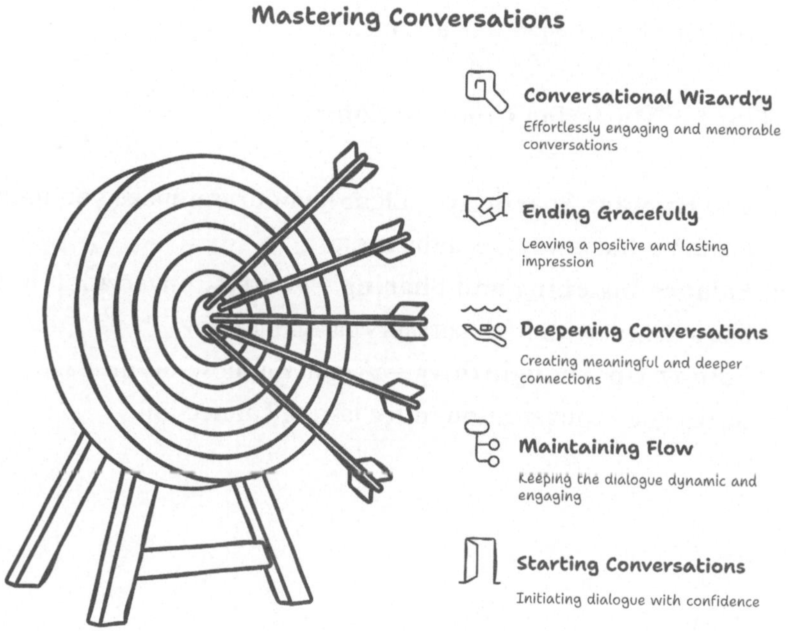

14. Following Up After a Great Conversation

If you had a particularly engaging conversation, don't hesitate to **follow up** afterward. A quick message saying, "I really enjoyed our chat—let's do it again sometime!" can strengthen the connection and open the door for future interactions. This follow-up is especially useful in networking or professional settings where maintaining connections can be beneficial.

15. Reflecting on What You've Learned

Every conversation is a chance to learn something new—about others, about the world, and even about yourself. **Take a moment to reflect on what went well** and what you can improve. This reflection will help you become even better at conversations, turning you into a conversational wizard over time.

Pro Tips for Mastering Conversations:

1. **Use Humour Sparingly** – Light humour can make you more relatable, but always read the room.
2. **Balance Listening and Sharing** – A great conversation feels like a dance, with both partners participating.
3. **Follow Up Thoughtfully** – A quick follow-up message can turn a good conversation into a lasting connection.

20

How to Deal with Social Exhaustion

Let's face it—**social exhaustion is real**, especially for introverts. Even if you've mastered the art of small talk, nailed first impressions, and become a conversational wizard, spending too much time around people can leave you feeling completely drained. It's like running a marathon without breaks: eventually, you just want to collapse on the couch with a cosy blanket and your favourite show.

In this chapter, we're diving into **strategies for managing social fatigue**, so you can recharge without feeling guilty. The goal isn't to avoid socialising but to find a balance that works for you. After all, you don't need to be "on" all the time to be a great friend, colleague, or party-goer.

1. Recognizing the Signs of Social Exhaustion

The first step to managing social exhaustion is simply **recognizing when it's happening**. Everyone's social battery runs out eventually, but the signs can be subtle. Maybe you start feeling irritable, your focus starts to slip, or you notice that you're zoning out in conversations. When you're socially exhausted, even the idea of another interaction can feel overwhelming.

Learning to recognize these signs early on helps you **take action before you're completely drained**. The moment you notice your energy dipping, it's a signal to step back and recharge.

2. Creating Personal Boundaries Around Social Time

One of the most effective ways to prevent social exhaustion is by **setting boundaries**. It's okay to say no to invitations or to leave events early if you're starting to feel drained. Instead of overcommitting, prioritise social activities that truly matter to you, and don't be afraid to decline the rest.

Example: If you're invited to multiple events in one weekend, consider choosing the one that's most meaningful to you and politely declining the others. This way, you can give your full energy to the interactions that count without spreading yourself too thin.

3. Finding Quick Recharge Strategies

Sometimes, social exhaustion hits in the middle of an event where you can't just leave. In these cases, having **quick recharge strategies** can make a big difference. Step outside for a breath of fresh air, take a few moments in a quiet room, or even head to the bathroom to decompress for a few minutes. These mini-breaks can help reset your energy so you can make it through the rest of the event.

You're doing great! Now that you know how to recognize social exhaustion, set boundaries, and take quick breaks to recharge, let's dive deeper into **long-term strategies** for managing your social energy. The goal here is to find a sustainable way to enjoy socialising without feeling completely wiped out afterward.

4. Embracing the Power of "No" Without Guilt

For many introverts, saying "no" can feel like a struggle, especially if you don't want to disappoint others. But here's the truth: **you don't owe anyone constant access to your time and energy**. Learning to say "no" confidently and without guilt is one of the most liberating skills you can develop. It's about respecting your own limits so that when you do say "yes," you can show up fully.

Example: If someone invites you to an event you're not up for, try responding with something like, "I'd love to, but I'm pretty booked this weekend. Let's catch up another time!" This way, you decline politely while keeping the door open for future plans.

5. Scheduling Downtime Before and After Social Events

One of the best ways to prevent social exhaustion is by **scheduling downtime** around social engagements. If you know you have a big event or party coming up, set aside some quiet time before and after to recharge. Think of it as "buffer time" for your social battery.

Example: If you have a party on Saturday evening, try spending Saturday afternoon doing something calming, like reading or taking a walk. Similarly, plan a relaxing activity for Sunday morning to help you decompress afterward.

6. Practising Self-Compassion

Finally, it's essential to practise **self-compassion** when it comes to social exhaustion. Feeling drained after socialising doesn't make you antisocial or a bad friend; it just means you're human. Be kind to yourself, acknowledge your limits, and remember that it's perfectly okay to take care of your needs first.

Whenever you start to feel guilty about needing time alone, remind yourself that recharging is essential for showing up as your best self. After all, a well-rested, happy version of you is much more enjoyable to be around than a burnt-out, exhausted one.

Great work so far! Now that you've mastered the art of setting boundaries, scheduling downtime, and practising self-compassion, let's explore some practical tips for **recharging effectively**. It's not just about taking a break; it's about making sure those breaks actually replenish your energy. Let's focus on how to make the most of your downtime so you can bounce back refreshed and ready for more social interactions.

7. Finding Solitude in Small Moments

One of the best ways to recharge is by **finding solitude in small moments**, even when you're in a social setting. You don't always have to wait until you're home to take a break. Stepping outside for fresh air, taking a quick walk, or simply sitting quietly with a cup of coffee can give you the breather you need to reset your social battery.

Example: At a busy family gathering, excuse yourself for a short walk around the block. The change of scenery and the quiet can help you feel refreshed and ready to re-engage.

8. Engaging in Solo Activities That Nourish You

Introverts recharge best through **activities that allow them to be alone with their thoughts**. Whether it's reading, painting, journaling, or gardening, find activities that genuinely nourish your soul. These hobbies not only help you unwind but also provide a sense of fulfilment and joy that can counterbalance the drain of socialising.

Example: If you're feeling drained after a long day of meetings, spend the evening reading a book you love or listening to your favourite music. These activities help restore your energy and put you in a positive mood.

9. Creating a Comfortable "Recharge Zone"

Having a designated space in your home where you can **fully relax and recharge** can be a game-changer. Make it cosy with items that comfort you—like soft blankets, scented candles, or calming music. Knowing you have a personal sanctuary to retreat to after social events can make them feel less daunting.

Example: Create a cosy corner with a comfy chair, a warm lamp, and your favourite book. Even just 20 minutes in this space can help you feel rejuvenated after a busy day.

You're doing an amazing job managing your social energy! Now that you know how to take quick breaks, engage in nourishing activities, and create your own recharge zone, let's focus on **strategies for long-term energy management**. This section is about building habits that help you maintain a steady social battery over time so you can enjoy social interactions without feeling constantly drained.

10. Practising Mindful Socialising

One of the best ways to prevent social burnout is by **being mindful of how you spend your social energy**. Instead of saying yes to every invitation, think about which events and people truly bring you joy. Prioritise gatherings that feel meaningful or energising, and don't be afraid to skip those that leave you feeling drained. It's all about **quality over quantity**.

Example: If a friend invites you to multiple events in one week, choose the one you're most excited about and politely decline the others. Let them know, "I'm really looking forward to [event], but I need some downtime around that time." This way, you can focus your energy where it matters most.

11. Setting Social Goals That Align with Your Needs

Socialising doesn't have to be an all-or-nothing experience. **Set small, achievable social goals** that align with your comfort level. For example, if you're working on being more social, aim to attend one event per week or make time for one-on-one catch-ups with friends. By setting realistic goals, you can gradually build your social stamina without overwhelming yourself.

Example: Your social goal for the month might be to attend one meetup or social gathering, and to reconnect with a friend over coffee. This approach ensures you're staying social, but in a way that feels manageable.

12. Embracing the "Social Detox"

Sometimes, even with the best strategies, your social battery can hit zero. That's when a **social detox** can help. Take a full day (or even a weekend) to unplug from social activities, turn off notifications, and focus solely on yourself. Use this time to rest, reflect, and do things that make you happy. The reset will leave you feeling recharged and ready to engage again.

Fantastic! You've reached the final page of this chapter on managing social exhaustion. Now that you've learned how to prioritise meaningful interactions, set social goals, and even take the occasional social detox, let's finish with some final strategies to ensure you're **fully recharged** and ready to enjoy your social life on your own terms.

13. Practising the Art of the "Gracious Exit"

Knowing when and how to leave social situations gracefully is an essential skill for introverts. If you start feeling drained, it's okay to **make a polite exit**. You don't have to wait until the party is over or force yourself to stay longer than you're comfortable with. Craft a few exit lines that feel natural to you, so you can leave without feeling awkward or guilty.

Example: You can say something like, "I've had such a great time, but I have an early morning tomorrow. Let's catch up again soon!" This way, you leave on a positive note while honouring your need for rest.

14. Incorporating Mindfulness and Relaxation Techniques

Social exhaustion isn't just physical—it's also mental. To fully recharge, consider incorporating **mindfulness practices** like deep breathing, meditation, or yoga into your routine. These activities help calm your mind and reset your energy after social interactions, making it easier to bounce back.

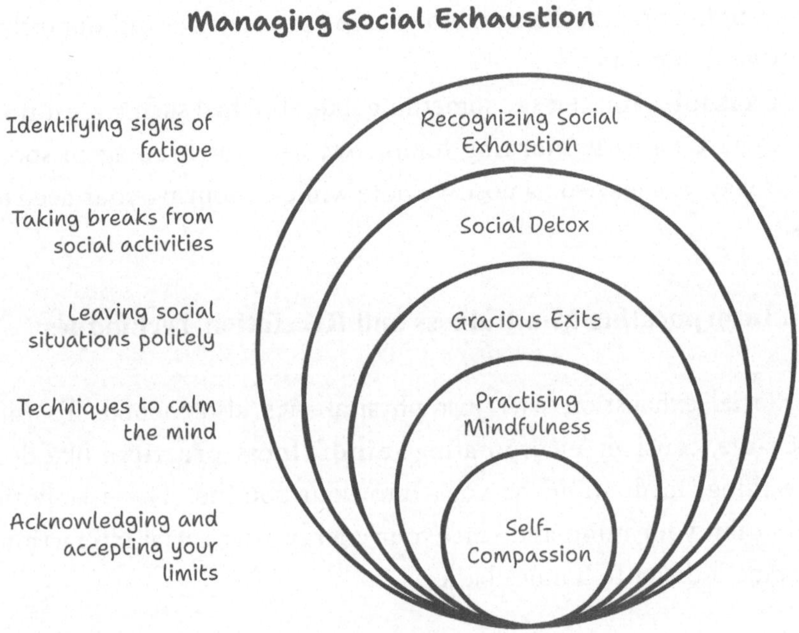

15. Being Kind to Yourself During the Process

Lastly, don't forget to **practise self-compassion** as you navigate your social life. It's okay to feel exhausted after a busy day of socialising—it doesn't mean you're antisocial or weak. Remind yourself that taking time to recharge is a healthy and necessary part of being an introvert. Celebrate the fact that you're investing in your well-being so that you can show up as your best self for the people and activities that truly matter.

Pro Tips for Managing Social Exhaustion:

1. **Take Small Breaks** – Step away for a few minutes to recharge during social events.

2. **Set Boundaries** – Prioritise meaningful interactions and don't be afraid to decline invitations.
3. **Be Kind to Yourself** – Social exhaustion is normal; give yourself permission to rest.

21

Building Confidence, One Awkward Moment at a Time

Let's be real—**confidence doesn't come naturally for everyone**, especially if you've spent most of your life feeling like the quiet observer in the background. But here's the thing: confidence isn't something you're born with; it's something you build, step by step, one awkward moment at a time. And yes, there will be awkward moments—plenty of them. But that's where the magic happens.

In this chapter, we'll explore how to **transform those cringe-worthy experiences into stepping stones for growth**. It's not about never feeling awkward or uncomfortable; it's about learning to embrace those moments and use them to boost your confidence. Let's dive in and discover how to make confidence-building a (mostly) enjoyable journey.

1. Embracing the Awkwardness

The first step to building confidence is **accepting that awkwardness is part of the process**. Trying new things, stepping out of your comfort zone, or speaking up in unfamiliar settings can be uncomfortable, but those moments are where the most growth happens. The goal isn't to eliminate awkwardness—it's to **reframe it as a sign that you're challenging yourself**.

Example: If you accidentally spill your coffee while meeting someone new, instead of cringing and apologising endlessly, laugh it off with, "Guess I'm just trying to break the ice—literally!" Embracing the awkwardness shows you're comfortable with yourself, which is a hallmark of confidence.

2. Starting Small to Build Momentum

Confidence doesn't come from grand gestures; it comes from **small wins** that build up over time. Start with low-stakes challenges, like striking up a conversation with a cashier, speaking up in a small meeting, or trying something new at a social event. These little wins **boost your self-assurance** and create momentum for bigger challenges.

Example: If the idea of public speaking terrifies you, start by sharing your thoughts in a small group setting. Gradually increase the stakes as you get more comfortable. Every small step builds your confidence muscle.

3. Celebrating Every Victory (Even the Small Ones)

Building confidence is a journey, and it's important to **celebrate your progress** along the way. Even if it feels like a tiny step, acknowledging your efforts reinforces your sense of accomplishment. Did you talk to a stranger? Celebrate it. Did you manage to get through a presentation without panicking? That's a win!

Example: Keep a journal where you jot down small victories each day. It could be as simple as "I made a new friend" or "I introduced myself to someone at work." Reflecting on these moments helps you see how far you've come.

Fantastic! You're starting to embrace the awkwardness, celebrate small wins, and take those first steps toward greater confidence. Now, let's explore some strategies for **tackling bigger challenges** without feeling overwhelmed. Building confidence is like levelling up in a game—you don't jump straight to the hardest level. Instead, you take on slightly more challenging tasks as you grow stronger.

4. Using Visualisation to Prepare for Nerve-Wracking Situations

One way to build confidence is through **visualisation**. Before entering a situation that makes you nervous—like a job interview, a party, or a presentation—take a few moments to visualise yourself succeeding. Picture yourself walking into the room confidently, having a great conversation, or delivering your points clearly. This simple technique can trick your brain into believing you've already succeeded, which helps reduce anxiety.

Example: Before a big meeting, find a quiet space, close your eyes, and visualise yourself speaking confidently, making eye contact, and receiving positive reactions. This mental rehearsal helps you feel more prepared and at ease when the moment actually comes.

5. Embracing Failure as Part of the Process

Confidence doesn't mean never failing. In fact, **embracing failure is one of the best ways to build confidence**. Each time you stumble, instead of seeing it as a setback, view it as a lesson. What went wrong? What can you do differently next time? Failure isn't the opposite of success; it's part of the journey.

Example: If you tried to network at a social event but ended up feeling awkward and retreating to a corner, don't beat yourself up. Reflect on what made you uncomfortable and set a small goal for the next event, like chatting with just one new person. It's all about progress, not perfection.

6. Practising Self-Affirmation

Sometimes, we're our own worst critics. If you want to build confidence, it's crucial to **be kind to yourself**. Self-affirmations are simple, positive statements that remind you of your strengths and capabilities. These statements help shift your mindset from self-doubt to self-belief.

Example: Start your day with affirmations like, "I am capable of handling any situation," or "I am growing more confident every day." Over time, these positive reinforcements can change the way you see yourself.

Excellent! You're doing an amazing job embracing the awkward moments, visualising success, and practising self-affirmations. Now, let's talk about **how to build confidence through consistent practice** and using every opportunity as a stepping stone. Confidence is like a muscle—the more you use it, the stronger it gets. Let's explore how to integrate confidence-building exercises into your daily routine.

7. Setting "Confidence Challenges" for Yourself

One of the best ways to grow your confidence is by **setting small challenges** that push you slightly out of your comfort zone. These can be everyday tasks that you wouldn't normally do but aren't too overwhelming. The idea is to keep pushing your boundaries incrementally so that each step feels achievable.

Example: Challenge yourself to compliment a stranger, speak up during a meeting, or try something new on your own like attending a class or event. These small wins will gradually build up, making you feel more capable over time.

8. Learning to Laugh at Yourself

Part of building confidence is realising that not everything has to be taken seriously. **Learning to laugh at yourself** when things don't go as planned can take the pressure off and make social interactions more enjoyable. People are often drawn to those who can laugh at their own mistakes because it shows humility and resilience.

Example: If you accidentally spill your drink at a party, instead of turning red with embarrassment, just smile and say, "Well, that's one way to make an entrance!" Embracing your mishaps with humour makes you more relatable and helps defuse any awkwardness.

9. Surrounding Yourself with Positive People

The company you keep can have a significant impact on your confidence. **Surround yourself with supportive, encouraging people** who celebrate your successes and lift you up when you stumble. Being around positive influences can help you feel more confident, especially when you're taking on new challenges.

Example: If you're trying to improve your social skills, find friends who are patient and understanding. They can provide a safe space for you to practise and grow without fear of judgement.

You're making great progress! By now, you've learned to embrace challenges, laugh at yourself, and surround yourself with positive influences. Let's now focus on strategies for **maintaining that newfound confidence** in real-life situations. Confidence isn't just about one-time wins; it's about consistently showing up for yourself, even when things get tough.

10. Turning Setbacks into Stepping Stones

No matter how confident you become, there will always be moments when things don't go as planned. Instead of letting setbacks shake your confidence, learn to **use them as stepping stones for growth**. Reflect on what you can learn from the experience, adjust your approach, and try again. Each setback is an opportunity to build resilience.

Example: Let's say you tried speaking up in a meeting but stumbled over your words. Instead of feeling defeated, take it as a chance to prepare better next time. Think about what you'd do differently and use that experience to improve.

11. Practising Self-Reflection

Confidence isn't just about outward actions; it's also about knowing yourself on a deeper level. **Take time to reflect on your achievements, your strengths, and even your areas for improvement**. Regular self-reflection helps you stay grounded and aware of your progress, reminding you that confidence is a journey, not a destination.

Example: At the end of each week, set aside a few minutes to write down three things you did well and one thing you'd like to work on. This simple exercise keeps you focused on growth rather than perfection.

12. Building a "Confidence Toolkit"

Lastly, consider creating a **personal confidence toolkit**—a collection of strategies, affirmations, and reminders that you can turn to whenever you're feeling unsure. This might include favourite quotes, pep-talk notes, or even a playlist of songs that pump you up. Having these tools on hand makes it easier to regain your confidence quickly, especially before challenging situations.

Example: Keep a folder on your phone with screenshots of encouraging messages, compliments you've received, or personal achievements. On tough days, revisit this folder to remind yourself of how far you've come.

Amazing work! You've reached the final page of this chapter on building confidence, and by now, you've learned how to turn setbacks into stepping stones, reflect on your progress, and create a confidence toolkit. Let's wrap up this chapter with some **final strategies to maintain and grow your confidence over the long term**. Confidence isn't a one-time achievement; it's an ongoing process that requires patience and consistency.

13. Practising the "Stretch and Rest" Approach

Building confidence is like working out—you can't do it all at once. The best approach is to **stretch your comfort zone, then take time to rest and recharge**. For example, if you push yourself to attend a social event or try something new, allow yourself some downtime afterward to decompress. This balance helps you avoid burnout while still making progress.

Example: If you've just given a presentation or attended a networking event, plan a relaxing evening afterward to unwind. This way, you can reflect on your progress and prepare for the next challenge without feeling drained.

14. Focusing on Progress, Not Perfection

It's easy to fall into the trap of thinking you need to be perfect to be confident. But the truth is, **confidence comes from recognizing your progress, not from achieving perfection**. Celebrate the small wins and focus on how far you've come rather than stressing over where you think you should be.

Example: If you've been working on your social skills, notice how much easier it's become for you to start conversations or speak up in meetings. Acknowledge the progress, even if it's slow, and remind yourself that every step counts.

15. Remembering That Confidence is a Lifelong Journey

Pro Tips for Building Confidence:

1. **Celebrate Small Wins** – Acknowledge your efforts and progress, no matter how small.
2. **Rest After Stretching** – Balance challenging yourself with downtime to recharge.
3. **Embrace the Journey** – Confidence isn't about reaching a final goal; it's about continual growth

22

How to Win Friends Without Losing Yourself

Friendships are one of the greatest joys in life, but sometimes, the pressure to fit in can make it feel like you're losing a bit of yourself in the process. For introverts, trying to be more social often comes with the fear of having to change who you are just to make connections. But here's the secret: **you don't have to compromise your true self to build meaningful friendships**. The key is to connect with others while staying authentic.

In this chapter, we're diving into how to **win friends and build genuine connections without losing yourself in the process**. It's about finding a balance between being open to new experiences and staying true to who you are. Let's explore how to navigate friendships without feeling like you have to put on a mask.

1. Knowing Your Boundaries and Sticking to Them

The first step to winning friends without losing yourself is by **setting clear boundaries**. Boundaries aren't walls; they're guidelines that protect your energy and well-being. When you're clear about what you're comfortable with—whether it's how much time you can spend socialising or what topics you're willing to discuss—you create space for more genuine interactions.

Example: If you enjoy meeting new people but need time to recharge afterward, let your friends know that you might need some downtime after a social event. This way, they'll understand that it's not personal if you decline an invitation occasionally.

2. Embracing Selective Socialising

As an introvert, you don't need a huge circle of friends to feel fulfilled. **Quality over quantity** is the name of the game. Instead of trying to be friends with everyone, focus on deepening connections with a few people who truly resonate with you. Selective socialising means choosing interactions that enrich your life rather than draining you.

Example: If you're invited to multiple gatherings in one week, prioritise the ones where you feel most comfortable or where you'll connect with people you genuinely enjoy. This helps you make the most of your social energy without feeling stretched too thin.

3. Staying True to Your Values

Friendships built on authenticity are the ones that last. **Stay true to your values**, even if it means walking away from people or situations that don't align with them. When you're honest about who you are and what you stand for, you attract friends who appreciate you for your true self. This approach not only feels better but also leads to deeper, more meaningful connections.

Excellent progress! Now that you've mastered the art of setting boundaries, embracing selective socialising, and staying true to your values, let's dig into some **practical ways to deepen these authentic connections**. Building friendships that last is about creating a strong foundation where both sides feel valued and understood. Here's how to navigate this without sacrificing your sense of self.

4. Practising Honest Communication

One of the keys to winning friends while staying true to yourself is by **practising honest communication**. It's tempting to say what you think people want to hear, especially when you're trying to make a good impression. But being straightforward, even if it's uncomfortable, builds trust and shows that you're authentic. This doesn't mean being brutally honest—just genuine.

Example: If a friend invites you to an event that you're not comfortable with, instead of making up an excuse, try saying, "I appreciate the invite, but I'm not really into [activity]. Let's hang out another time." This way, you're respecting both your friend and yourself.

5. Balancing Giving and Receiving in Friendships

Introverts can sometimes fall into the trap of being the "listener" in friendships, always there to support others but rarely sharing their own thoughts and feelings. **Healthy friendships are a balance of give and take**. Don't be afraid to open up and let others support you too. Sharing your own experiences, even if they're small, deepens the connection and shows that you trust your friends.

Example: The next time a friend asks how you're doing, instead of the usual "I'm fine," try opening up a bit more: "I've actually been working through [something personal]—it's been a bit challenging." This invites your friend to offer support and creates a deeper bond.

6. Creating "Friendship Rituals"

One way to build lasting friendships is by creating **rituals or traditions** together. These don't have to be anything elaborate—just something you both enjoy that becomes a recurring event. Whether it's a monthly coffee date, a favourite TV show you binge together, or a shared hobby, rituals create a sense of continuity and make friendships feel special.

Example: If you and a friend love trying new restaurants, make it a monthly ritual to explore a new spot together. These shared experiences strengthen the bond and give you something to look forward to.

Great! You're doing an amazing job learning how to build deep and authentic friendships while staying true to yourself. Now that you've explored honest communication, the balance of giving and receiving, and creating friendship rituals, let's focus on **maintaining these meaningful connections over the long term**. Friendships, like any relationship, require nurturing, but that doesn't mean you have to lose yourself in the process.

7. Practising Active Appreciation

In any friendship, it's easy to take each other for granted over time. **Actively showing appreciation** is a simple yet powerful way to keep the connection strong. Let your friends know how much you value them—not just during special occasions but in everyday interactions. A little gratitude goes a long way in making people feel seen and valued.

Example: Send a quick message to a friend saying, "I just wanted to say thanks for always being there. I really appreciate your support." These small gestures create a positive vibe that keeps the friendship thriving.

8. Giving Each Other Space to Grow

One of the best parts of a healthy friendship is **allowing space for personal growth**. Sometimes, your friends might be going through phases where they're busy, focused on personal projects, or just need some alone time. Respecting their need for space shows that you value their well-being. True friendships don't require constant contact to stay strong.

Example: If a friend is going through a busy period, check in occasionally without expecting a long response. A simple, "Hey, just thinking of you—hope everything's going well!" let them know you care without adding pressure.

9. Knowing When to Walk Away

Not all friendships are meant to last forever, and that's okay. Sometimes, you may find yourself in a friendship that no longer aligns with your values or brings you joy. **Recognizing when it's time to step back** is crucial for your own well-being. It doesn't mean there's bad blood; it's simply about making room for connections that truly enrich your life.

Example: If you notice a friendship has become one-sided or feels draining, it might be time to have an honest conversation or gradually distance yourself. It's okay to prioritise your mental and emotional health.

You've done an incredible job so far, learning how to nurture friendships while staying true to yourself. Now that you understand the importance of appreciation, giving space, and knowing when to walk away, let's explore **how to navigate the inevitable ups and downs** of friendships. Friendships aren't always smooth sailing, and being able to handle conflicts gracefully is a key part of maintaining strong, healthy connections.

10. Handling Conflicts with Empathy

Conflicts in friendships are bound to happen—it's a natural part of any close relationship. The key is to **handle disagreements with empathy**. Instead of getting defensive or shutting down, try to understand the other person's perspective. This doesn't mean you have to agree, but showing that you're willing to listen can help resolve issues without damaging the friendship.

Example: If a friend says something that upsets you, instead of reacting immediately, take a deep breath and respond with, "I understand where you're coming from, but here's how I feel." This approach keeps the conversation open and respectful.

11. Repairing and Rebuilding Trust

Sometimes, misunderstandings or miscommunications can cause a rift between friends. If that happens, it's important to **address the issue and rebuild trust**. Acknowledge your part in what happened, apologise if needed, and be patient as the friendship heals. The willingness to repair a friendship shows that you value it.

Example: If you had a disagreement with a friend, reach out afterward and say, "I've been thinking about what happened, and I'm really sorry if I hurt you. I value our friendship and would love to talk it through." A genuine apology can go a long way in mending fences.

12. Knowing When to Let Go with Grace

While it's important to work through conflicts, sometimes the healthiest choice is to **let go of a friendship that no longer serves you**. This can be difficult, especially if you've shared a lot of history, but clinging to a draining or toxic relationship can be more harmful than beneficial. Letting go with grace means appreciating the good times you've had, learning from the experience, and moving on without resentment.

Example: If you've been feeling drained after every interaction with a certain friend, it might be time to take a step back. You can communicate something like, "I think we're growing in different directions, and that's okay. I'll always appreciate the memories we've shared."

Congratulations! You've reached the final page of this chapter, mastering the art of authentic friendships, handling conflicts with grace, and knowing when to let go. Now, let's wrap up with some final strategies to help you **maintain meaningful friendships** while staying true to yourself. These last tips will ensure that your connections remain strong, fulfilling, and mutually beneficial.

13. Practising Self-Care Within Friendships

Friendships are a two-way street, but it's essential to remember that **taking care of yourself** comes first. If you're not feeling your best, it's okay to take a step back and focus on your own well-being. Real friends will understand that you need time to recharge. Practising self-care within friendships means knowing when to engage and when to rest.

Example: If you're feeling socially drained but a friend wants to hang out, it's okay to say, "I'd love to catch up, but I need some time to myself right now. Let's plan for next week instead." This keeps the friendship healthy while prioritising your own needs.

14. Celebrating Each Other's Successes

A key part of winning friends and maintaining lasting connections is learning to **genuinely celebrate each other's wins**. Whether it's a new job, a personal milestone, or a small achievement, showing enthusiasm for your friend's successes strengthens the bond and creates a positive atmosphere in your friendship.

Example: The next time a friend shares good news, make an effort to celebrate with them. It could be as simple as sending a congratulatory text or planning a small get-together to toast their achievement. This keeps the friendship vibrant and supportive.

15. Embracing Friendships as an Evolving Journey

Finally, remember that **friendships are a journey, not a destination**. People change, circumstances shift, and friendships can ebb and flow. Embracing the natural evolution of friendships without clinging to how things "used to be" allows you to appreciate the present moment and the value each connection brings to your life.

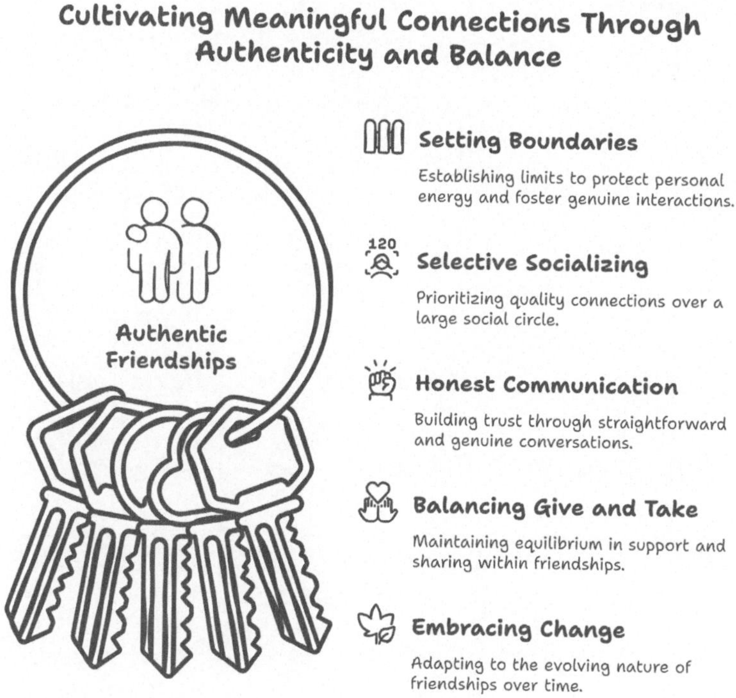

Pro Tips for Maintaining Authentic Friendships:

1. **Be Honest About Your Needs** – Communicate openly about your boundaries to keep the friendship healthy.

2. **Celebrate and Support** – Show genuine joy for your friend's successes to create a positive dynamic.
3. **Embrace Change** – Let friendships evolve naturally and appreciate each phase for what it bring

23

Dealing with Rejection – Because It's Inevitable

Let's be real: **rejection sucks**. Whether it's not getting that job you wanted, being ghosted after a date, or feeling left out of a social circle, rejection can sting. For introverts, the fear of rejection can sometimes feel like a paralysing force that stops us from putting ourselves out there. But here's the thing: rejection is a part of life, and it's **inevitable**.

In this chapter, we're going to flip the script on rejection and explore how to **deal with it like a pro**. We'll cover why rejection isn't as bad as it seems, how to build resilience, and even how to use rejection as a tool for growth. By the end, you'll see that getting rejected doesn't mean you're not good enough—it just means you're one step closer to finding the right fit.

1. Understanding the Nature of Rejection

The first step to handling rejection is understanding that **it's not a reflection of your worth**. More often than not, rejection is about fit and timing rather than a personal failing. Maybe that job wasn't the right match for your skills, or that social group just didn't align with your interests. Recognizing that rejection is often situational can help take the sting out of it.

Example: If you didn't get the job you applied for, instead of thinking, "I'm not good enough," try reframing it as, "It wasn't the right fit for me. Something better is out there."

2. Embracing the "Next!" Mentality

One of the best ways to bounce back from rejection is by adopting a **"Next!" mentality**. Instead of dwelling on what didn't work out, focus on what's next. Whether it's sending out another job application, going on another date, or finding a new group of friends, moving forward is the best antidote to rejection.

Example: If someone declines your invitation to hang out, don't take it personally. Just think, "Okay, next! Who else might be up for coffee?" This keeps you proactive and prevents you from getting stuck in a rejection rut.

3. Reframing Rejection as Redirection

Sometimes, rejection is the universe's way of pointing you in a better direction. **Reframe rejection as redirection**, a nudge toward something that's a better fit for you. Often, what feels like a closed door is just an opportunity to explore a new path.

Example: If a project you were passionate about gets rejected, consider it a chance to refine your skills, approach it differently, or focus on a new project that might bring you more satisfaction in the long run.

Great job embracing the reality of rejection! Now that you understand it's often about fit, not worth, and that a "Next!" mentality can help you bounce back, let's explore some practical ways to **build resilience**. Dealing with rejection isn't about avoiding it but learning how to recover quickly and keep moving forward.

4. Practising Self-Compassion

One of the most important skills you can develop when dealing with rejection is **self-compassion.** It's easy to beat yourself up after a setback, but being kind to yourself is crucial for bouncing back. Remember, everyone experiences rejection, even the most successful people you admire. Treat yourself the way you'd treat a friend who's feeling down after a rejection.

Example: Instead of saying, "I messed up" or "I'm not good enough," try telling yourself, "It's okay. This happens to everyone, and it's just part of the journey." This shift in mindset helps soften the blow and keeps you motivated to try again.

5. Turning Rejection into a Learning Opportunity

Every rejection comes with a silver lining if you're willing to look for it. **Use rejection as a chance to learn and grow**. Reflect on what happened, what you can improve, and how you can approach similar situations in the future. This mindset not only helps you get better but also takes some of the sting out of rejection because you're gaining something from it.

Example: If you didn't land that job you interviewed for, ask for feedback if possible. Even if you don't get a response, take some time to reflect on what you could improve for the next interview—whether it's refining your resume, practising your answers, or tweaking your approach.

6. Celebrating Your Effort, Not Just the Outcome

One of the best ways to build resilience against rejection is by **celebrating your effort** rather than focusing solely on the outcome. It takes courage to put yourself out there, whether it's applying for a job, asking someone out, or joining a new group. Give yourself credit for taking action, regardless of the result.

Example: If you muster up the courage to introduce yourself to someone new, celebrate that effort, even if the conversation doesn't go as planned. It's a step in the right direction, and each attempt makes the next one a little easier.

You're doing great! By now, you've learned how to practise self-compassion, turn rejection into a learning opportunity, and celebrate your efforts. Let's take it a step further by exploring **how to build emotional resilience** and handle rejection like a pro. This section will focus on transforming your mindset so that rejection no longer feels like a roadblock but rather a stepping stone.

7. Building a Support Network

Rejection can feel isolating, especially if you're handling it alone. One of the best ways to bounce back is by **leaning on your support network**. Whether it's close friends, family, or even an online community, sharing your experiences and hearing encouraging words can make all the difference. Sometimes, just knowing someone's got your back can ease the sting of rejection.

Example: If you're feeling down after a rejection, reach out to a trusted friend and say, "Hey, I'm feeling a bit discouraged—do you have a few minutes to chat?" Often, a fresh perspective or some encouraging words can help you feel more hopeful.

8. Practising the "Rejection Reframe"

The next time you face rejection, try a technique called the **"rejection reframe"**. Instead of focusing on what went wrong, reframe the experience as a positive challenge. Ask yourself, "What can I learn from this?" or "How can I use this experience to grow?" This shift in thinking transforms rejection from a failure into an opportunity.

Example: If you didn't get accepted into a program you were excited about, instead of thinking, "I wasn't good enough," reframe it as, "This gives me time to explore other opportunities or improve my skills for next time."

9. Taking Rejection Less Personally

One of the hardest parts of dealing with rejection is not taking it personally. It's easy to fall into the trap of thinking, "What's wrong with me?" But the truth is, rejection often says more about the other person or situation than it does about you. **Learning to depersonalise rejection** helps you bounce back faster and keeps your confidence intact.

Example: If you don't get a response after reaching out to someone, remind yourself that it could be due to their busy schedule or other priorities—it's not necessarily a reflection of your worth or effort.

Awesome! You're becoming a pro at turning rejection into something positive. Now that you've learned how to lean on your support network, practice reframing rejection, and avoid taking it personally, let's talk about **long-term strategies for resilience**. These final techniques will help you build a mindset that not only handles rejection but also thrives on it, turning setbacks into comebacks.

10. Focusing on What You Can Control

One of the most empowering ways to handle rejection is by **focusing on what you can control**. You can't control other people's decisions, but you can control your own actions, reactions, and mindset. By shifting your focus to what's within your power, you'll feel less helpless and more proactive.

Example: If you didn't get a response after applying for your dream job, don't dwell on why you were passed over. Instead, focus on updating your resume, refining your interview skills, or applying to other positions. This approach keeps you moving forward.

11. Using Rejection to Fuel Your Motivation

Instead of letting rejection discourage you, use it as **fuel for your motivation**. Many successful people—from writers to entrepreneurs—faced countless rejections before they made it big. Let rejection be the fire that drives you to keep pushing forward. Each "no" gets you closer to the "yes" you're looking for.

Example: If a pitch or idea gets turned down, remind yourself that even bestselling authors like J.K. Rowling and Stephen King faced multiple rejections before their works were accepted. Keep refining your skills and trying again—it's all part of the journey.

12. Practising Gratitude for the Experience

It might sound strange, but **practising gratitude for rejection** can be transformative. Every experience, even the negative ones, teaches you something valuable. By being grateful for what you've learned from rejection, you change the narrative from failure to growth.

Example: After being turned down for an opportunity, take a moment to reflect on what you've gained. Maybe you learned how to improve your presentation skills or discovered a new area to focus on. This gratitude helps shift your mindset toward positivity.

Fantastic progress! You've now learned how to turn rejection into motivation, focus on what you can control, and even practise gratitude for the experience. As we close this chapter, let's dive into some final strategies to help you **move forward confidently** after experiencing rejection. The goal is to not only bounce back but to come back even stronger.

13. Creating a "Rejection Resilience Plan"

One of the best ways to handle rejection is by **preparing yourself in advance**. A "rejection resilience plan" is a set of steps you can take when you're feeling down after a rejection. This might include reaching out to a supportive friend, practising self-care, or diving into a hobby you love. By having a plan, you're less likely to spiral into self-doubt and more likely to bounce back quickly.

Example: Your plan could be as simple as: "If I get rejected, I'll take a 15-minute walk, call my best friend, and treat myself to my favourite dessert." Knowing you have a go-to strategy can reduce the emotional impact of rejection.

14. Treating Each Rejection as a Numbers Game

Sometimes, handling rejection is about changing your perspective. **Think of rejection as a numbers game**—the more you put yourself out there, the closer you get to a "yes." Every "no" is just another step toward your goal. By focusing on the bigger picture, you'll realise that each rejection is part of the process, not the end of it.

Example: If you're applying for jobs, set a goal to send out 20 applications rather than pinning all your hopes on one. Each rejection becomes less significant when you know you have multiple irons in the fire.

15. Reminding Yourself That Rejection is Temporary

Finally, remember that **rejection is just a temporary setback**. It doesn't define your future or your abilities. The most successful people are often those who faced the most rejection but kept going anyway. Keep your eyes on your long-term goals and trust that the right opportunities will come your way.

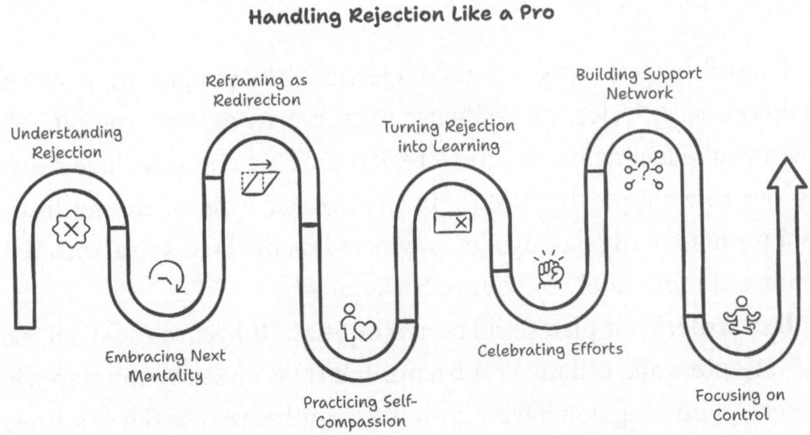

Pro Tips for Handling Rejection:

1. **Create a Rejection Resilience Plan** – Have steps in place to bounce back quickly.
2. **See Rejection as a Numbers Game** – The more you try, the closer you get to a "yes."
3. **Remember It's Temporary** – Every rejection is a stepping stone, not a dead end.

24

Navigating Group Dynamics Like a Pro

Ah, group dynamics—the ultimate test of social skills! Whether it's a team meeting, a family gathering, or a group outing with friends, **navigating group settings can feel like a high-wire act** for introverts. You're trying to stay engaged, contribute to the conversation, and avoid feeling like a wallflower all at once. But here's the thing: mastering group dynamics doesn't require you to change who you are. It's about **understanding the unwritten rules** and learning how to flow with the group while staying true to yourself.

In this chapter, we're going to explore how you can **thrive in group settings without feeling drained**. You'll learn practical strategies to engage with others, manage social energy, and even enjoy being part of a group (yes, it's possible!). Let's get started!

1. Finding Your Role in the Group

One of the best ways to feel more comfortable in a group setting is by **finding your natural role**. Not everyone has to be the centre of attention or the life of the party. Maybe you're the thoughtful listener, the one who asks insightful questions, or the supportive encourager. Embracing your unique role helps you feel more at ease and allows you to contribute meaningfully without pretending to be someone you're not.

Example: If you're in a team meeting, instead of trying to dominate the discussion, focus on listening carefully and chiming in with thoughtful comments. This way, you're still participating, but in a way that aligns with your strengths.

2. Using "Micro-Contributions" to Stay Engaged

In group settings, it's easy to feel lost in the shuffle, especially if you're more reserved. One way to stay involved without overwhelming yourself is by making **micro-contributions**—small, meaningful comments or questions that show you're engaged. This could be something as simple as agreeing with someone's point, adding a quick thought, or asking a clarifying question. These small contributions keep you in the conversation without draining your social battery.

Example: If someone in a group conversation mentions an upcoming event, you could add, "That sounds interesting—how did you hear about it?" This shows you're paying attention and keeps the conversation going without putting the spotlight on you.

3. Managing "Social Spotlight" Moments

Let's face it—there are times in group settings when the spotlight unexpectedly turns on you. Maybe someone asks for your opinion, or you're asked to share an update. **Instead of panicking**, take a deep breath, smile, and share your thoughts concisely. Remember, people aren't expecting a perfect response; they're just interested in your perspective. By keeping your response brief and to the point, you can contribute confidently without feeling overwhelmed.

Great job navigating through the first steps of group dynamics! By understanding your role, making micro-contributions, and handling the social spotlight, you're already on your way to feeling more at ease in group settings. Let's build on that by diving into **strategies for keeping your energy levels steady** so you can engage fully without feeling drained.

4. Balancing Listening and Speaking

Group conversations can sometimes feel like a verbal tug-of-war, where everyone's vying to get a word in. But as an introvert, one of your greatest strengths is **listening**. Use it to your advantage! While others may focus on talking, your thoughtful listening can help you pick up on what's truly being said. However, balance is key—make sure you're also contributing when you have something meaningful to add.

Example: If you've been listening for a while and notice a pause in the conversation, seize the opportunity to share a thought or observation you've been holding onto. It's a great way to make your presence known without interrupting the flow.

5. Using Body Language to Communicate Engagement

Sometimes, engaging in group dynamics isn't about what you say, but rather **how you show up**. Your body language can communicate just as much as your words. Make eye contact, nod to show agreement, and lean slightly forward when someone is speaking. These small gestures signal that you're present and interested, even if you're not speaking much.

Example: If a colleague is presenting an idea in a meeting, nodding and maintaining eye contact shows you're engaged. It encourages them to keep speaking and makes you appear approachable, even if you're more reserved.

6. Taking "Mini-Breaks" to Recharge

Group settings can be overwhelming, especially if they're lengthy. To prevent burnout, it's helpful to **take mini-breaks** whenever you need a breather. This could be as simple as stepping away for a glass of water, taking a quick walk outside, or even just excusing yourself to the bathroom for a few moments. These small breaks allow you to recharge your social battery and return feeling refreshed.

Example: At a long social event or work gathering, take a moment to step outside for a breath of fresh air. This brief pause can help you gather your thoughts and re-center before rejoining the group.

Fantastic progress! Now that you've learned how to balance listening and speaking, use body language effectively, and take mini-breaks to recharge, let's explore some **techniques for navigating group dynamics when conversations get intense or challenging**. The goal here is to help you feel confident and stay grounded, even when the conversation heats up or feels overwhelming.

7. Steering Conversations with Strategic Questions

One way to navigate challenging group dynamics is by using **strategic questions** to guide the conversation in a positive direction. If the discussion becomes tense or starts to veer off into topics you're uncomfortable with, asking a well-timed question can help redirect the focus. This technique is particularly useful in meetings or social gatherings where tensions can run high.

Example: If a conversation at a social event starts to get overly heated about a controversial topic, try interjecting with a neutral question like, "That's interesting—what do you think we can do to find common ground on this issue?" This approach shifts the focus to solutions rather than conflict.

8. Creating "Connection Points" to Deepen Engagement

In group settings, it's easy to feel like you're just skimming the surface of conversations. To build deeper connections, focus on **finding common ground** with others. These "connection points" can be shared interests, experiences, or even a mutual appreciation for something. Highlighting what you have in common can help you feel more engaged and less like an outsider.

Example: If you're at a group dinner and someone mentions they love hiking, and you're into nature too, chime in with, "I've been trying to find new trails recently—any recommendations?" This not only shows genuine interest but also deepens the interaction.

9. Handling Overlapping Conversations with Confidence

In larger groups, conversations often overlap, with multiple people talking at once. For introverts, this can be overwhelming. Instead of trying to force your way into a crowded conversation, **focus on smaller, side discussions**. This way, you can engage more comfortably without feeling like you're competing for attention.

Example: If a group discussion gets too chaotic, turn to the person next to you and start a quieter conversation on a related topic. This lets you contribute in a way that feels more manageable and enjoyable.

Amazing progress! You've now mastered the art of using strategic questions, finding connection points, and handling overlapping conversations with confidence. Let's take it a step further by exploring **how to navigate difficult group dynamics, such as dealing with dominant personalities or managing social anxiety**. These are often the trickiest parts of group interactions, but with a few strategies, you can hold your own without feeling overwhelmed.

10. Handling Dominant Personalities Gracefully

In group settings, there's often someone who loves to dominate the conversation, leaving little room for others to speak. Rather than trying to compete for airtime, you can **navigate around dominant personalities by using tactful techniques** to insert yourself into the conversation. One effective strategy is to wait for a brief pause, then jump in with a concise comment or question.

Example: If someone is monopolising a meeting, you might say, "That's a great point—could we also consider [your idea]?" This shows respect while also shifting the conversation to include your perspective.

11. Managing Social Anxiety in Group Settings

Even if you're equipped with all the strategies, **social anxiety can still creep up** in group settings. The key to managing it is preparation and grounding techniques. Before entering a group situation, take a few moments to breathe deeply, visualise a positive outcome, or remind yourself of your strengths. If anxiety starts to build during the event, focus on small, manageable interactions, like talking to just one person at a time.

Example: If you feel your anxiety rising during a group event, excuse yourself for a quick break. Go to a quiet corner, take a few deep breaths, and remind yourself, "I'm here to enjoy this experience, not to be perfect." This simple reset can help you re-enter the group with a calmer mindset.

12. Using the "Tag-Team" Strategy for Support

If you're attending a group event with a friend, **use the "tag-team" strategy** to support each other. Agree in advance that if one of you feels overwhelmed or stuck in a conversation, the other can step in to help. This technique provides a safety net, making group interactions feel less daunting.

Example: If you're stuck talking to someone and starting to feel drained, your friend can join the conversation and either shift the topic or gently steer you away. Knowing you have backup can reduce social anxiety and boost your confidence.

Excellent work reaching the final page of this chapter! By now, you've learned how to handle dominant personalities, manage social anxiety, and use support strategies like the "tag-team" method. As we wrap up this chapter, let's discuss some **final techniques for thriving in group settings while maintaining your energy and authenticity**. These last strategies will help you confidently navigate any group scenario without feeling drained or overwhelmed.

13. Setting Personal Goals for Group Interactions

Sometimes, group settings can feel like a chaotic free-for-all, especially for introverts. To keep yourself grounded, **set personal goals** before entering a group situation. This could be as simple as contributing one thoughtful comment, having a meaningful conversation with one new person, or simply staying present and listening. Having a clear, achievable goal can give you a sense of purpose and help reduce social anxiety.

Example: Before attending a networking event, set a goal like, "I'm going to introduce myself to two new people and ask them about their work." This focus gives you a concrete objective, making the event feel more manageable.

14. Knowing When to Exit Gracefully

There's nothing wrong with **knowing when it's time to leave** a group setting, especially if you're starting to feel drained. Learning how to exit gracefully can help you preserve your energy while still leaving a positive impression. Simply express your appreciation for the conversation and politely excuse yourself.

Example: If you're feeling exhausted at a party, say something like, "It's been great catching up, but I have an early morning tomorrow. Let's connect again soon." This way, you leave on a positive note without overstaying your welcome.

15. Reflecting on What Went Well

After navigating a group interaction, take a few moments to **reflect on what went well**. Acknowledge your wins, whether it was speaking up in a meeting, making a new connection, or simply staying engaged. This reflection not only builds your confidence but also helps you improve for future group situations. It's a way to celebrate your progress and reinforce the positive experiences.

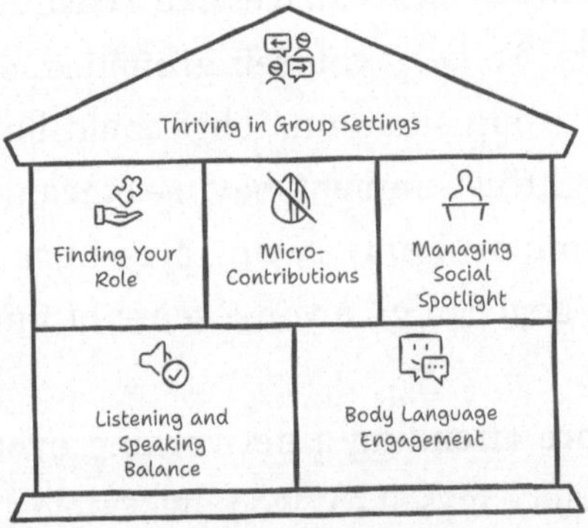

Pro Tips for Navigating Group Dynamics:

1. **Set Personal Goals** – Focus on achievable interactions to stay grounded.
2. **Exit Gracefully** – Know when to leave to protect your energy.

3. **Celebrate Small Wins** – Reflect on what went well to build confidence for the future.

25

Mastering the Art of Listening

(Because It's Underrated)

Listening—it seems like such a simple concept, but it's one of the most **underrated social superpowers** out there. In a world where everyone is eager to talk and be heard, being a good listener can set you apart. For introverts, this is great news because listening is often one of your natural strengths. But how do you turn it into a tool that helps you connect better with others, build deeper relationships, and even gain influence?

In this chapter, we're going to explore how to **master the art of listening**, turning it into a skill that not only improves your social life but also boosts your confidence. Let's dive into how listening can make you the most interesting person in the room—without you having to say much at all.

1. Understanding the Power of Active Listening

Most people think they're good listeners, but the truth is, **active listening is a rare skill**. It's not just about nodding your head and waiting for your turn to speak; it's about being fully present in the moment and truly absorbing what the other person is saying. Active listening involves giving your full attention, asking thoughtful questions, and reflecting back what you've heard.

Example: The next time someone shares a story, instead of jumping in with your own experience, try saying, "That's really interesting. What happened next?" This simple response shows that you're genuinely interested and encourages them to open up more.

2. Using Silence to Your Advantage

One of the most powerful tools in your listening arsenal is **silence**. It might feel uncomfortable at first, but letting a brief silence hang in the air gives the other person space to think and often leads them to share more deeply. People are naturally inclined to fill silences, so when you give them that space, they're likely to keep talking, often revealing more than they intended.

Example: If someone pauses while talking, resist the urge to jump in right away. Instead, let the silence stretch for a few seconds. You'd be surprised how often they'll continue with even more valuable insights.

3. Reflecting Back What You Hear

One of the best ways to show someone you're truly listening is by **reflecting back what they've said**. This doesn't mean parroting their words verbatim but summarising their thoughts to show that you understand. This technique not only helps clarify the conversation but also makes the other person feel truly heard.

Example: If a friend is venting about a stressful situation at work, you might say, "It sounds like you're feeling really overwhelmed by everything on your plate right now." This simple reflection helps them feel validated and opens the door for a deeper conversation.

You're off to a fantastic start! Now that you understand the power of active listening, using silence effectively, and reflecting back what you've heard, let's take it further by learning how to **deepen your connections through the art of listening**. Listening isn't just about hearing words—it's about making people feel valued, understood, and appreciated.

4. Listening Beyond the Words

True listening involves **tuning into more than just the words being spoken**. Pay attention to the other person's tone of voice, facial expressions, and body language. Often, what someone isn't saying is just as important as what they are saying. By being aware of these non-verbal cues, you can gain a deeper understanding of what's really going on beneath the surface.

Example: If a friend says, "I'm fine," but their tone is flat and they avoid eye contact, it might be a sign that something is bothering them. A gentle follow-up like, "Are you sure? You seem a bit off today," shows that you're truly paying attention.

5. Asking Open-Ended Questions to Encourage Sharing

One of the most effective ways to keep a conversation flowing is by **asking open-ended questions**. These are questions that can't be answered with a simple "yes" or "no," and they encourage the other person to share more deeply. Open-ended questions show that you're genuinely interested in their thoughts and feelings, which builds trust and rapport.

Example: Instead of asking, "Did you like the movie?" try asking, "What did you think of the characters in the movie?" This invites a more thoughtful response and keeps the conversation engaging.

6. Practising Empathetic Listening

Empathetic listening is about **putting yourself in the other person's shoes** and truly understanding their emotions. It's not just about hearing their words but also feeling their feelings. When you listen with empathy, you create a safe space where people feel comfortable opening up and sharing their true selves.

Example: If a friend is talking about a tough day, respond with, "That sounds really challenging—I can see why you're feeling frustrated." Acknowledging their feelings shows that you're not just listening but also caring about their experience.

You're becoming a master of the listening arts! By now, you've learned how to listen beyond the words, ask open-ended questions, and practise empathetic listening. Let's build on those skills by exploring how to **enhance your listening abilities in different social situations**. Whether it's a one-on-one conversation or a group setting, these techniques will help you connect with others on a deeper level.

7. Listening in Group Conversations

Group conversations can be tricky because they're often fast-paced and filled with overlapping voices. **Active listening becomes even more important** in these situations. Focus on the person speaking, and avoid the temptation to plan your response while they're talking. By giving your full attention, you'll catch more nuances and be able to contribute more meaningfully when it's your turn to speak.

Example: If you're in a group discussion and someone is sharing a story, nod along to show you're engaged. When there's a pause, you can add something like, "I loved that point you made about [topic]—can you tell me more about it?" This shows you were paying attention and are genuinely interested.

8. Listening Without Judgment

One of the biggest barriers to effective listening is the tendency to **judge or form opinions while someone is speaking**. This can prevent you from fully understanding their perspective. Practice listening with an open mind, especially if the topic is something you don't agree with. You don't have to change your viewpoint, but being open to understanding theirs can lead to more meaningful conversations.

Example: If someone expresses an opinion that you disagree with, instead of immediately countering, try saying, "That's an interesting perspective—can you share more about why you feel that way?" This not only shows respect but also helps you gain a deeper understanding of their viewpoint.

9. Using "Active Affirmations" to Show You're Engaged

A simple yet powerful technique to enhance your listening skills is by using **active affirmations**—small verbal cues that show you're paying attention. Phrases like "I see," "That makes sense," or "I hadn't thought of it that way" encourage the speaker to continue sharing while letting them know you're actively engaged.

Example: If a friend is sharing a personal story, you might respond with, "Wow, that must have been tough. I can't imagine how you managed that." These affirmations keep the conversation flowing and show that you're truly invested in what they're saying.

Fantastic! You're mastering the art of listening in both one-on-one and group conversations. Now that you've learned to listen without judgement and use active affirmations, let's dive into techniques for **listening in emotionally charged conversations**. These situations require a different level of focus and empathy, especially when the other person is feeling vulnerable or upset.

10. Creating a Safe Space for Difficult Conversations

When someone is sharing something deeply personal or emotional, it's important to **create a safe and supportive environment**. This means minimising distractions, giving your full attention, and offering a non-judgmental presence. Let them express themselves fully before responding. Sometimes, just being there to listen can be more valuable than offering advice.

Example: If a friend is opening up about a difficult experience, resist the urge to jump in with solutions right away. Instead, say, "I'm really glad you felt comfortable sharing that with me. I'm here to listen." This lets them know they're safe to continue sharing.

11. Reflecting Emotions, Not Just Words

In emotionally charged conversations, it's crucial to **reflect the emotions behind the words** rather than just summarising what's being said. This shows that you're truly connecting with how they feel, not just what they're saying. Acknowledging emotions helps the speaker feel validated and understood, which can be incredibly healing.

Example: If someone says, "I'm so exhausted from trying to keep everything together," instead of just repeating their words, respond with, "It sounds like you're feeling really overwhelmed and drained." This reflection shows empathy and helps them feel seen.

12. Knowing When to Just Listen

Sometimes, people aren't looking for advice or solutions—they just need to vent. In these moments, the best thing you can do is **just listen**. Offering unsolicited advice can make them feel like you're not truly hearing them. Instead, ask, "Do you want advice, or would you like me to just listen?" This question shows respect for their needs and lets them guide the conversation.

Example: If a friend is sharing frustrations about their job, instead of jumping in with suggestions, simply nod, make eye contact, and say, "I'm here for you—keep going." Letting them know you're there to listen, without judgement, can be incredibly comforting.

You're doing an incredible job mastering the nuances of listening, especially in emotionally charged conversations. Now that you've learned to create a safe space, reflect emotions, and know when to simply listen, let's wrap up this chapter with **final strategies to enhance your listening skills in everyday life**. These last tips will help you become the kind of listener people remember and appreciate.

13. Practising Mindful Listening

One of the best ways to improve your listening skills is by practising **mindful listening**. This means being fully present in the moment, putting away distractions like your phone, and focusing solely on the conversation. Mindful listening not only helps you absorb what's being said but also makes the other person feel valued and respected.

Example: The next time you're having a conversation, make a conscious effort to put your phone face down or away and focus on the speaker. This simple act shows that you're fully invested in the interaction, which can strengthen your connection.

14. Ending Conversations on a Positive Note

Listening doesn't stop when the other person finishes talking. **Ending the conversation on a positive note** reinforces that you appreciated the exchange. Whether it's thanking them for sharing, acknowledging the conversation's value, or simply expressing that you enjoyed talking with them, these small gestures leave a lasting impression.

Example: After a meaningful conversation, try saying, "I really appreciate hearing your perspective—it gave me a lot to think about." This shows that their words had an impact on you, making them feel heard and valued.

15. Turning Listening into a Daily Habit

Like any skill, listening improves with practice. Make it a goal to **practise your listening skills daily**, whether it's with friends, family, colleagues, or even strangers. The more you practise, the more natural it will become, and soon enough, you'll notice the quality of your conversations improving.

Example: Try setting a daily challenge for yourself, like actively listening to someone without interrupting for at least 5 minutes. It could be during a phone call, a casual chat, or even a meeting. By turning listening into a habit, you'll become a trusted and valued conversational partner.

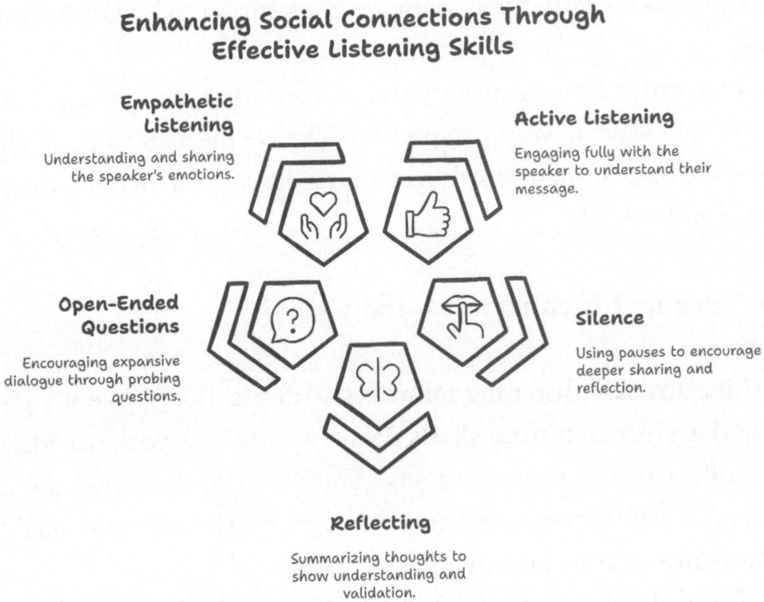

1. **Practise Mindful Listening** – Put away distractions and focus on being fully present.
2. **End on a Positive Note** – Acknowledge the value of the conversation to leave a lasting impact.
3. **Turn Listening into a Habit** – Make a conscious effort to listen actively every day.

26

How to Stop Overthinking Every Social Interaction

Let's talk about **overthinking**—that annoying little voice in your head that second-guesses everything you say, replaying social interactions like a bad movie on repeat. For introverts, overthinking can be a constant companion, turning even the simplest social interactions into a mental minefield. Did you say the right thing? Did you come off as awkward? What if they're judging you?

In this chapter, we're going to tackle **how to break free from the overthinking loop**. The goal isn't to become immune to self-doubt (because hey, we're all human), but to learn how to quiet that inner critic and move forward with confidence. Let's explore practical strategies to help you stop over analysing every conversation and start enjoying your social interactions.

1. Recognizing the Signs of Overthinking

The first step to stopping overthinking is **recognizing when it's happening**. Overthinking often shows up as replaying conversations, obsessing over what you said, or worrying about how others perceived you. If you find yourself mentally rehashing a conversation hours later, it's a sign you're stuck in the overthinking loop.

Example: After a party, if you're still wondering whether you said something wrong to someone, pause and remind yourself that most people are too busy thinking about their own lives to scrutinise every word you say.

2. Practising the "So What?" Technique

One of the simplest ways to break free from overthinking is by using the **"So what?" technique**. When you catch yourself obsessing over something you said, ask yourself, "So what?" This helps you put things in perspective. If the worst-case scenario isn't life-changing, then it's not worth wasting your mental energy on it.

Example: If you're worried you made an awkward joke at a social gathering, ask yourself, "So what if it was awkward? Will anyone remember it in a week?" The answer is usually no, which helps you move on.

3. Shifting Your Focus to the Positive

Overthinkers tend to focus on the negatives: what went wrong, what could have been better, or what might happen if things go awry. Instead, try **shifting your focus to what went well**. For every interaction you're overthinking, challenge yourself to find at least one positive aspect. This simple shift can help rewire your brain to focus on the good rather than the bad.

Example: After a networking event, instead of obsessing over the one conversation that felt awkward, remind yourself of the person who complimented your insights or the new connection you made. Focusing on these positives helps you feel more confident and less critical of yourself.

Great progress! By now, you've learned how to recognize the signs of overthinking, using the "So what?" technique, and shift your focus to the positive. Now let's explore **how to break the overthinking**

cycle in real-time, so you can enjoy your social interactions without getting lost in your head. These strategies will help you stay present and focused, making conversations more enjoyable.

4. Using Grounding Techniques to Stay Present

Overthinking often happens when you're **stuck in your head**, replaying past conversations or worrying about future interactions. One of the best ways to break this cycle is by using grounding techniques that bring you back to the present moment. Simple methods like focusing on your breath, feeling your feet on the ground, or noticing sensory details around you can help you stay connected to the here and now.

Example: If you're in a conversation and notice your mind starting to spiral, take a slow, deep breath and focus on the texture of the chair you're sitting on or the sound of the other person's voice. This brings you back into the moment and helps quiet the overthinking.

5. Embracing the "Good Enough" Mindset

Perfectionism is a huge driver of overthinking, especially for introverts who may worry about making the perfect impression. Instead of aiming for perfection, try adopting a "**good enough**" **mindset**. Accept that not every interaction has to be flawless—it's okay to have an off day or say something awkward now and then. In fact, these moments often make you more relatable.

Example: If you're overthinking an email you sent to a colleague, remind yourself, "It's good enough. The point was made, and they're not expecting Shakespeare." This shift in perspective can help you move on without obsessing over every detail.

6. Practising the "One-and-Done" Rule

To stop yourself from obsessing over past conversations, practise the **"one-and-done" rule**: once you've replayed the interaction in your mind once, let it go. Instead of mentally dissecting every word, give yourself permission to review it once, learn from it if necessary, and then move on. The more you practise this, the easier it becomes to break free from the overthinking loop.

Example: After a challenging meeting, allow yourself one mental review. After that, say to yourself, "I've reflected on it, and now it's time to move on." This approach prevents you from getting stuck in a cycle of overanalysis.

You're doing a fantastic job! Now that you've mastered grounding techniques, embraced the "good enough" mindset, and started using the "one-and-done" rule, let's take it a step further by exploring how to **change your relationship with overthinking**. It's not about eliminating it entirely (because let's be real, everyone overthinks sometimes), but about **managing it in a healthier way**.

7. Practising Self-Compassion

One of the reasons overthinking can be so draining is because we're often our own worst critics. If you tend to beat yourself up over every social faux pas, practising **self-compassion** can help break this cycle. Remind yourself that it's okay to make mistakes, and that no one is judging you as harshly as you're judging yourself. Treat yourself with the same kindness and understanding that you would offer a friend.

Example: If you find yourself ruminating over a conversation where you stumbled over your words, pause and say to yourself, "It's okay—I'm human. Everyone makes mistakes, and it's not the end of the world." This gentle reminder can help you move on faster.

8. Turning Overthinking into Productive Reflection

Not all overthinking is bad; sometimes, reflecting on past interactions can help you improve. The trick is to **turn overthinking into productive reflection**. Instead of obsessing over what you did wrong, focus on what you can do differently next time. This shifts your mindset from self-criticism to self-improvement.

Example: If you're replaying a conversation where you felt awkward, instead of asking, "Why did I mess up?" ask yourself, "What could I do next time to feel more comfortable?" This turns overthinking into a constructive exercise rather than a self-punishing one.

9. Using Humor to Diffuse Overthinking

Sometimes, the best way to break the cycle of overthinking is to **laugh it off**. Humour can be a powerful tool for gaining perspective. When you find yourself spiralling, try to see the situation from a humorous angle. Imagine it as a funny scene in a sitcom—suddenly, it doesn't seem so serious.

Example: If you're worrying about a cringe-worthy moment at a party, imagine how it would play out in a comedy show. Picture yourself as the lovable character who always finds themselves in awkward situations. This helps you lighten up and realise that, in the grand scheme of things, it's not a big deal.

Fantastic progress! Now that you've learned how to be self-compassionate, turn overthinking into productive reflection, and use humour to diffuse anxious thoughts, let's explore **ways to prevent overthinking before it starts**. These proactive strategies can help you manage your social interactions with more ease, so you can focus on enjoying the moment instead of second-guessing yourself later.

10. Setting a "Time Limit" for Overthinking

One effective way to keep overthinking in check is by **setting a time limit** on how long you allow yourself to ruminate. Give yourself, say, 10 minutes to replay a conversation in your mind. Once that time is up, it's time to let it go and move on. This strategy helps you process your thoughts without letting them spiral out of control.

Example: After a stressful meeting, set a timer for 10 minutes and allow yourself to analyse what happened. Once the timer goes off, take a deep breath and shift your focus to a new task. This keeps you from getting stuck in a loop of overanalysis.

11. Replacing "What Ifs" with "What Is"

Overthinking often involves a lot of "**what if" questions**: What if they didn't like me? What if I said something wrong? Instead of getting caught up in hypothetical scenarios, try shifting your focus to "**what is**"—the reality of the situation. This helps ground you in the present and prevents your mind from wandering into worst-case scenarios.

Example: If you're worried about how you came across in a conversation, ask yourself, "What is the actual evidence that things went badly?" Often, you'll realise that your fears are based on assumptions, not facts.

12. Creating a "Social Interaction Debrief"

A great way to combat over thinking is to **create a quick debrief** after social interactions. This doesn't have to be a long process—just take a moment to jot down a few thoughts on what went well and what you might improve for next time. By turning it into a structured activity, you give your mind a way to process the interaction without spiralling into overthinking.

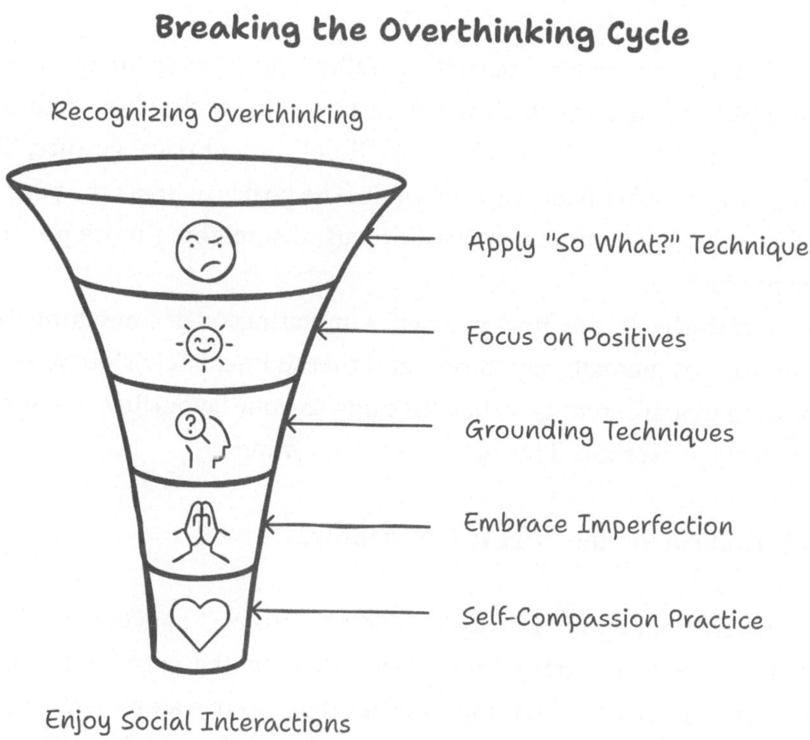

You've reached the final stretch! By now, you've mastered strategies like setting time limits for overthinking, focusing on "what is" instead of "what ifs," and using debriefs to reflect constructively. Let's wrap up this chapter with **final techniques to transform overthinking into a tool for growth**. These strategies will help you turn those anxious thoughts into opportunities for self-improvement, so you can leave overthinking behind and step into every social situation with confidence.

13. Practising "Thought Stopping" Techniques

When you catch yourself spiralling into overthinking, **use thought-stopping techniques** to interrupt the cycle. This might involve a quick mental command like "Stop!" or a physical gesture, like snapping a rubber band on your wrist. The goal is to break the pattern of overthinking and redirect your focus to something more positive or productive.

Example: If you find yourself ruminating over something you said earlier, mentally say "Stop!" and then immediately shift your attention to a different task, like listening to your favourite song or doing a quick exercise. This helps reset your mindset.

14. Embracing the "Let It Go" Mantra

Overthinking often involves holding onto past conversations, social missteps, or minor interactions that, in the grand scheme of things, don't matter. Developing a **"let it go" mantra** can help you release those thoughts. Find a phrase that resonates with you, like "Let it go," "It's not that deep," or "Onward and upward." Repeat it whenever you notice your mind wandering back to past worries.

Example: After a stressful social interaction, remind yourself, "It's over, and it doesn't define me." This helps you focus on the present rather than getting stuck in the past.

15. Celebrating Your Wins, No Matter How Small

One of the best ways to combat over-thinking is to **focus on your successes** instead of your perceived mistakes. At the end of each day, take a few moments to reflect on what went well. Did you make someone laugh? Did you handle a conversation smoothly? Did you step outside your comfort zone? By celebrating these small wins, you build confidence and reduce the urge to dwell on the negatives.

Example: Keep a journal where you jot down one positive social interaction from the day, no matter how small. Over time, you'll start to see that you're doing better than you give yourself credit for.

Pro Tips for Overcoming Overthinking:

1. **Use Thought-Stopping Techniques** – Interrupt the cycle and redirect your focus.
2. **Adopt a Let It Go Mantra** – Remind yourself that it's not worth holding onto minor worries.
3. **Celebrate Your Wins** – Focus on the positives to shift your mindset from self-doubt to self-confidence.

27

A Crash Course on Humor

(Because Everyone Loves a Good Laugh)

Let's talk about humor—it's the ultimate social lubricant, the secret weapon that can turn an awkward interaction into a memorable one. For introverts, mastering the art of humor can feel like a daunting task, especially if you're more reserved. But here's the great news: **you don't have to be a stand-up comedian** to be funny. Humor isn't just about cracking jokes; it's about finding the funny side of everyday life, connecting with others, and making social situations more enjoyable.

In this chapter, we'll explore how to **infuse humor into your social interactions**, so you can relax, have fun, and build stronger connections. Whether it's learning how to laugh at yourself, finding the right moment for a witty comment, or simply bringing a lighthearted attitude to your conversations, we've got you covered.

1. Understanding the Different Types of Humor

Not all humour is the same, and the good news is that there are many **different styles** to choose from. Whether you're into dry wit, playful teasing, observational humour, or just a good pun, there's a type of humour that fits your personality. Understanding the different types can help you find your own comedic voice and use it to connect with others.

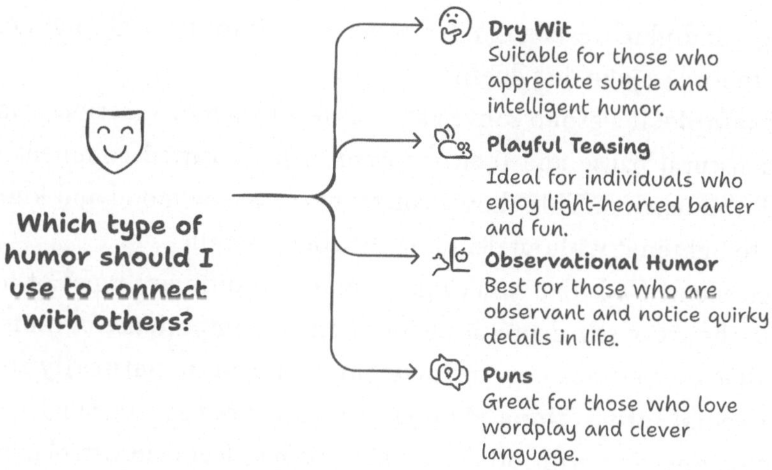

2. Learning to Laugh at Yourself

One of the best ways to disarm social tension and make people feel comfortable around you is by **laughing at yourself**. Self-deprecating humour can be incredibly endearing when used in moderation. It shows that you don't take yourself too seriously and are comfortable in your own skin. Just remember, there's a fine line between light-hearted self-teasing and putting yourself down—keep it fun and positive.

Example: If you trip over your words during a conversation, you could say with a smile, "Oops, looks like my brain is buffering again." This shows you can roll with the punches and helps lighten the mood.

3. Timing is Everything

Humour is all about **timing.** A well-timed joke can turn an ordinary conversation into a memorable one, while a poorly timed comment can fall flat. The key to good timing is reading the room and being mindful of the context. It's better to wait for the right moment than to force a joke that doesn't fit.

Example: If a group conversation is feeling a bit too serious, wait for a natural pause and then throw in a lighthearted comment to break the tension. This shows you're aware of the mood and know how to lighten it without derailing the conversation.

Excellent! Now that you've got a grasp on different types of humour, the art of self-deprecating jokes, and the importance of timing, let's dive deeper into how to **incorporate humour naturally into your social interactions**. Humour isn't just about getting laughs; it's about connecting with others, making people feel comfortable, and turning everyday moments into opportunities for fun.

4. Finding Humor in Everyday Situations

You don't have to be the life of the party to be funny. Sometimes, the best humour comes from simply **noticing the funny side of everyday situations**. This could be something quirky you noticed on your way to work, a funny interaction you had with a stranger, or even an amusing thought that popped into your head. Sharing these lighthearted observations can be a great way to break the ice and get people laughing.

Example: If you're at a coffee shop and the barista messes up your name, instead of getting annoyed, you could joke, "I guess 'Steve' is my new identity today." These kinds of comments show that you don't take things too seriously and are willing to have a laugh about it.

5. Using Humour to Handle Awkward Moments

Awkward moments happen to everyone, but **humour is a fantastic way to turn them around**. When you find yourself in an uncomfortable situation—like saying something awkward, dropping your drink, or forgetting someone's name—using humour can diffuse the tension and make everyone feel at ease. The trick is to acknowledge the awkwardness in a lighthearted way.

Example: If you forget someone's name shortly after being introduced, you can say with a smile, "I'm so sorry—I have the memory of a goldfish. What was your name again?" This not only breaks the ice but also shows that you're not afraid to laugh at yourself.

6. Finding Common Ground Through Shared Laughter

One of the most powerful aspects of humour is its ability to **create a sense of connection**. Shared laughter is like social glue—it brings people together and helps build trust. If you can find something that everyone in the group can relate to, you've hit comedy gold. Whether it's a funny comment about the weather, a shared frustration, or a light-hearted joke about the situation you're all in, finding common ground through humour is a great way to bond.

Example: If you're stuck in a long line with others, you could say, "By the time we get to the front, it'll be next year!" A little exaggeration and shared commiseration can turn a boring moment into an opportunity for laughter.

You're doing an amazing job embracing the art of humour! By now, you've learned how to find humour in everyday moments, use it to handle awkward situations, and create connection through shared laughter. Let's take it further by exploring how to **use humour as a tool to navigate social interactions more confidently**. Humour can be your secret weapon for breaking down barriers, relieving tension, and making memorable impressions.

7. Practising "Playful Teasing" (The Right Way)

Playful teasing can be a great way to bond with others, but it needs to be handled with care. The trick is to **keep it lighthearted and always positive**. Tease about things that are obviously unimportant—never touch on sensitive topics. When done correctly, playful teasing can create a sense of camaraderie and show that you're comfortable enough to have fun with the other person.

Example: If a friend is always late, you could say, "Ah, right on time... 10 minutes behind schedule, as usual!" This kind of playful ribbing is fun without being mean-spirited, and it can strengthen your bond.

8. Using Humor to Lighten Up Serious Conversations

Humour isn't just for social gatherings—it can also be a powerful tool in more serious settings. Knowing when to inject a little lightheartedness can **break tension** and help everyone relax. The key is to be subtle and read the room carefully. If people seem stressed or tense, a well-timed joke can shift the mood and make the conversation more enjoyable.

Example: If a meeting at work is dragging on, you could say something like, "At this rate, we'll need to order dinner." It shows you're aware of the situation while adding a bit of levity.

9. Embracing "Situational Humour"

Situational humour is all about **making the most of what's happening around you**. It's spontaneous, based on the context of the moment, and often comes off as more authentic. This type of humour can be particularly effective in making social interactions feel more natural and fun.

Example: If someone's phone rings loudly in a quiet room, you might say, "Ah, they're playing our song!" It's a light, situational joke that acknowledges the interruption without making anyone feel uncomfortable.

Awesome progress! Now that you've embraced playful teasing, mastered using humour to lighten serious conversations, and are making the most of situational humour, let's focus on **how to use humour as a confidence booster**. Humour isn't just a tool for connecting with others; it's also a powerful way to feel more at ease in social settings. When you can make yourself (and others) laugh, you create a positive energy that makes interactions more enjoyable for everyone involved.

10. Using Humour to Overcome Social Anxiety

If social situations make you anxious, using humour can be a great way to **ease your nerves**. By focusing on the lighter side of things, you shift your mindset from fear to fun. It's easier to relax when you're not taking everything too seriously. Even if you're feeling a bit awkward, a well-timed joke can help break the ice and put both you and others at ease.

Example: If you feel your nerves building up before speaking in front of a group, you could start with a light-hearted comment like, "I'm glad to see you're all here today... even if it's just for the free coffee!" This can help loosen you up and make the audience smile.

11. Embracing "Self-Deprecating Humor" (In Moderation)

We've touched on self-deprecating humour before, but it's worth revisiting because it can be such a **powerful tool for building rapport**. When you're willing to laugh at yourself, it shows that you're confident and don't take yourself too seriously. However, it's important to use this type of humour sparingly. Too much self-deprecation can come off as insecurity, so keep it light and positive.

Example: If you trip over your words during a presentation, you might say, "Sorry, my tongue decided to take a nap halfway through that sentence." This light-hearted comment shows you're comfortable enough to poke fun at yourself without losing confidence.

12. Practising "Humor Warm-Ups"

If you're heading into a social event and feeling a bit rusty, try using "**humour warm-ups**" to get yourself in the right mindset. This could be watching a few minutes of your favourite stand-up comedian, listening to a funny podcast, or even recalling a hilarious memory. Priming yourself with laughter beforehand can put you in a lighter, more relaxed mood, making it easier to engage socially.

Example: Before a big social event, watch a few clips of your favourite comedy show. The laughter will help ease your nerves, and you'll walk in with a smile, ready to share that positive energy.

You've done an incredible job mastering the art of humour! By now, you've learned how to use it to lighten up conversations, boost your confidence, and even overcome social anxiety. Let's wrap up this chapter with some **final strategies to make humour a natural part of your social toolkit**. Humour doesn't have to be forced or scripted—it can flow naturally when you're relaxed and enjoying yourself.

13. Creating a "Humor Bank"

One way to feel more comfortable using humour is by building a "**humour bank**"—a collection of funny stories, jokes, or anecdotes that you can pull from in conversations. This doesn't mean you have to memorise one-liners, but having a few go-to stories that reliably get a laugh can make you feel more confident in social situations.

These stories can be personal experiences, funny observations, or even light-hearted jokes you've heard from others.

Example: If someone asks about your weekend, instead of saying, "It was fine," you might share a funny story about how your dog tried to chase a squirrel up a tree and ended up tangled in the leash. These little anecdotes are great conversation starters and can instantly lighten the mood.

14. Learning to "Read the Room" for Humor

Not every moment is the right time for a joke. One of the most important aspects of using humour effectively is being able to **read the room**. If people are stressed, tense, or dealing with something serious, a light joke might not land well. But in a relaxed setting, a little humour can go a long way in breaking the ice. The key is to be mindful of the mood and adjust your approach accordingly.

Example: If you're at a work meeting that's getting heated, it's probably not the best time for a joke. But if you're at a casual gathering and the conversation is lagging, a funny comment can be just the thing to lift everyone's spirits.

15. Remembering to Have Fun

At the end of the day, **humour is about having fun**. Don't put pressure on yourself to be the funniest person in the room. Instead, focus on enjoying the moment, being present, and letting humour flow naturally. When you're genuinely having fun, it shows, and others will be drawn to your positive energy.

Example: If you're at a party, don't stress about trying to be funny. Just relax, enjoy the conversation, and let your sense of humour come out naturally. The best jokes are often the spontaneous ones that happen when you're genuinely enjoying yourself.

Pro Tips for Mastering Humor:

1. **Build a Humor Bank** – Keep a few funny stories or jokes ready to share.
2. **Read the Room** – Be mindful of the mood before injecting humour.
3. **Have Fun** – Let humour be a natural extension of your personality.

28

Embracing Your Inner Ambivert

The Best of Both Worlds

If you've been following along, you've probably noticed that you don't fit neatly into a box labelled "introvert" or "extrovert." That's because **most people fall somewhere in between**—and that's where the ambivert comes in. Being an ambivert means you've got the best of both worlds: the ability to be social and outgoing when the situation calls for it, and the comfort of retreating into your own space when you need a break. So let's dive in and explore how embracing your inner ambivert can lead to a more balanced, fulfilling social life.

1. Introduction to Ambiversion: Finding the Sweet Spot

Let's start with the basics: **what is an ambivert?** If introverts are the quiet thinkers and extroverts are the social butterflies, ambiverts are the chameleons of the social world. They're not confined to one end of the spectrum—they can shift between introverted and extroverted traits depending on the situation. Think of it like having a superpower that lets you adjust your social energy on demand.

But here's the kicker: **being an ambivert isn't about being perfectly balanced all the time**. It's about knowing when to lean into your social side and when to pull back, depending on what you need. It's like having both a turbo button and a "chill out" button, and knowing when to use each.

Example: Think of ambiverts as being like those rare individuals who can enjoy a lively party one night and then be perfectly content to stay in with a good book the next. They're the best of both worlds, and they know how to make each side work for them.

2. Recognizing Your Own Social Spectrum

So, how do you know where you fall on the social spectrum? The first step is a bit of **self-reflection**. Take a moment to think about your typical social behaviour. Do you find yourself craving interaction, but also needing regular breaks to recharge? Do you enjoy spending time with others, but feel exhausted after too much socialising? That's your ambivert side shining through.

Let's try a few **self-reflection exercises**:

- Think about your favourite social scenarios. Are you the life of the party until you hit a wall? Or do you enjoy being with close friends but get drained after large gatherings?
- Reflect on how you feel after social interactions. Do you feel energised, drained, or somewhere in between? Understanding your natural rhythms can help you plan your social life more effectively.

Real-life examples of ambiverts include people like Oprah Winfrey, who can be charismatic on stage but also values her downtime. Or Elon Musk, who can command a room when needed but is known for his introspective side. These are people who've mastered the art of switching between social modes based on the situation.

3. Strategies for Balancing Social Interactions and Alone Time

Now that you've identified where you fall on the introvert-extrovert spectrum, let's get practical. **How can you manage your social energy effectively?** It's all about knowing when to push yourself to be social and when to lean into your need for alone time.

Here are some **practical tips**:

- **Listen to your body and mind**: If you're feeling drained, it's okay to take a step back. Cancelling plans occasionally to recharge is not a crime.
- **Plan "buffer days"**: After a big social event, give yourself a day to decompress. It's like letting your social battery recharge so you can be ready for the next adventure.
- **Practice saying "yes" and "no" strategically**: Lean into social events that excite you, but don't be afraid to decline invitations that feel more draining than fun.

Example exercise: Create a "social energy budget" for yourself. If you know a busy week is coming up, plan some downtime before and after big events to recharge. It's like planning a financial budget but for your social energy!

You've recognized your ambivert tendencies and learned how to balance your social interactions with alone time. But there's more to embracing your ambivert superpowers—like knowing how to **adapt your social style to different situations**. This adaptability is what makes ambiverts so effective in social settings. They can turn up the charm when needed and dial it back when it's time to recharge. Let's dive into how you can leverage these skills in various social contexts.

4. Leveraging Ambiversion in Different Scenarios

One of the greatest strengths of being an ambivert is your ability to **adapt your social style** based on the situation. Whether it's a networking event, a casual hangout, or a team meeting, ambiverts can intuitively adjust their approach. This flexibility makes you more effective in diverse social settings and allows you to thrive where others might struggle.

Here are some practical ways to **play to your strengths** as an ambivert:

- **In large gatherings or networking events**: Tap into your extroverted side by starting conversations with new people. Focus on asking questions and showing genuine interest, which takes the pressure off you to perform.
- **In one-on-one meetings**: Use your introverted strengths to listen actively. Let the other person do most of the talking while you absorb the details. This not only makes you appear more engaged but also builds stronger connections.
- **In group settings**: Balance your energy by participating actively when needed, but don't be afraid to step back and let others take the spotlight. Knowing when to contribute and when to observe is your secret weapon.

Case study of an ambivert in action: Imagine Sarah, who's attending a work conference. During the daytime sessions, she uses her extroverted side to network and exchange ideas with colleagues. But when the evening social events roll around, she taps into her introverted side to take some quiet time in her hotel room, so she's refreshed for the next day.

5. Strategies for Knowing When to Switch Gears

Being an ambivert means you can **shift between social modes**—but how do you know when it's time to switch gears? It's all about listening to your internal cues. Here are a few strategies for recognizing when to lean into your introverted or extroverted side:

- **Monitor your energy levels**: If you're starting to feel drained, that's your signal to pull back and take a breather. Conversely, if you're feeling isolated or restless, it might be time to seek out social interaction.
- **Assess the environment**: Different settings call for different approaches. If you're at a lively party, channel your social energy. But if you're in a more intimate setting, it's okay to be quieter and focus on meaningful conversations.
- **Use social "warm-ups"**: If you're about to enter a high-energy situation, take a few minutes to get into the right mindset. Listen to upbeat music, watch a funny video, or practise some deep breathing to centre yourself.

Example exercise: Try this the next time you're heading into a social event: take a quick "social pulse" check before you walk in. Ask yourself, "Do I have the energy to engage fully right now, or do I need to ease into it?" Adjust your approach based on your answer.

6. Embracing the Power of Flexibility

The beauty of being an ambivert is that you're **not locked into one way of being**. You can adjust your social style to fit the moment, which is a superpower that many people envy. Embrace the fluidity of your personality and recognize that it's perfectly okay to switch between your introverted and extroverted sides as needed. This adaptability is what gives you the best of both worlds.

Real-life example: Think of an ambivert like a Swiss Army knife—versatile, adaptable, and ready for any social situation. Whether you need to be the life of the party or the quiet observer, you have the tools to handle it all.

Fantastic work embracing your ambivert strengths! Now that you've explored how to adapt to different social situations and recognize when to switch gears, let's talk about the **power of self-acceptance**. You've navigated this entire journey of social growth, but the real secret is learning to embrace who you are while allowing space for growth.

7. The Power of Self-Acceptance and Growth

As an ambivert, you have the unique ability to **thrive in both social and quiet spaces**. However, it's important to remember that being an ambivert doesn't mean you have to be "on" all the time. It's about knowing yourself, honouring your needs, and finding a balance that works for you. Self-acceptance is the foundation for true social confidence.

Embracing both sides of yourself:

- Accept that it's okay to enjoy a lively party one day and crave solitude the next. You're not being inconsistent; you're being true to your needs at the moment.
- Recognize that social growth doesn't mean transforming into someone you're not. It's about **expanding your comfort zone**, not abandoning it. Growth happens when you stretch yourself just enough to challenge your boundaries without breaking them.

Example: Imagine you've been pushing yourself to attend more social events to build your confidence. But suddenly, you feel drained. Instead of forcing yourself to keep going, listen to that inner voice saying, "Hey, it's time to recharge." Give yourself permission to take a night off—it's all part of the balance.

8. Personal Growth Happens Outside Your Comfort Zone

Let's face it—comfort zones are cosy, but **growth rarely happens there**. The beauty of being an ambivert is that you can step out of your comfort zone without feeling completely lost. Every time you challenge yourself to be more social or to embrace solitude, you're growing. And sometimes, it's those quiet moments of reflection that lead to the most powerful insights.

- **Push yourself gently**: If you're naturally more introverted, set a small social goal—like starting a conversation with a new colleague or attending one social event this month. If you're more extroverted, challenge yourself to spend a quiet evening alone with your thoughts.
- **Celebrate the small wins**: Every time you step out of your comfort zone, even if it's just a little, acknowledge it. Growth is a process, not a destination.

Real-life example: Let's say you usually avoid public speaking. One day, you decide to volunteer for a short presentation at work. You feel nervous, but after it's done, you realise it wasn't as terrifying as you thought. That's growth in action, and it's something to be proud of.

9. Letting Go of the Pressure to Fit In

One of the biggest challenges for ambiverts is feeling like you need to **choose a side**—introvert or extrovert. But here's the truth: you don't have to fit into anyone else's definition. The beauty of ambiversion is that it's all about flexibility. You get to define what social success looks like for you.

- **Be unapologetically you**: Whether you're the quiet one at the party or the person cracking jokes in the corner, embrace it. There's no one right way to be social.
- **Ditch the labels**: Stop trying to fit yourself into a box. Sometimes you're outgoing, sometimes you're introspective, and that's perfectly okay. You're not being inconsistent—you're being versatile.

Example: The next time someone asks, "Are you an introvert or an extrovert?" feel free to say, "I'm a bit of both—depends on the day." It's a great conversation starter and shows that you're comfortable embracing your true self.

You're almost at the finish line! Now that you've embraced your ambivert flexibility and let go of the pressure to fit into labels, let's explore how to **leverage your ambivert strengths in everyday life**. Whether you're navigating social interactions, managing relationships, or focusing on personal growth, embracing both sides of your social spectrum can open up new opportunities and enrich your life.

10. Leveraging Ambiversion in Relationships

Being an ambivert gives you a unique advantage in your personal and professional relationships. You can **adapt to the needs of different people** and situations, making you a great friend, partner, or colleague. Knowing when to listen deeply and when to step up and take the lead can make all the difference.

Practical tips for relationships:

- **With extroverted friends**: Channel your social energy to match theirs when needed, but don't hesitate to set boundaries when you need alone time.
- **With introverted friends**: Use your listening skills to connect on a deeper level, and create safe spaces for meaningful conversations without overwhelming them.

Example: If you're in a relationship where your partner is more extroverted, plan activities that balance social outings with quiet, one-on-one time. This keeps both of you happy while honouring your own energy needs.

11. Using Your Social Flexibility in the Workplace

One of the greatest benefits of being an ambivert is your ability to **adapt to different work environments**. Whether it's brainstorming with a team or working solo on a project, you can adjust your approach to suit the task at hand. This makes you a versatile and valuable asset in any workplace.

How to leverage your ambivert strengths at work:

- **Networking events**: Use your extroverted side to make connections, then follow up later in a quieter setting to build deeper relationships.
- **Team projects**: Balance contributing ideas with listening to others, ensuring that everyone feels heard.
- **Solo tasks**: Lean into your introverted tendencies to focus deeply and produce high-quality work.

Example: Imagine you're leading a meeting. Start by engaging your team with questions to get everyone involved, then shift into listening mode to absorb their ideas. This balanced approach encourages collaboration while also showing that you value everyone's input.

12. The Secret to a Fulfilling Social Life: Embracing Both Sides

At the end of the day, being an ambivert isn't about being **perfectly balanced** all the time. It's about **knowing when to embrace your introverted or extroverted side** based on what the moment requires. By tuning into your inner compass, you can enjoy the best of both worlds without burning out.

Embracing the flow:

- Don't pressure yourself to be more social than you're comfortable with, but also don't shy away from opportunities to connect with others.
- Remember, growth happens in both the quiet moments of introspection and the lively energy of social gatherings. Embrace both as part of your journey.

Real-life example: Picture this—you've been feeling drained from socialising all week, so you decide to take a quiet Saturday to yourself. But then, you get invited to a casual get-together that you're genuinely interested in. Instead of forcing yourself either way, listen to your energy levels and choose what feels right in the moment.

You've made it to the final page of the final chapter! By now, you've learned how to embrace your ambivert tendencies, leverage them in relationships, and thrive in both social and professional environments. Let's wrap up with some final words on the **power of self-acceptance, continuous growth, and embracing your unique journey**. As your sarcastic mentor, it's time to deliver a few parting thoughts with a wink and a nudge.

13. The Power of Self-Acceptance and Embracing Growth

Let's get one thing straight: the goal of all this isn't to "fix" yourself or transform into someone you're not. It's about **recognizing and embracing the strengths you already possess**. Growth doesn't mean forcing yourself to become a social butterfly overnight or retreating into a hermit's cave forever. It's about expanding your toolkit so you can navigate life's social situations with confidence and ease.

Here's the deal:

- Give yourself permission to be both quiet and loud, outgoing and reserved. The beauty of being an ambivert is that you don't have to choose.
- Remember, **social success isn't a one-size-fits-all formula**. It's about finding what works for you and owning it, unapologetically.
- Celebrate the quiet victories (like initiating a conversation) and the bold leaps (like attending that party you were dreading).

Real-life example: Think of it like training for a marathon. Some days you sprint, other days you walk, and sometimes you just need to rest. It's all progress, and it's all part of your journey.

14. Your Final Challenge from Your Sarcastic Mentor

Alright, ambivert hero, you've learned a lot—now it's time to put it into practice. I challenge you to **step out of your comfort zone** just a little bit more this week. Try saying yes to something you'd normally shy away from or take a moment to retreat when you're feeling overwhelmed. The goal is to keep experimenting, keep learning, and keep growing.

- **Push yourself** to speak up in that meeting.

- **Accept that invite** you're unsure about.
- Or, on the flip side, take that well-deserved solo day to recharge.

Parting advice: Remember, nobody's watching your every move as closely as you think they are. So go ahead, trip over your words, laugh at yourself, and have fun with it. Life's too short to overthink every interaction.

15. Conclusion – Go Forth, Ambivert Hero

Before we wrap up, let's take a moment to acknowledge how far you've come. You've navigated the maze of social interactions, learned how to balance your energy, and discovered that you're pretty amazing just as you are.

Here's your final call to action:

- **Embrace your ambivert superpowers** and use them to live a more balanced, joyful, and connected life.
- Share your journey with others—whether they're introverts, extroverts, or fellow ambiverts. We're all figuring this out together.
- And, of course, don't forget to keep laughing, connecting, and living life on your own terms.

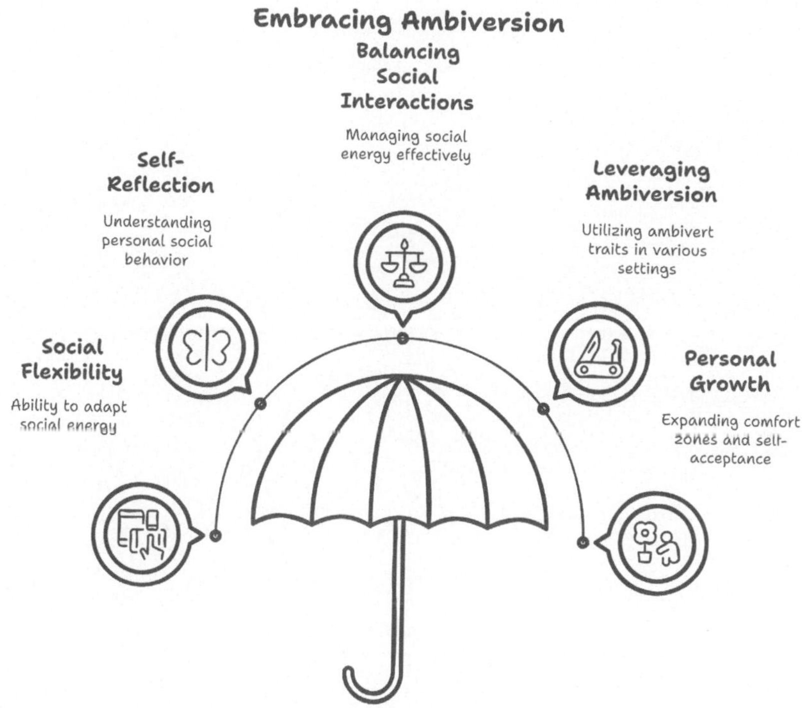

Pro Tips for Embracing Ambiversion:

1. **Be Yourself, Unapologetically** – Embrace both your social and quiet sides.
2. **Challenge Yourself Gently** – Step out of your comfort zone, but don't force it.
3. **Celebrate Your Journey** – Recognize your growth, however small it may seem.

The End – But Just the Beginning of Your Journey!

Thank you for sticking through this guide with me. Now it's your turn to take these tips, embrace your inner ambivert, and start living a balanced, fulfilling life. And remember, if all else fails, there's always humour to fall back on!

Printed at Repro India Ltd.